Roy' Hal, wanted this Book! I a do so. Your Noble to your— your State & Country. God Bless! Enjoy my crazy Ride!

Pete

ONE HELL
OF A RIDE

Pierre "Pete" Charette

3/3/ 23

A key figure in the take-down of the heroin
organization known as *The French Connection*

ONE HELL OF A RIDE

INVESTIGATIVE UNDERCOVER
LIFE OF A DEA AGENT

Pierre A. Charette

LitPrime
"Your story is our priority"

LitPrime Solutions
21250 Hawthorne Blvd
Suite 500, Torrance, CA 90503
www.litprime.com
Phone: 1-800-981-9893

Published by LitPrime Solutions   01/28/2022

ISBN: 978-1-955944-55-7(sc)
ISBN: 978-1-955944-56-4(hc)
ISBN: 978-1-955944-57-1(e)

Library of Congress Control Number: 2022901627

CONTENTS

DEDICATIONS

This book is dedicated to the loving memory of my parents, Philorum and Emilienne, whose support, love, integrity, and, and worries for my constant safety made me have one of the greatest careers in law enforcement worldwide.

To my beautiful and loving wife, Paula, who inspired me to write this book, which at times, I questioned my purpose to do this, but she stood by me. She made me see that my story needed to be told for our grandchildren.

To Dr. Mark Salsbury and his staff at The Wellstar Medical Group Urgent Care, Acworth, Georgia who by the grace of God, brought me back to life with the assistance of his great emergency staff when I died of cardiac arrest in the emergency room. They refused to accept this and succeeded in bringing me back to life.

To our wonderful loving family, the Charette Family: Gilles and Tassy, Phillip, Marie, Timothy, Marie, John and Georgia, Michael, Christopher, Bobby, Danielle, Marielle and David Klapp, Celine and Myron Underwood, Madison, Liam, Ava, Louis and Kristen, Britney, Bernard and Patty. The McCullum Family: Ron, Helen, Paula, Ronald and Joanie, Erik, Sean, Perry and Ray, Myles Andrew, Annie, Dana and Marjorie, Tyler, Candace, Ava, Meghan, Jennifer and Jason LaForte, Madison, Gianna, Rhonda and Andy Mohammed, Andrew, Keira, Tracy and Billy Connors, Billy Jr., Mason.

To Sean McCullum, my nephew, a special thanks for designing the picture covers of my first edition book. You are an amazing photographer.

Special thank you to Seth Woods, of Colorado, for being one of my editors on this book.

I struggled to find a title for this book, and one day after talking with Tom Cash after his wife's funeral, Tom said, "Pete, she had a beautiful funeral and you know Peggy and how crazy she was to be around with! Well she made me promise her to put one comment on her tombstone; you'll never guess what she made me put on it?"

"Knowing Peggy, it's got to be good! What?"

"She told me to put 'It's been one hell of a ride' on it."

Laughing, I knew at that moment I had my book title. Peggy will always be in my heart and will never be forgotten.

Later I told him of my decision, for which he thanked me and for honoring her!

REST IN PEACE. LOVE YOU, PEGGY!

+ + + + + + +

To all of my DEA family and law enforcement colleagues worldwide, especially to those who lost their lives, there are too many to name, I wouldn't have been able to accomplish all I did without your involvement with me. This was not a one man's accomplishment; it was a team effort. I am honored to tell my story and to have been a part of this famous ride with you, because it has been yes, one hell of a ride!

AUTHOR'S NOTE

D ue to the nature of my work, I must ensure that people with whom I have worked and who are still alive are protected from anyone who may wish to harm them. This is all new to me; therefore, I must make sure their safety comes first.

Since the time I became involved in law enforcement, my career for sure was not a normal and standard work that most officers experience. I pushed myself to "PROTECT and SERVE" the people of this country, and I took this OATH seriously regardless of the day-to-day dangers that came with the job. The job changed fast for me and resulted in my being involved in undercover work that took me around the world. I would have never accomplished what I did in 33 years without the tremendous support from my law enforcement colleagues and friends all over the world.

Because of this, I have been advised that there are certain restrictions imposed on an author about various disclosures of people's names and photos without permission. That being said, I assure all of my tremendous colleagues that your names will be referred to with a "PN" short for Pseudo Name. You know who you are, and I will not reveal names without having had written authorized permission. These accounts are real and not fabricated or enhanced. What you read is what I did, and I have nothing but pride to have been supported by so many.

TESTIMONIALS

Dr. Carlton E. Turner, PH.D.,
Former Drug Czar to President Ronald Reagan

"In my 78 years of life, God has provided me many opportunities most of which a country boy from rural Alabama could not have dreamed, much less lived. Along the way from the farm to the White House, I met extraordinary people. One was Pete Charette. Pete is a natural storyteller and writer. As an instructor for the Bureau of Narcotics and Dangerous Drugs (BNDD) and the Drug Enforcement Administration (DEA) from 1970 to 1981, it was my privilege to meet key members of both organization from the agents on the street to the Directors and Administrators. From my vantage point, Pete was the best. His language skills allowed him to go places few could go. His natural ability to survive in the drug underworld, combined with an uncanny ability to communicate his experience provided us with an understanding of the dangers a drug enforcement agent faces each day. You may find Pete's experiences unbelievable but believe me they are real. Your view of drug enforcement agents will change."

B. Boykin Rose
Associate Deputy Attorney General of the United States Department of Justice (retired)

"If you want to experience vicariously the exhilarating and daring life of an undercover DEA agent with a storied career, look no further than this book. Pete Charette accomplished what few others could in the dark and sinister war against narcotics trafficking through sheer willpower, unflinching bravery and cunning. He possessed a singularity of purpose, integrity and vision coupled with an ability to lead a diverse group of federal, state and local law enforcement officials in a way that was not common at the time.

I had the privilege of serving as Associate Deputy Attorney General in the United States Department of Justice. In that role, I worked with many law enforcement professionals. I found them to be honorable people working in an admirable profession. Yet in life, there are always standouts. Pete was most assuredly one such person. His intellect, passion, fearlessness and leadership made him a powerful weapon in the fight against organized crime. Doing a good job satisfies most people. Pete was driven by a ferocity that commanded respect, awe and admiration, achieving unprecedented results. So, for those of you who are drawn to stories of courageous people who win against all odds, who never despair and carry on, this book is for you."

◆◆◆◆◆

John B. Brown III
Deputy Administrator (retired), U.S. Drug Enforcement Administration

"Pete Charette has not only been a trusted colleague and Brother Agent – he was even once my boss – but for nearly half of a century, he has been a tremendous friend!

Many of us met Pete for the first time on that cold January morning in 1972 when we reported to the headquarters of the former U.S. Bureau of Narcotics and Dangerous Drugs (BNDD) at 14th and "I" streets in downtown Washington, DC. We were to become BNDD Basic Agent Training Class #23, and if we made it through training successfully, we would become Federal Narcotics Agents.

"Pete stood out right from the beginning. A bundle of French energy whose personality was as big as his smile, Pete became fast friends with everyone. Our classmates had backgrounds as diverse as any you could imagine. Some of us had prior law enforcement experience, many had been teachers, sales personnel, whatever – a few even had very mysterious backgrounds that no one ever talked about. Pete came to the BNDD academy after already having had a stellar career as a detective in South Florida, where he worked tough narcotics cases - and even tougher official corruption cases. In BNDD #23, Pete did what he always has done – he relied on his experience and perspective and reached out to give a helping hand to some of our classmates to make sure they made it through training.

"In his book, Pete takes us along as he works as a Special Agent to bring down some of the largest criminal organizations ever known. Nobody worked harder than Pete – not that Pete even had to work hard – not with all his experience, ingenuity and expertise. But I have always believed that Pete's true legacy – even greater than what he accomplished as a Special Agent - will be what he has done as a Supervisor and Manager to mentor, guide and support other Agents and Officers – just as he did back in basic training – to make certain that the job got done the right way, and that everyone went home safely in the end."

• • • • • •

SAIC Thomas Cash
Retired Special Agent in Charge, Drug Enforcement Administration, Miami, Florida

"Pete Charette had a most interesting life and very interesting cases. More so than average agents because of time and circumstances surrounding his assignments. His assignments were aided by his ability to speak fluent

French in a critical time. It was known in France and other countries in Europe, as the "Agent Provocateur" law and such activity by a French Police officer or Agent was viewed as totally illegal in French Courts. Actually, cases were not prosecuted when such activity occurred as the alleged "provoking agent's" conduct led to the acquittal of the heroin trafficker or any other criminal. The acquittal was valid inasmuch as the officer or Agent was" luring innocents to commit the crime of heroin production." DEA however could do the meetings, the surveillances, the visits and pose as anyone they could get away with pretending to be. So that is where Pete Charette came in and that is part of what you will read about in this book.

"So, to combat that heroin scourge, you needed a young French speaking man or woman to do what became known as the "Undercover" work because the French could not do the enticing informative work necessary to discover the crime of heroin trafficking. It was made for Pete Charette and he did it often and successfully working out of our Paris office. Fluent French was what made his undercover act believable. Plus, he looked like a young French criminal which made his act all the more successful.

"In my later career I too worked in Paris as Assistant Regional Director and Pete was still seen as the icon of the Paris office who began our success working with the French National Police. DEA would do what the French could not do, and DEA could testify in French Court as they were accredited to France through the Embassy. Without such undercover operations, the French would have been buried in heroin.

"Later in my career as I was the Special Agent in Charge of the Miami Field Division and assigned him to the Caribbean Offices where his French came into play in many of the French speaking islands. Just remember that truth is stranger than fiction. DEA Special Agents serving around the globe have had some amazing results not all of which have been categorized. Perhaps Pete's book with an amazingly true title will inform you of some of the cases that can now be revealed."

———— ✦✦✦✦✦ ————

Special Agent Steve Murphy *(retired DEA), Co-Founders and Keynote Speakers, DEA Narcos*

"Pete Charette is another of America's unsung heroes, someone that dedicated his life to protecting others as well as his country, someone who didn't ask for, nor seek attention or glory, someone who had a loving wife and family who understood when the call of the job had to come first. He was a DEA Special Agent who knew the job and proactively worked it, an Agent who set an example for others to follow, an Agent who became a leader and mentor, and an Agent who is my friend.

"In today's society, the word 'hero' is thrown around freely with little regard to the actions or circumstances involved. But Pete earned that title, although he'll never use that title or admit it. But isn't that one of the traits of a true hero?

If you want to learn what life as a DEA Agent can be like, the dangers, the excitement, staying focused on your mission, this is the book for you. Pete doesn't tell stories about what others did while he sat back and watched. He lays out firsthand knowledge of how he worked undercover in a seedy and violent world when any day could realistically be his last. This isn't Hollywood, this is real life from a man who lived it!!!

"I had the pleasure of working under Pete while stationed in Miami. His enthusiasm was contagious, his advice was sought, and we always knew he had our backs. Pete was instrumental in supporting me for assignment to Colombia. We maintained contact which resulted in us working on some of the first Colombian heroin cases. And of course, Pete was always there to support us in the Pablo Escobar investigation.

Pete, thanks for your commitment to duty and honor, and for always supporting us "baby" Agents!!! God bless you and your family my friend!"

Kenneth (Mac) McCarron *(Retired Supervisory Special Agent)*
U.S. Drug Enforcement Administration, U.S. Department of Justice,
Miami Field Division, Miami, Florida

"I met Pierre "Pete" Charette in 1985, when I was a Special Agent with the United States Drug Enforcement Administration (DEA) in Miami, Florida. Having the opportunity to not only meet Pete, but to work for and with Pete was very instrumental and benefited me greatly in becoming a successful Special Agent and Supervisory Special Agent with the DEA. Pete recruited me to manage a multi-agency Ad Hoc Task Force responsible for the pursuit, investigation, arrests and convictions of significant co-conspirators responsible for the manufacture and distribution of marijuana throughout the State of Florida. The investigation proved successful and the experience and knowledge I acquired while I worked as Pete's Case Agent proved successful the rest of my 37 years in the field of law enforcement. The supervisor, partner and brother I was blessed to have in my life is Pete Charette, who has always honored, cherished and protected the shield he wore."

———— ⋅⋅✦✦✦⋅⋅ ————

Kevin Studer
Program/Operations Manager, DSoft Technology Engineering and Analysis,
Inc.

"It is rare in one's life that you come face to face with a real-life patriot. I have had such a privilege. Pete Charette has been one of if not my best friends for the last eight years - and I've never met a better human being. He has been a loving father, a dedicated husband, a brilliant storyteller, with a deep core of compassion and empathy, who's continually put himself in harm's way for his country, his community, and those he loves. Pete is a genuinely selfless man who's made an enormous impact in my life. It was an honor to have him in my wedding party. His stories about his time in the DEA were the kinds of things I thought were pure 'creative embellishment' when I first met him. But as I've gotten to know him, and talked with those that have known him, I've realized just how much of a wild ride his life has been. He has always been willing to pass on his stories, experiences, and wisdom in the most unassuming manner to not only myself but also to those that he works with in our company. I'm sure he's got a few more wild adventures in him - and I have no doubt they'll be one hell of a ride!"

1

My Ride Begins in Canada

My adventures began in 1943 in a small town in Valleyfield, Canada, where I grew up with my three brothers Giles, John, Bernard. My parents were owners of the Victoria Restaurant. I had a normal upbringing and my parents always taught us to be honest and helpful to others.

My adventure actually began on a winter day while walking from my Catholic elementary school to my father's restaurant as we normally did with my brothers Gill and John. On the way, I observed a police officer talking to a woman with a child. My eyes focused on this stalwart man, and I was in awe of his black uniform and shiny buttons, perfectly fit hat and glistening shield on his chest. My oldest brother Gill asked, "What are you looking at?"

I said to him, "Someday I will be a police officer" and kept on walking. I was only seven years old, but that image was imprinted in my mind from that moment, later to repeat itself when we moved to the United States in 1955.

Growing up in Canada was totally different from my life in the United States. As a kid, my favorite sport was hockey, and I received a great education in this sport. My father's best school friend was Toe Blake, who became the coach for the Montreal Canadians in the early fifties.

I was the youngest of the three brothers at this time. My fourth brother was born in Florida in 1962. We grew up in a neighborhood that mainly had two-story apartment buildings, and only three family houses existed on our block. My father's business was very successful, and our neighbors either worked at the cotton mill or the Canadian Schenley Whiskey factory, which was directly behind our property.

In 1955 we moved to the United States as a result of my father's health, necessitating a move to a warmer climate. Ultimately, he decided to move to Florida, specifically Hollywood when I was nine years of age, and neither my brothers nor I could speak one word of English, except for my dad and my mom. Shortly after our relocation, my father purchased a small motel on US 1.

Growing up in the U.S. was exciting, but my first day in school was a frightening experience. I remember asking Dad, "If I am asked something, what do I say?"

He replied, "Simple. If it sounds right, just say 'YES' and if it sounds wrong, 'NO.'" Those were the only English words I knew for at least six months until I slowly picked up more English. I remember being laughed at when the teacher asked for us to make a phrase using the word Potato and pointed to me. I thought for a second and proudly spurted out, "I grow potato in my backyard" with a French accent, and everyone began laughing. I didn't understand why the laughter.

The teacher responded, "Pierre, you have a beautiful accent."

Unlike today, my parents held us to a strict standard and Dad told my brothers and me that being here in the United States, we must only speak French in the house and outside of the house "You will only speak English." He further warned that if he ever caught us not speaking English outside, there would be severe consequences with the administration of belt spanking. Despite his stern warnings, he caught us on several occasions, and we quickly learned just how serious he was.

I believe that this was the best way for us to become Americans and looking back, it's a shame that foreign parents don't use this standard. To be honest, I love my country and wish that all of us, as citizens should only speak English in public when in the United States

2

Why I Chose This Ride!

Growing up in Hollywood, Florida, was great! We ended up having a fifth brother named Louis. My dad had been a successful businessman in Canada and became successful again in Florida, Hollywood specifically, as the owner of a chain of motels.

As I mentioned earlier, seeing my first police officer in Canada had made a huge impression on me. The second vision of my possible future occurred while I was attending McNicol Middle School. One day in my seventh-grade social studies class, our teacher announced that students who were interested in becoming a school safety patrol officer should go to the principal's office and apply. On the wall of the class hung a poster of a boy with his white safety patrol cross belt with a badge, standing at an intersection alongside a police officer helping kids across the intersection. This poster inspired me so much that at the class break, I made a beeline to the principal's office. I walked in and told the principal's secretary, who was a neighbor of ours, that I needed to see him immediately!

When I walked in, he greeted me with, "Bonjour, Pierre."

I said immediately, "I want to be a safety patrol officer and become a police officer when I grow up."

He started laughing and said, "You know, there are others who also wanted the job!"

I was so determined to get this and thinking quickly thought, *force yourself to have a tear!* Suddenly few tears formed, and I said, "I want this, please. I will be the best you ever had."

He gave me a funny look and smiled and answered, "I believe you will be!" He told me the position was mine and called his secretary in and told her to get me a safety patrol belt and badge, and I was sworn in on the spot. My insides were churning with pride, and I knew that this was my future. Looking back on what I did, I now realize that this was my first 'undercover' role by way of faking my emotions.

I proudly reported to the Hollywood police officer at the crossing that afternoon, and he became my mentor. I was full of questions about police work, and this smiling Irish cop took his time to make me want to be the best officer ever. I was a safety patrol officer for three years. Eight years later, I returned to see him and proudly pulled up to his home across from the school in my Broward County Sheriff's patrol car on my first shift to thank him for assisting me in becoming a deputy Sheriff. Needless to say, we were both emotional!

Events in my senior year at South Broward High School in 1963 caused me to have to make a decision that made my dream of being in law enforcement come true. I was the president of the Diversified Continuing Education Training Program which allowed us to go to school half a day and work half a day. Two weeks before graduation, our teacher, Mr. Marion West *(deceased)*, approached me about wanting to meet me with my parents at home in order to discuss a private matter. We agreed and met one evening at my house, where Mr. West told my parents that each year the DCE Program is given a college scholarship for the University of Florida, and that he had chosen me to receive this.

My parents were so proud of this, and I was stunned. After discussing this, my dad asked me what I wanted to do. I asked to be excused, went to my room, and sat on my bed wondering what to do. As I sat there, I remember looking into the bedroom dresser mirror and seeing my safety patrol belt hanging along the side. I stared at it for several minutes and remembered talking to my oldest brother Gilles who was serving in Viet Nam as an air police officer in the Air Force. I had discussed with him without my parents' knowledge that I wanted to go into the

Army and asked his advice as to what to do. Gilles told me the best job was to be a military police officer. He told me it was exciting and could lead to a great career in law enforcement. Remembering that conversation convinced me that I had to pursue this dream, and so my decision was made.

I came back into the room and told my dad and Mr. West that I was honored to be considered, but I would have to turn it down because I was enlisting in the Army after graduation. My dad understood and told me to follow my dream. Mom was in shock to hear that I was doing this since both of my oldest brothers were already in the Air Force. My brother John had joined after Gilles had joined a year later. This was the best decision that started my one hell of a ride in law enforcement, filled with risk, danger, excitement, honor, highs and lows, and working with the most amazing brotherhood of men and women in the world.

3

The Beginning of the Ride

In July of 1963, I enlisted into the U.S. Army as a military police officer during the Vietnam War. I received Boot Camp training at Ft. Jackson, South Carolina. After Boot Camp, I began my MP Training in Ft. Jackson at Augusta, Georgia. My orders upon completion of MP School was for me to be sent to Viet Nam to be a French Translator. The date of graduating MP School was one I will never forget. On that day I was advised that my orders had been changed, and I was not going to Vietnam but to Albuquerque, New Mexico to Sandia Base, assigned to the Defense Atomic Support Agency (DASA). This was an all Armed Force Base.

I flew out on November 22, 1963, an unforgettable day. As I flew to Dallas, Texas to catch a flight to New Mexico, 30 minutes before landing, the pilot announced on the intercom, "Ladies and gentlemen I have been informed that the President of the United States has been shot in Dallas." People started crying and a short time later we learned that he had died. We finally landed in Dallas and all military personnel were told to immediately report to the Military Airport office. I was told that I was to be assigned to the airport police immediately until things were determined if this was an act of war. Five hours later, I was released and left for New Mexico.

My MP career at Sandia Base was exciting, and I made great friends.

My roommate who is still my best friend is from New Jersey. A singer in a rock and roll band, he was drafted and served two years. He and I had wild adventures both at work and off. He retired as a police Captain and to this day he is like a brother to me.

I learned a lot about the MP work and was eventually promoted to a Specialist E-4 Rank and assigned to be the head of the MP Town Patrol Office at the Albuquerque Police Department. My duty was to do MP patrol with the police, looking for Military AWOLs and ensuring that soldiers conducted themselves in a proper order in bars and night clubs.

Being proud of my assignment and to prove myself worthy of this post, I quickly learned that you never enter a bar where there is a brawl involving military and civilians until everything is calm. My first education occurred when we responded at a Country Western Club. The officers were dispatched and advised that soldiers and civilians were involved in a brawl.

Upon arriving the Sergeant asked," Who wants to go in first?" I immediately volunteered! That was a big mistake!

I learned later that my police department friends were testing me to see if I was a stand-up guy. The fighting and crashing of furniture could be easily heard outside. I took a deep breath, took out my nightstick and opened the door, took two steps in and received a fist in the face, knocking me backward and out cold on the pavement! Yes! LESSON LEARNED!!! When I came to, my nose bleeding, the cops patted me on my back, laughed and said, "Frenchy, you are now one of us." With a half weak smile, I felt as if I had been crowned as a cop!

During my MP career I was approached by my company commander and First Sergeant and asked if I would be willing to represent our company in the 4th Army Sandia Base Command, Military Police Officer of the Year Award Program. I was honored to accept and for two months I studied Military Justice, MP Code of Conduct and Military Police Enforcement Administration Procedures. I had to appear before a Provost Marshall Board where I was quizzed, tested and named Military Police Officer of the 4th Army Command in 1965. My first honor and award as a law enforcement officer.

At the same time when I was asked to re-enlist and was preparing to do this, I received a call from my mother who advised me that the Sheriff of the Broward County Sheriff's department, Allen B. Michell (*deceased*) wanted me to call him immediately. I asked myself why the Sheriff wanted me to call him. My mother furnished me with his phone number. Curiously, I called and his secretary, who was his wife, answered and immediately advised me he was waiting for my call.

The Sheriff came on the line and asked, "How are you doing?" He continued, "You know, I was an Ex-Provost Marshall in the MP and read in the Army Times that you were named Military Police Officer of the 4th Army Sandia Base command." We talked a bit.

"Thank you, sir, for your interest."

"Pierre," he said, "what are your plans with the Army? Are you going to re-enlist?

I responded, "I am up for re-enlistment and was offered a $25,000 Bonus if I did."

"No, you're not," he interrupted. "You're coming to work for me. I have a job for you as a deputy Sheriff!"

An uncomfortable silence followed! I thought, *This is what you have been waiting to do. Go for it!* Finally, I spoke and said, "Sheriff, I have three months to go and would be honored and accepted the offer!"

"See you in three months, Pierre. I'm proud to have you in my department!"

I was baffled and excited. Now I had to get ready for another hell of a ride. This one would launch me in the most amazing ride and career that anyone could have.

I was proud to have served in the Army as an MP, and I am constantly reminded of it whenever I see a military funeral and hear taps being played. My first Sergeant somehow had found out that I played a Coronet and asked me to report to him. He said, "Frenchy, I hear you play the trumpet, is that right?"

"Yeah, Sarge, why are you asking?"

He responded, "We need a bugler for military funerals once a month in Santa Fe, New Mexico and you are now our bugler!" I agreed and was honored to do this! Little did I know how this would impact me for the rest of my life.

Wendy, David, and Bonnie Lehman and Pete Playing the Bugle

We were detailed with six other MP's to be the Honor Guard for the burial ceremony of returning Viet Nam fallen heroes. My first funeral sadly arrived, so we all traveled on an Army bus to Santa Fe, New Mexico, with me as the driver. On the way, we passed the time telling stories and reading. Once there, silence ensued accompanied with butterflies in my stomach. As we arrived at the gravesite, we solemnly exited the bus and saw an open grave waiting to receive its hero. While waiting for the hearse, I surveyed the area to find the best spot to play taps! I finally decided that rather than standing at the gravesite to play, I broke rank and went up a small hill overlooking the burial site. I said to myself, *Pete, do this right and do it for David Lehman, my childhood best friend, who was shot off a navy patrol boat and died in Viet Nam.*

As I waited, the guys were lined up for the 21-gun salute, as the funeral convoy and family came around the bend. I felt sick to my stomach as reality kicked in! I observed this soldier's mother exit the car. She was being held and weeping uncontrollably as she was escorted to the gravesite. Slowly the funeral pall bearers removed the hero. The honor guard assumed the attention position with rifles, and I saluted our hero at attention, bugle tucked under my left arm. After the final prayers, I said a silent prayer. "Please Lord, help me do it right with your love and guidance to send him to your loving arms!" From that time on, I said this prayer for over 200 funerals of fallen heroes.

Suddenly, the order to raise arms was given, and I watched all seven of my colleagues fire the first volley, then the second volley, and finally the last. Slowly, I raised my bugle and took a deep breath, lips against my mouthpiece, trembling. Suddenly the notes flowed from my body into the air, reverberating on each note until the final note flowed out and held for 15 seconds! I slowly lowered my horn tucked under my left arm and saluted as tears flowed down the sides of my cheeks. David, God bless! Suddenly I heard a scream and the mother of this hero threw herself on top of the coffin weeping and wrapping her loving arms around the casket. She was slowly removed by the family and led back to the awaiting car. This picture still remains vivid each time I hear taps. Yes, I was proud to have honored our heroes by being a part of their services; however, when I left the Army, I put my bugle away for good.

⁘⁘⁘

While at Sandia Base, not all was sad and solemn. There were some amusing times on the base. While on patrol one day with a new MP driving on Main Street, the main gate guard sent a radio transmission that a Cadillac convertible had just run the gate and was heading toward the Officer Club Road.

I radioed that I had the vehicle in sight and was proceeding to stop it. It was occupied by a civilian dressed driver and a blond female. I blue-lighted the vehicle which pulled over, then exited my vehicle and checked the windshield as I approached to see if it had a Blue Officer Decal. It did not. The top of the convertible was down, and I overheard the blond say, "Go ahead, Honey, show them who's the boss."

"Sir, you ran the base gate entrance without stopping. Could you please step out of the car?" I asked.

He stepped out and replied, "Soldier, you don't address me without saluting me first."

"Sorry, but I don't see an officer's decal on your vehicle. So, show me some ID."

"Soldier, you stand at attention when you address me. I'm a Full Bird Colonel!"

I persisted. "Until I see ID, I don't care who you are. Let's see some ID now or you're under arrest."

I noticed his fist went into a clinch grip, and I figured he wanted to take me on, which would be his biggest mistake. The New MP who was a Golden Glove Boxer started to move forward and as the 'colonel' started to swing at me, my partner delivered one quick right hook, grinned and knocked him out with one punch.

Next, we handcuffed him while the female screamed at us. When we stood him up and came too, he said, "I will have your asses court-martialed. I'm an advocate judge, and my ID is in my wallet!"

I looked at my partner who was grinning at him but restrained myself from laughing. Sure enough, his ID proved he was a Full Bird Colonel JAG Officer!

"Oh, Hell! Watch him. I'm calling the lieutenant to come to the scene now," I said.

"1-0-1 to Base, need the CO to come to Club Road ASAP."

"Frenchy, I'm on my way!"

"10-4, Sir!"

Within minutes the first lieutenant pulled up and heard the incident. He responded, "Frenchy, there's never a dull moment when you're on duty. I got to call the colonel to meet us at the MPO (Military Provost Marshal's Office). This is going to get hot!"

"No problem, Sir! This so-called officer is going down and we aren't backing down, understood?"

"Got it."

When we got to the MPO, the Provost Marshal was already there. "Lieutenant Frenchy, in my office. Give it to me quick and fast."

"Yes, Sir." I filled him in, then he called my partner ordering me not to say anything until he got his side of the story. It was exactly as I said.

"Lieutenant, get me the Base Commandant on the phone now!" commanded the provost marshal.

"Sir, the admiral is on the phone!"

The PM briefed the admiral. "Sir, this so-called officer attempted to strike my man, and he got a surprise. We are taking him to the stockade now, where he can appear before you in the morning. Have a great evening, Sir!"

The PM met the JAG Officer, who demanded that he immediately put us under house arrest. The PM said, "You're a disgrace to your uniform, and the only person under house arrest is you!"

"Frenchy, you and the Lieutenant take this so-called officer out of my sight and lock his ass up at the stockade, and you guys write your report and bring him to the admiral's office at 10:00 a.m. tomorrow. Good night! And Oh, by the way, nice shiner!" With a smirk on his face, he saluted us and left.

The next morning, we were at the admiral's office, where each one of us told him our story. The JAG had his assigned representative. We all waited for two hours when finally, the PM appeared and said, "The admiral found him guilty of attempted assault on two enlisted MPs and gave him a choice of losing one rank with an apology to both of you or full military court-martial and dishonorable discharge. He took the demotion in rank! You guys did a great job in handling this," then added with a wink, "Love the shiner!"

The funniest incident of my MP career happened on a hot summer weekend when we were told that we were having a military parade review on the parade grounds on a Saturday in over 100-degree heat!

On parade day, the Army, Air Force, Navy and Marines, all in dress uniforms, lined up on the parade grounds. The reviewing stand consisted of uniformed officers whose wives were dressed in their summer's best along with the admiral in his white uniform and his wife with her summer white brim hat and white summer dress.

While waiting for the order to march in review, some of the troops in over 100-degree heat began to pass out! Finally, the order to march in revue was given while the band played. Once the revue was completed, the only thing left to do was for the MPs near the flag post to receive the order for a 21-gun salute and to fire the two cannons!

The 21-gun salute was given and executed. Then it happened! Both cannons were shot, but to everyone's surprise, the cannons were loaded with black gun powder, not clear powder!

All you could see was a cloud of black powder being blown by a small wind, directly into the bleachers, and yes, just like in the movies, black powder covered everyone's white uniforms and dresses!

"Oh shit," was our first Sergeant's comment as we all tried not to laugh.

The order was given to dismiss. Needless to say, there were no more summer parades, and a full-blown investigation was made. No one was ever identified as the culprit. Of course, the word spread that we, the MPs, were the most likely suspects, and for days every time we walked by the first Sergeant's office, we still could hear him laughing! Yes, we were a tight group.

I was proud to have had the opportunity to serve my country, but I wanted more adventure! Little did I know that I would be on one hell of a 33-year ride!

4

Arresting My Lieutenant On My First Day On Patrol

My Broward County Sheriff Department adventures started in 1966 thru 1971. July 1, 1966, was a great day for me. Discharged from the Army, I flew back home to start my lifelong dream to be a civilian law enforcement officer. I couldn't wait to call the Broward County Sheriff's Department, Sheriff Alan B. Michell, to start what would turn out to be an adventure that would take me all over the world for the next 33 years. I was told to report to the Fort Lauderdale Police Department to attend a 16-week police academy. Our class was in a small room at the police department and was attended by police recruits from the police departments of Pompano, Fort Lauderdale, Hollywood, Oakland Park and the Broward Sheriff's Department. The training was basic knowledge of Florida laws and arrest techniques, patrol techniques, and physical PT training, which was conducted on the side of the police department on a patch of grass no larger than 75 square feet.

The first week consisted of the issuance of uniforms and basic orientation. We were told that we would have to purchase our own guns, handcuffs, leather belts, holsters and nightsticks. In those days departments did not provide you with any material except your badge and uniform.

My starting salary was $6800 per year, and after taxes in those days, left me with around $5,500 per year. I learned quickly by officers and mentors that low salaries, unfortunately, caused some to become open to corruption.

I was living at home with my parents as a young bachelor and confided in my dad about what I was learning. I remember saying to my dad, "It's scary to hear that low salaries leave some officers to become dirty! I promise you that I will never take a dime. EVER!"

"I've always raised you boys to always be honest, and I believe you, Pierre! Just remember one thing—never lose your integrity. If you do, you are then marked for life, and you will be worse than the criminals you arrest!"

I lived by my dad's words for my entire career, and I am proud to say with honor that I never took a penny in my 33 years. (Later, I will discuss the several attempts to bribe me, and I will describe how those who tried ended up getting a surprise by me and went straight to jail, did not pass go, or get $200!)

My first weekend Dad and I went for a ride to the gun store to buy my first weapon. I chose a Cross Draw Gun Holster and picked out a nickel-plated .38 Caliber Smith & Wesson 6-inch barrel, six-shot pistol. When I was given the cost for everything, I started to pay, but Dad stopped me and said, "No, this is my gift to you for having made me so proud of who you are." Charettes tend to be very emotional. As a result, my eyes teared up, and it took everything I had to hold back. Dad knew that I didn't need to say anything.

This weapon became very special in our family. I qualified with this weapon and carried it for six years. My brother Gill (*deceased*) left the Air Force after 16 years and asked me if I could help him get a job with the Sheriff's department. I met with the Sheriff, who hired him immediately. He borrowed my gun to qualify with it also. Next to use it was my stepson Mark Goggans who was hired by the late Sheriff Nick Navarro (*deceased*), one of my best friends and mentor, and to whom I owed my life. My stepson later had my gun framed as a retirement gift.

On September 26, 1966, I was advised to report to the Fort Lauderdale Police Department located on Broward Boulevard for the start of my police academy training. In 1966 Broward County, Florida, did not have a police academy, and all police agencies in the county sent their new officers to be trained at this department.

We did not have uniforms and reported to class in casual clothes. The class was restricted to 22 officers from various police agencies mentioned earlier. The training lasted three months, and we graduated on December 22, 1966. The classroom was a small conference-sized room, and all of our physical training and defensive tactic training was held on the north corner of the police department building on a patch of grass approximately 75 square feet. Unlike the 12 weeks of training, graduation day at the police academy in those days was short and sweet. The academy head simply called each one of us to the front of the class and presented us with certificates of completion. Afterward, we took a class picture and were told to report to our department's patrol office.

On December 20, 1966, I received a memo from the commander of the BSO Road Patrol, instructing me to report for duty on Friday, December 23, 1966.

Report to duty — December 23, 1966

On December 23, I reported for duty to begin my wild ride. The Sheriff's department at that time was on the eighth floor of the Broward

County Courthouse in Fort Lauderdale, Florida. I was directed upon arriving to report to my Patrol Sergeant Bob Richards (PN). When I walked into the office, he said, "You got to be Frenchy."

Smiling, I answered, "Yes! Pleasure to meet you, sir!"

He replied jokingly, "Sir? Do you see any bars on my collar? You call me sarge and that's good enough for me." He inspected me up and down. "How old are you?"

"I replied, "twenty-one."

He replied, "You look like a teenager! Be prepared to be taken on by some of these bad-asses in Zone One, where you're working. I got to be straight with you, Frenchy, the south end of the zone's four to twelve shift is always busy, and you ride alone! Unfortunately, Broward County only has five deputies per shift for the whole county. This map here on the wall shows that you cover from the Dade/Broward County line south to State Road 84 North."

I stood there for a couple of minutes thinking, *What the hell have I done*? Then I said,

"That's about 20 miles wide, right?"

"You got it. Don't worry. If you need help, the zone guy north of you will always head your way if he isn't tied up, and you're dispatched on a call. You'll do the same for him if he's on a call. We cover one another always!"

"Got it!" I said.

"Here's your ticket book and box for report forms and call signs card. Over here is your dispatcher's office." He took me over to introduce me to Mary, our dispatcher.

"He's just a kid," she said. "Welcome to hell!" We both laughed! She was our den mother, and no one messed with her guys. After she briefed me on calls, she added, "Now you need to know our private signal code." I looked at her puzzled and she explained, "When the Brass hits the road, I will sneeze on the radio and say sorry about that! That's your alert that the Brass is out prowling around, so be on your toes!" Right there and then I knew she had our back!

Sarge continued my orientation. "Frenchy, the motor pool is next door, so go ahead and get your patrol car. You will be fine. Head south to Pembroke Road and relieve the deputy. Just give him a call, and he will tell you where to meet and will give you his end-of-shift briefing. Be safe!"

I picked up my car, checked the shotgun, hooked it up to the dashboard, a shell in the chamber and ready to be used if need be. I checked the trunk for the oxygen tank, first aid kit, blanket, road flares, animal rod, and body tarp. As I was doing my radio check to dispatch and give my first Unit 101 is 10-8, which is the radio code for 'on duty,' I observed an unmarked car pulling up to the gas pump.

A tall, husky man with the face of a bulldog got out of his car. He looked at me standing outside my patrol car with my radio mike in my hand and gave me a stern look, and said with a raspy voice, "Hey, kid! How ya doing? I'm Lieutenant Cecil Stewart (*deceased*) of the vice squad. You're new, and I guess you must be 21?" He began to laugh!

"Yes, Sir, pleasure to meet you." I introduced myself and shook his hand.

"Can I talk to you in private for a minute?"

"Yeah, sure," I answered, and we walked away from the motor pool manager.

"What I am going to ask you is confidential and not to be discussed with anyone. That's an order!" he said, pointing at me. "Understand?"

"Yes, Sir." *What in the hell is going on?*

"I need you to do something for me at exactly 7:00 p.m. You're going to call in and tell your Sergeant that your car is overheating, and you need to come in and change cars. Understand?"

"Yes, Sir!"

"Once you get here, you go upstairs, and at exactly 7:15 p.m., you walk into the office across from the dispatcher's office and tell the shift commander that you have orders to arrest him and handcuff him and take him to the booking desk downstairs. Tell them Lieutenant Cecil Stewart ordered you to arrest him. That's all. I got to go, and I'll see you when you get off at midnight. Have a great evening, and remember, no one is to know!"

"Yes, Sir!" That was all I could say.

Speechless, I watched him leave and could not believe what had just happened. How in the hell did I get into this mess? Why me?

With butterflies in my stomach, driving, and scared shitless, I drove south, calling the zone deputy. He responded, "Frenchy, I've been waiting to meet you. Meet me at the Hollywood Stock Car parking lot, off 95 and Griffin Road."

"Ok,10-4. Be there in a few minutes!"

Pete Charette ready for work

As I pulled up, standing outside his car was a 6'1", 220 pound, all muscle, black deputy, smiling and shaking his head! "Son, you nothing but a kid! We need to talk! I heard about you already from the man himself, the Sheriff, who told me about you! MP of the Year! Great honor, Frenchy."

He briefed me on this area which, was called Carver Ranch, an all-black small community with great people, but it had a small group of car thieves and troublemakers. He advised me that to the north was the Hollywood Davie PD, to the west was Miramar and Pembroke Pines PD, and to the southeast was Hallandale PD.

He told me that he had already gotten word from one of his sources that the punks in the ranch were aware of a new guy on the block this evening, and the head of the pack, a black male with a front gold tooth, let it be known that he would test me this evening. I felt my stomach churning, then he said, "Frenchy, that little son of a bitch is right now at Pembroke Road and 55th Avenue at the chicken place. You need to stop in and introduce yourself! Don't worry, I will be here with my binoculars watching. If I see that they are taking you on, then I'll come in and I will be whipping asses!"

"Roger that! I'm on my way."

He got his binoculars out as I drove off, scared. When I pulled up and parked, facing me were six punks. He had described Gold Tooth to me. There he was, wearing a black leather cap, grinning and sporting a gold front tooth shining in the sun! I got out of my patrol car and put on my Texas hat (The only thing missing was the music from *High Noon*!) Soaked and wet, I weighed 130 pounds, a skinny 5'10" rookie, but I was ready to make it known that I was in charge of this area for the people living here.

They kept looking at me laughing when Gold Tooth said, "Hey, there's the honkey! We heard you're the new guy." He began laughing.

"Yes, I am, and you must be Gold Tooth."

"What if I am?"

"I got the word that you possibly wanted to test me? Well here I am!"

He tightened up and approached me with his left fist clenched ready to give me a left hit to the face. Big mistake! Little did he realize that I had been in some altercations as an MP. I placed my right hand behind my right leg, where I had sewed a pocket to hold my police slapper, which in those days was authorized. I was holding it ready! Before he knew it, with one quick pull and slap with my lead slapper to the jaw, he went screaming to the ground. I looked around at his boys and said, "Next?"

The boys all took off running around the corner, leaving the punk on the ground. There were some customers there, and unexpectedly I heard someone yell, "YEAH! Thank you!"

He had one hell of a sore mouth. I picked him up and placed him in the caged unit, advising him that I could charge him for attempted assault of a police officer, or I could drop him off at home. He decided on the latter.

I drove back to meet with the deputy who was waiting, laughing. He said, "Frenchy, you passed the test. Have a great evening!" Then he turned to Gold Tooth and said, "If I was you, I wouldn't mess with this crazy Frenchman! Next time he will mess you up bad! Looking back to me, he said laughing, "See you, my man! Have a safe tour!"

I took Gold Tooth home and met his mother. She apologized for him, and right in front of me, she hauled off and popped him right across his mouth and said, "When your daddy gets home, he is going to whip your ass!"

Laughing, I told her it was a pleasure to meet her, and we became good friends. I would always stop and have coffee with her during my shift. She was a hard-working motel maid.

I loved working Zone One. There was never a shortage of excitement. I was not satisfied to do just patrol duty and let this job become complacent for me. I always looked for things that seemed out of place, which always led me to uncover illegal activity.

Riding around, I was terrified about my assignment to arrest an officer on my first day on the job. *What the hell! I will probably get fired on my first night.* But an order is an order, and as my first Sergeant used to say, "Yours is not to question why. Yours is to do or die."

5

Calm Being Shot At! The Arrest

The time was 6:30 p.m. I picked up my mike and said, "1-0-1 to Base."

"Go ahead 1-0-1."

"Can you notify Unit 1-0-0 that I need to come in? My car is overheating, and I need to change units."

"1-0-0 to 1-0-1, Go ahead, come in, Frenchy. I'll cover Zone One. Make it fast."

"1-0-1, 10-4."

All the way to Fort Lauderdale, I reviewed in my mind my scenario for the arrest, repeating "Why Me?"

"1-0-1 to Base, be 10-7 (off the radio) motor pool.

"10-4."

I proceeded to the courthouse, timing myself to arrive at the office exactly at 7:00 p.m. On the elevator, my hands were shaking, and I was breathing deeply. I repeated, "Shit, why me?" over and over.

I arrived on the eighth floor, went down the hall to the office, and walked in. The shift commander looked up from his desk and asked, "What do you need?"

"I don't know what's going on, but I have orders to arrest you and book you downstairs!"

"What is this, a fucking joke?" he questioned as he stood up and placed his hand on top of his holster.

"No joke. Put your hand behind your back, NOW!"

I drew my gun and ordered him to turn around as I aimed my gun on him. The dispatcher who could see what was happening let out a scream and called Unit 100 to come to the office immediately, saying, "Frenchy is arresting the shift officer."

"You son of a bitch. I'll have your ass," he spit out as I handcuffed him."

"I'm sorry, but I was ordered by Lt. Cecil Stewart of the vice squad to do this and book you downstairs. That's all that I know."

The look on his face dropped, and his head slumped down. Not another word came out of his mouth. I took him downstairs to the booking desk, and when I walked in, the desk Sergeant looked up and said, "What the hell is going on?"

"Sarge, I got orders from Lt. Stewart to arrest this officer and to book him. That's all I know."

"Oh hell! Ok, kid! We'll take him. Go back to work!"

"Yeah, thanks."

I walked out trembling and went to get my car as Sarge pulled up. He got out of his car and said, "Frenchy, this better be good."

"Sarge, Lt. Stewart ordered me to arrest him. I don't know what the hell is going on, and I was ordered not to tell anyone."

"Oh hell, Frenchy, this has got to be big. Relax, you're Ok! I'll call Stewart and find out what's going on! Go back to work! Oh, Frenchy, good job!"

"Thanks, Sarge!"

Back on the road, I could hear radio communications from Lt. Stewart asking the dispatch to send a couple of paddy wagons to transport female prisoners, and that the Cat House raid was successful and to advise the Sheriff.

At midnight, I ended my shift, waiting at the motor pool was Lt. Stewart, who was smiling as he approached me and said, "So, they call you Frenchy?"

"Yes Sir."

"Thank you for a hell of a good job and for scaring the hell out of our dispatcher." He laughed. I was briefed that the vice squad had been working a house of prostitution in Hollywood run by a madam, and that the officer was running tags for the madam, to make sure that the clients weren't undercover vice cops!

Now it all made sense, and the buzz around the courthouse was that a new rookie deputy had arrested the officer at gunpoint! Needless to say, I got a lot of looks and recognition for a few days! Little did I know that this incident would lead me to my promotion as a vice detective several months later, becoming the youngest detective in Broward County.

After this undercover arrest, I had several recognizable incidents and arrests while on patrol. My first big incident still as a uniform patrol deputy occurred one night, around 10:00 p.m., as I was driving south on Hallandale Road from State Road 7 with traffic nowhere to be seen. Passing by a used car dealership, out of the corner of my left eye, I noticed a male figure ducking behind a car facing the road. I kept on driving toward I-95 East, and once out of sight, I turned around with lights off and parked my car near the rock pit lake. I took out my binoculars and saw a male entering the dealership, which was closed. I got on the radio and called my Sergeant, who was in the area and asked him to meet me at the warehouse area near State Rd. 7. I had a burglary and possible car theft in progress.

When he arrived and I told him what I had, we worked our way on foot to the Channel 4 tower near the car dealership and observed that now two-car haul trailers were parked off the road in front of the dealership. Cars were starting to be loaded on it. Sarge said, "We will get Hollywood PD and Hallandale PD to help us and take them down now!"

"No, wait till they load both trucks, and then we take them down. this will increase the number of car theft charges against them!"

Sarge looked at me, smiled and said, "I like the way you think."

After all cars were loaded, we took them down. The arrest broke one of the largest car theft rings in Florida.

There is never a dull moment making the rounds, and the public sometimes forgets that this profession is dangerous. Many incidents occur to cops that are never mentioned in the media, which for us, is considered to be part of the job.

For example, during another shift, as I was driving north on State Road 7 nearing State Road 84 going to meet a deputy for coffee, an oncoming pickup truck approached and as I looked at the driver and passenger, the driver had his hand out of the window with a gun pointed at my car shooting at me twice. Luckily, he missed, and I did a 180-degree spin, called it in on the radio. The next zone deputy responded on the radio saying, "I'm on my way, Frenchy," with siren blaring over the air.

I continued to pursue the individual who pulled off the road onto an empty dirt lot. I jumped out with gun drawn and ordered both passengers out with hands up. As I approached them, the next zone deputy came in sliding to halt. He handcuffed the passenger, and as I started to handcuff this redneck, he started to fight. I grabbed my nightstick, and just as I started to hit him in the head with a downward full speed blow, the deputy was in the process of coming at him with a flying tackle. WHAM! My club hit him in the head and sent him flat face to the ground! Reacting fast, I said to this guy who I was still struggling with, "You're going down, and fast."

With two fast taps with my night-stick to the skull and face, the SOB developed a permanent headache and was handcuffed. The deputy staggered up and said, "Frenchy, you son-of-a-bitch, you hit me."

Laughing, I apologized and said, "You dove in with your head as I was going to nail him." Sarge, who had pulled up and saw it happen, was laughing his ass off. Needless to say, this was the talk of the department. The two rednecks were charged with aggravated assault. The gun used to fire at me was a .357 Magnum. I know that God had watched out for me that day. Just another day in the life of a cop!

There are times that I look back and know that God was always there because some of my experiences could have turned out badly. Cops on patrol have, at times, pulled pranks on each other and funny stories come out of it. I'm truly convinced that, if cops pooled their stories together, a best seller book could easily be written.

This brings up the one incident that happened on a quiet night, where I was working the north zone near Pompano Beach, Florida, off Power Line Road and Hammond Ville Road by the labor camp.

Dispatch called a silent alarm call at a liquor store at this intersection. The zone deputy responded, and I, with another deputy, backed him up. When we arrived on the scene, we proceeded to check the outside of the building doors and found no signs of any attempted forced entry. Searching of the outer perimeter and bushes also failed to find anyone. So, we called dispatch and cleared the call.

While having small talk in front of the store, the zone deputy said, "Guys, give me a boost. I want to check the roof."

"You're crazy! Nothing is up there." Still, we boosted him up where he was able to grasp onto the ledge of the roof, leaving him dangling.

He yelled, "Come on, help me." We started throwing small rocks at him, jokingly! As he lifted himself up and looked over the edge, he yelled, "Oh shit!" He dropped to the ground on his ass, drew his gun and yelled, "There are guys up here!"

We all drew our guns and took cover behind our vehicles as we yelled warnings. "Come down with your hands up now. You're surrounded. If you don't, you're dead!"

Sure enough, three white males appeared with their hands up, one holding a ladder as they began to come down one by one.

All suspects were placed in the caged cars, and we all looked at each other in disbelief, even more so when we went up and, on the roof, discovered two guns and the beginning of an entry being cut by them to enter through the roof.

At the end of the shift, we all agreed that in future, when a silent alarm comes in, make sure to check on top of the roofs. Yes, we could have been shot while joking around! This deputy would later become a great Chief of police for the Davie, Florida Police Department.)

As time passed, things started to change and no longer was a new cop put on the job without any training by another seasoned officer. New deputies had to be trained with one seasoned officer before being released on the job. It didn't take long to learn the ropes by yourself as a new deputy. You could get in trouble really fast and regret it if you couldn't adapt!

6

New Deputy, New Deputy Training

As always, we reported on duty and reported to the squad room where the Sergeant briefed everyone as to what occurred on previous shifts and what to look out for. We were briefed about any new intelligence developed by the detective bureau as to what was happening in all the zones in the county for that prior shift.

After three months passed, the Sergeant advised me that I was going to have to train a new cadet who was in the briefing room and identified him to us as Rookie (PN)! The Sergeant said, "Frenchy, Deputy Rookie is riding with you. Make sure you break him in right and go easy on him. We need all the new help we can get."

"Got it! Don't worry, Rookie!" I said. "You will learn really fast. This zone is a piece of cake. Only one or two fights per night and maybe a shooting once or twice."

He said, "Seriously, Frenchy?"

The guys broke out laughing and Sarge said, "He's busting your balls. Maybe one shooting and a couple fights only. Now get out of here, guys. By the way, careful and remember if someone's got to die, it's the bad guys!"

Rookie headed out to the motor pool, where I showed him how to do his routine checkup and to make sure his car had the proper equipment all in good working order. As we entered, I said, "Tradition for your first time on duty is you get the honor to call in to dispatch your first 10-8."

He gave me a big smile, proudly grasped the microphone and said, "Unit 1-0-1 is 10-8."

"1-0-1, that's a big 10-4 and welcome on board, kid! Be safe! His first response was followed by calls from Units 1-0-0,1-0-2,1-0-3,1-0-4, each one ending with "Be safe!"

I added, "You will never forget this, and you will do Ok!"

I showed him our area of patrol along with all our bad characters' hangouts and where the quickest way in and out was if needed or if things escalated into a possible dangerous situation where backups were needed and where our staging areas were for any outbreaks that could turn into small riots. I told him, "Never establish a regular routine patrol. By doing that, you provide a profile for bad guys who are constantly monitoring your patrol patterns so they can be ready to do their nasty deeds."

On our patrol, we came up at a traffic light at 56th Avenue and Pembroke Road. The light turned red as I came to a stop behind a Dodge Charger. I learned quickly to always look at the driver of any car in front of you when stopped for any nervous signs by the driver looking back in his mirror. Two black males were seated in the Charger, and the driver kept looking at me and staring desperately for the light to change. Breaking the silence, I said, "Grab the mike. Don't hold it to your mouth and call this tag in ASAP. We got a stolen car in front of us."

"Ok. 1-0-1 to dispatch. Request an immediate license plate check."

"10-4, 1-0-1. We have a stolen Car. BOLO (Be On Lookout) on this one from Hollywood PD, 20 minutes ago".

"10-4."

"Strap in! We are going for a wild ride. He's getting ready to jump the light as soon as it's yellow on the other side. NOW!"

"Oh shit!" he said as I floored the gas pedal and the SOB took off like a bat out of hell! "Tell dispatch we are in hot pursuit heading west to 441 and this SOB will turn right north toward Davie. Tell dispatch to get Hollywood PD rolling. We will be approaching Hollywood Boulevard in about one minute, going north on 441!"

"1-0-1 to dispatch, have HPD (Hollywood Police Department) go to 441 ASAP." He was holding the mike in his hand trembling and with a wide stare as we were reaching 90 miles per hour. The siren was blaring with blue lights flashing. As we crossed Hollywood Boulevard, two HPD cars dropped behind us in hot pursuit. I saw Johnson Street coming up and suspected that the driver would make a left turn onto it to head west. Just as I suspected, he did exactly what I wanted him to do. At this point, we screeched left doing 80 mph, and saw unit 100, the Sergeant, drop behind with the Zone 2 deputy in pursuit also. I knew that this street was a dead end with a dairy farm at the end of the road, and he could only go left unto a side street.

"Tell 100 I'm going to TAP (A military name given for the bugle call to formation of soldiers in the field dating back to the 1880s) him when he turns left to flip him into the ditch. Hang on because we may roll too."

"Fuck, are you fucking crazy? Are you real? I don't believe this! 1-0-1 to 100 Frenchy says he's going to TAP him at the end of the road when he turns left!"

"100 10-4."

"1-0-2,10-4. Dispatch, notify HPD."

"Dispatch, 10-4."

"You're mine, punk!" As he started to turn left, I gunned it and caught his left rear bumper, tapped it then made a quick turn left braking at the same time.

"Oh shit," the rookie said, as a cloud of dust exploded in front of us and we slid sideways into a ditch. The patrol car tilted on its side to a stop in the ditch. The suspect car was observed doing a couple of rolls into the dairy field.

"Frenchy, are you all right?" the Sergeant hollered as I slowly crawled out of the car that was lying on its side, dust settling, and the rookie was also crawling out repeatedly saying, "He's crazy! He's crazy!"

Laughing, I looked into the field and saw the suspected car lying on its side with the dust settling No one, however, could see any of the suspects in the car. We kept looking when an HPD Dog Unit had arrived. A big German Shepherd was picking up the scent and followed it to a big oak tree. We all started looking up, and to our amazement, we spotted two black males. One of them said, "Sir, sir, please don't cut that dog loose, we coming down!"

We all broke out laughing, while the suspects were taken away by HPD.

"Frenchy?"

"Yeah, Sarge?"

"Great job! That was one hell of a ride!" Then turning to the rookie said, "You doing all right, kid?" He began laughing.

"Yes, sir. He's nuts, you know that?"

"You're with the best! Let's get this car back up, and we'll get it towed out of here. We got another unit coming to replace this one."

"Ok, Sarge."

"Great job! This is one you will always remember, rookie!"

We eventually went back to work, and the rookie became a great deputy Sheriff. Later on, he was promoted to a BS (Broward Sheriff Office) detective.

There are too many stories to tell, but all I can say is that patrol work is one of the most exciting there is because every new day on duty is an unknown adventure. Being alert and adept will make this profession totally unique and exciting. As I illustrated, there can be fun times, and cops really do have a great sense of humor, but if you let it get the best of you, you are doomed and will eventually get yourself in trouble or get one of your fellow officers hurt.

Another funny memory that has always stuck in my mind was the time when I got a complaint call in Davie, Florida, about a woman who called in a house break-in. I responded to the call and met with a pleasant black lady, who reported that she had observed two young boys running away from the back door of her house when she was returning from grocery shopping. She described them to be around 12-13 years of age, wearing blue jeans and short sleeve Polo shirts, one blue and one yellow. She reported that she had found a money jar on the kitchen counter tipped over and suspected they might have taken some money from the jar. I advised her I would check the area for them.

The boys were last seen running across a field from her home. I drove around the area and observed the two boys sitting by the Davie Canal in town. I pulled up and told the boys to get in the back of the patrol car. They were both nervous and scared out of their wits. I told them why I stopped them, but both denied doing anything wrong. I told them that I suspected them of breaking into this house, which they denied while looking at each other. I told one of them to sit in front and calmly said, "Ok, what's your name?"

"Eddie." (PN)

"Eddie, you know if you lie to me, you're in big trouble, right?"

"Yes, Sir."

"I'm going to give you a polygraph test. It's a test that will tell me if you're lying to me. Now I'm going to wrap this microphone cord around your arm and ask you questions, See this light here on this box? Well, it's green, and if you lie to me, it will turn red. Do you understand?"

"Yeah!"

"Ok, I'm wrapping this around your arm. Now, what's your first name?"

"Eddie."

"See? You're telling the truth. The light stayed green. Now, what's your friend's first name?"

"Steve."

"Right! See, the light is still green. Good job! Now comes the tough question, "Did you guys break into that house across the field?"

"N-NO."

Holding the mike down by my leg, I keyed the mike button and the red light came on. Eddie's eyes opened wide and with a scared look on his face. I said, "You're lying to me!"

"Yes! We're sorry!" The other boy immediately yelled out crying. "We're sorry, sir. We will never do it again. Please don't take us to jail. I promise we will never do it again."

It took everything I had to keep from laughing out loud. These two boys just did a crazy thing, and I could tell they had the crap scared out of them. I told them I was taking them back to this lady's home, and they needed to apologize to her. They both agreed. While crying, they apologized, emptied their pockets, and gave her back her change. She winked at me and smiled, and I told the boys that we were going for a ride to their homes to drop them off to their parents.

Both boys received a severe punishment from their parents, but all turned out well. Yes, I had some fun running a polygraph on kids, and other deputies adapted my technique and loved it.

7

Lesson Learned

From time to time, officers are rotated from zone to zone in order to prevent complacency. On reporting to work, I was advised that I had to patrol Zone 2, which was State Road 85 North to Oakland Park Boulevard and had a new recruit who I called Ding Dong to train on the job. I was introduced to this deputy who was around 6'3" and was a perfectionist with a slight lisp. He seemed too eager to learn, but I realized he was very gullible. I have to admit I did play a few pranks on him.

He was full of questions, and I sensed that he didn't like to be told how to do things. He was so overanxious to learn, so I quickly realized that he had to be dealt with immediately, or he could be a danger to himself and to other fellow officers if he wasn't set straight. An incident arose that brought this to light quickly, which could have turned out badly and cost me my life.

While on patrol, we received a call that a woman was threatening to kill herself in front of her sister and kids. I advised Ding Dong that this could end badly, and he was to follow my lead and cover me carefully as I would attempt to talk her out of it. Nervously, he agreed, but I told him to calm down.

Upon arriving at the house, the sister was outside crying with the kids and I could hear her sister inside the house screaming, "I swear

I'm going to kill myself" over and over. The sister said she was in the living room by a fireplace holding a .38 pistol to her head.

As we walked into the house, the living room was located to the left where the girl was crying and holding a silver .38 pistol to her head. I advised the new deputy, "Stay behind me and cover me while I walk slowly towards her so I can get her to drop the gun or take it from her."

He stuttered, "Oh, Ok!"

"Just relax and don't make any sudden moves." Then I entered the living room and slowly approached the girl. "Hi! I'm Deputy Charette. I know that you're upset and have some problems that can be worked out! Can I get you to please put the gun down, and let's resolve this problem? Ok?"

"I want to kill myself. I can't take it anymore!"

"Ok, let's see if we can talk about it! Ok?"

Slowly walking toward her, I was about two feet from her when I got a feeling that I was alone. Slowly, I turned to look back, and sure enough, he was no longer behind me. I suddenly realized that now I had to act. Looking out the living room window, I saw him sitting in the police unit talking on the radio. Later I learned that he was telling dispatch everything was 10-4 Ok.

The anger in me set in because of this stupid move by my so-called partner, and my instinct took over very quickly. *Do something quickly*!

With that thought, I turned and said, "Look" in a stern voice of command and pointed to the left toward the window in order to distract her attention for a second. As she looked out, in one swift motion, I grabbed the gun, pulled downward and yanked it out of her hand. I then pushed her fast to the floor and handcuffed her while I had my knee on her back.

I heard my Sergeant's voice as he was rushing in and said, "Frenchy, are you Ok!"

"Yeah! Just keep the ding dong away from me, or I might be brought up on charges."

Thank God it turned out Ok! I was able to regain my composure, and the rookie was man enough to apologize to me after he realized that his failure to cover me could have been deadly the deranged sister or me. This was a lesson learned that strong communication between partners during a life-threatening experience is a must.

A few days later, I had an opportunity to get a fun revenge against Ding Dong. We received a call that a floater had been found in a canal in Davie, Florida. As we arrived on the scene, people were standing on the top of the canal bank, observing a male body lying face down in the water by the edge of the bank. The body was bloated and appeared to have been there for several days.

I instructed dispatch to send the medical examiner and a detective to the scene. I instructed the rookie to get a plastic tarp out of the trunk of the patrol car, and that we would have to slip it under the body and pull it partially up onto the bank until the medical examiner arrived. First, I took out my camera and took pictures of everything. Then I partially got into the water and put the tarp under the body. That's where the fun part began. "When I say pull, you grab his right arm that is out of the water, and I'll grab his left arm that's out of the water. We pull on three!" I told him, "One, two, three, pull!"

With everyone watching, the rookie pulled hard on the right arm. To his amazement, he fell backward with a totally separated arm dangling in his hand and lying in his back screaming! Needless to say, I almost pissed myself laughing wildly! While he was close to passing out and white as a sheet, I said, "This is a lesson to be learned. Floaters, after a few days in the water, have limbs that easily come off if pulled. Let that be a lesson!"

Needless to say, he knew he had been had, but he took it in stride and started to stay calm. He later became a juvenile detective in the Sheriff's department and a damn good detective!

There are times as a patrol officer, you have incidents that test your ability to maintain restraint on the job. On one particularly beautiful day, I was enjoying my patrol shift when the dispatcher called my unit number.

"1-0-1, proceed to the Day Motel. Lady needs assistance, possible child molestation.

"1-0-1,10-4!"

"1-0-1, 1-0-2, on my way to assist!"

"10-4."

This motel was a 10-unit motel whose clientele was mainly people seeking employment or passing through for the night in an area known to be high in drifters and troublemakers.

My backup was an ex-highway patrol officer who was a hell of a good cop and great friend. He was built like a linebacker and when challenged, you knew that the attacker was about to get an ass beating if his left eyebrow suddenly cocked up on his forehead. Trust me, you did not want to be on the receiving end of the blow when he launched it!

We arrived at the motel at the same time when I observed a lady who looked mortified with tears streaming down her face and who was waiting for us. As we approached her, she said in a quivering voice, "My little girl was molested by a man two doors down. she's slightly retarded and told me that the man asked her to come in his room to show him her baby doll."

"Did he do anything to her?" I asked.

The mom said, "He asked her to take her panties off."

"Ma'am, can we talk to her?"

"Yes, she is in our room!"

We entered the room and this beautiful six-year-old little girl smiled as we both said, "Hello!"

Rebel said, "Hi! You are so pretty, and I love that beautiful dress!"

"Thank you. Are you policemen?"

"Yes, we are. Can I ask you a question?"

"Yeah."

"Did a man ask you to see your baby today?"

"Yes," she replied, looking down with a sad face!

"It's Ok. Did he ask you to come in his room?"

"Yes."

"Did he ask you anything else?"

"He ask me to see my underwear and take them off!"

"What color were they?"

"Pink, he put them under his bed, and he touched me on my tee tee!"

I immediately tightened up and looked at Rebel and the left eye was cocked! I asked her, "Did he say anything else to you?"

She replied, "Yes. He said don't tell anyone about this. It's our secret, Ok?

Then he told me to go now and play and he opened the door, and I left, and I told my mommy that I met a nice man who kept my panties."

My backup and I told the mother who was trembling and hugging her little girl that we would confront this man. "We'll return shortly. Stay in your room."

Immediately, we proceeded to the room in question. We could hear a tv playing as we knocked on the door. A man opened the door and with a frowning look, we asked if we could come in. He agreed.

Without hesitating, my backup spoke and said, "You have a right to remain silent and a right to have an attorney…" continuing as he advised this piece of crap of his Miranda Rights.

The suspect started to run out the open door, and like lightning, Bobby threw a right hook at him, sending him flying across the bed, saying, "You scum! You're under arrest for child molesting and resisting arrest!"

"Fuck you! I know my rights," he shot back with a bloody lip and a swollen jaw all red from the powerful punch.

I immediately lifted the bed and saw a pink little girl's underwear. It took everything I had to restrain myself from giving this guy the beating of his life!

We transported this scum bag to jail and on the way back, he let go with a big glob of spit aimed at me, just as a dog was crossing in front of my car, causing me to immediately hit my breaks and throwing the suspect into the metal cage, slamming his face into the metal screen cage unit. The guy had an imprint of the caged unit on his face but, thank God, the dog was not hit!

When I booked the individual, the booking Sergeant looked at the suspect and said, "Another loose dog in the road again?"

Months later, the suspect pled guilty, and we learned that this was his third offense of child molestation.

Until this day, I am a firm believer that the law should be changed to castrate sex offenders or put them out of their pitiful misery by sentencing them with the death penalty.

I know that some will resent my feelings on this issue, but without actually seeing the pain and lifetime hurt to someone's loved one, then it's impossible to understand what this is really all about!

My backup later became my partner as a Detective in the Vice and Narcotic Division. There are times for police officers when they will encounter incidents that will test their personal integrity on the job!

8

Test of My Integrity

My first incident strangely occurred when I observed a white Cadillac convertible with two males and two females go through a red light at the intersection of State Road 84 and 441 in Fort Lauderdale. The vehicle turned left, heading east toward Port Everglades. I put my blue light on and when I fell behind the car, I observed it had a Quebec, Canada tag.

Getting out of my car, I overheard the driver saying to his male friend who was seated in the front seat say in French, "I know what he wants. Watch this!" He reached for his wallet and pulled out his driver's license along with a 20-dollar bill, holding it in his left hand.

I greeted the driver and advised him that he ran a red light and asked for his driver's license. The driver smiled and handed me his license with $20 behind it. I told him that I only needed his license, to which he said, "That's Ok! It's for you. You know what I mean?" Then he winked!

I responded, "Ok! Wait here. I need to get my Sergeant." Smiling, I walked to my car.

Even from that distance, I overheard him say in French," He was getting his partner so he can cash in also. I know how these cops work, I'll give him a bill also, and we are out of here!"

I radioed my Sergeant saying, "100, I need you for a backup, got a Canadian who just bribed me with a 20 and I advised him I was calling you, and he's ready to bribe you also! I'm taking this guy down for bribing a police officer. Just play along when you get here!"

"10-4, Frenchy. Almost there, just coming around the corner!"

"10-4."

The Sarge pulled up, and we both approached the vehicle. I addressed the driver and said, "This is my Sergeant. The driver reached out to shake his hand with a $20 in the palm of his hand! As he did, I said in French, "I hate to tell you this, but you are under arrest for bribing two police officers, smart ass! Get out of the car, now!"

His face went pale with total disbelief, hearing my French-Canadian accent and words. I placed him in the back of the police cruiser, and he pleaded for a break, telling me how sorry he was. After booking him and conferring with the Solicitor's Office, it was agreed that the charge would be reduced to Misdemeanor Attempted Bribery with a stiff fine.

This was a test of my integrity, but unfortunately, some officers have been known to accept this sort of bribe on a daily basis. Needless to say, I was praised by my Sergeant, and the word got around fast about this!

I'm a firm believer that any officer who lowers himself to accepting any money is a worse offender than the one doing the bribing and deserves to go to jail and removed from law enforcement.

One of the programs with the Sheriff's department was the Citizens Auxiliary Deputy Program, which allowed private citizens to ride with deputies once cleared by a background investigation. This program gave additional manpower resources to us, and the riders were given training as to their supporting role with deputies and were a welcome rider, especially on weekends.

My first encounter with one assigned to me was a professional businessman who became a friend and a regular with me for numerous months.

On a Friday night, he was waiting at the motor pool for me, and after our normal car check, we headed south to Carvers Ranch. As the evening passed, we had several calls of drunk and disorderly individuals at the Stock Car Racetrack, resulting in arrests! Returning back to the area from booking a drunk male, we received a call from the dispatcher advising us about a report of fighting outside the Stock Car complex on Pembroke Road involving several black males. Upon arriving with siren and blue light on, we observed a crowd surrounding two black males engaged in a knife fight! I advised my deputy rider that we needed to separate them and get them to drop their knives, with our police batons in hand!

We got out and ordered about 15 males and females to move aside, to which they immediately complied. I yelled at the two males, "Knock it off and drop the knives!"

To my right stood the auxiliary deputy. The male on his right complied, dropped his knife and backed off.

Suddenly, a bystander started to mouth off at me, and I turned to him and said, "One more word out of your mouth, you're going to jail!" With my back to the deputy, the second male to my left still with the knife lunged at me with a stabbing motion. The deputy reacted quickly, grabbing the attacker's knife hand and yelling, "Look out Frenchy!" I spun around and drew back as he took him to the ground, holding his arm with the knife. My next instinctive reaction to keep him from now injuring him, was a swift kick to his head, just like a football punter, kicking for a field goal! Needless to say, I nearly got stabbed and could have lost my life that evening if it hadn't been for the auxiliary deputy. This individual resisted arrest and was charged with aggravated assault on a police officer.

Every officer that I know always remembers his first close call and learns a hard lesson: Always be on guard. In those days, we were looked up to. Unfortunately, things are very different now, and police officers don't have the support of their community as we used to have. It's not everywhere, but where it does happen, it makes our job of law enforcement more difficult. Hopefully, the situation will return to how it was, once communities see that we are there for their protection.

9

The Ride Changes Again – Promotion to Detective – October 16, 1967

Patrol work was a great career, but deep down inside, I knew that I wanted more for myself and felt that one day I would have the opportunity to advance my career in law enforcement.

Never did I realize that my wish would come true so soon. Little did I know that my career was about to take me on a whole new adventure!

Stormy nights on patrol create numerous accidents to cover and lots of paperwork. This night was a heavy rainy night as I drove into Zone 2. I rounded the corner off Sunrise Boulevard into the Washington Park area of Fort Lauderdale. The rain made it extremely difficult to see.

As I was making a pass by a popular black bar that was known to have illegal dice gambling on the side of the building and frequent brawls, I suddenly observed a figure lying in a gutter along the curb in front of the bar. I immediately stopped so as not to run over him.

Cautiously, getting out of my patrol car, I could see a dirty looking male lying in the street alongside the curb where rainwater was gushing on his torn, grubby coat. He was holding a half-empty bottle of Jack Daniel in his dirty left arm, his body facing in the direction of the bar. Two black male door guards were standing under a covered door canvas roof, watching me and laughing. One said, "That son of a bitch is drunk and been there for the past hour!"

I leaned down, shook the drunk and said, "Get up, pal. You're going to get run over. You hear me?"

Softly in a whisper, he said, "I'm a cop. Leave and let me be! Get out of here now!

Suddenly I reacted and kicked him and said, "You piece of shit! If you won't get up, then stay there and get run over for all I care!"

I'm out of here. It's raining too hard for me to mess with you, asshole!"

Shaking my head, I walked away and got into my patrol car and drove off, avoiding running over him.

As I rode out of the area, I asked myself, *"Who in the hell was that?" I hope that I reacted Ok. Should I go back or not?* I decided not to and to wait and see in an hour if he was still there. I carefully listened on the radio to see if anyone called the dispatch about this, but nothing came over the air while I rode around until the end of my shift.

I kept going over that scene in my mind until finally, I pulled in the motor pool to sign off duty. As I pulled in, I observed the drunk, standing next to a dirty Ford sedan, smiling as he yelled at me and said, "Hey kid, I want to speak with you." He walked towards me, extending his left hand out to shake my hand. "I'm Detective Joe Clark (*deceased*) of vice and narcotics. I want to thank you on your quick thinking and reaction when I told you to get the hell away from me earlier. That was some quick thinking, and you saved me from being exposed. I was working undercover on the bar, doing a surveillance for a drug deal that went down after you left. I arrested two pukes who were selling heroin after you left."

Looking at him in disbelief and with total amazement, I was in awe of this and felt great that I had not blown this guy's undercover role. I said, "I'm glad I did not blow your cover and glad to know you!"

"How old are you, kid?" he asked as he looked up and down at me. "I'm 21, Sir!"

"Don't call me Sir! Do I look like I got bars on my shoulders?" He was laughing.

"No, you don't, but I just got out of the Army. I was an MP, and it's force of habit, Sir!" Now I was laughing.

"You were in the MPs. I'm a Korean vet. That's how I got this dangling right arm that almost got blown off in a battle during the Korean War."

"I'm sorry to hear that!"

"Don't be. It makes my UC cover real good. Bad guys never suspect me to be a cop with this arm flailing around."

"Wow! That sounds like exciting work! I would love to do that someday!"

"Well, kid, thanks again, and I liked the way you quickly adjusted to what you heard, and I think you have a future with us! Have a good one, and I will see you soon," he said as he smiled, got into his car and drove off.

When I went upstairs to the patrol room to do my reports, my Sergeant came up to me and said, "Frenchy, I just got a call from Detective Joe Clark of the Vice Squad. He told me that you did a great job tonight by not blowing his cover. He said that he will be in touch with you soon, and he won't forget this night! Good job, Frenchy! Joe is the best this department has. He has balls of steel, but he's never called me about any of my guys before. You're the first! Good job!"

"Thanks, Sarge!"

The Sheriff's Department in Broward County in the sixties was small. Promotions from patrol officer to detective were rare because at least five years' experience on the road patrol was required to even be considered for a promotion, or the officer had to have a damn good hook to move up or be a great ass kisser.

There were occasions when the kiss asses got promoted, but they were on the shit list by those of us who earned our stripes the proper way–with great work ethics and hard-earned work. One of the problems was when elections for Sheriffs occurred, whoever was in power expected his employees to be loyal to him, and if they didn't support him and he was re-elected, then those who opposed him were out of a job the night of the election.

I never thought that I would be a detective until I had my time in, and I was never one to suck up and kiss ass in my entire career to get ahead in any department.

One year had gone by since my being sworn in as a deputy Sheriff, and a day I will never forget. It was October 16, 1967, as I was coming to work as usual. I walked into the squad room while our Sergeant was holding his shift change meeting when our Captain walked in and said he had an announcement to make. He said, "I wanted to meet with you all to say that I'm proud to announce that Pete Charette has just been promoted to detective and has been assigned to report for work to Lt. Cecil Stewart head of the BSO Vice Squad effective immediately. This promotion comes directly from Sheriff Michell. Pete, I personally want to congratulate you for this promotion. This makes you the youngest detective to be promoted in this department."

I stood there frozen still and did not know what to say as the squad applauded and guys shouted, "Way to go, Frenchy!"

The Captain asked me to come to his office and presented me with the transfer memo from the Sheriff. With a smile, he said, "Frenchy, I'm proud of you. I never had anyone get promoted so fast, and you did it on your own merit, with hard work and an unbelievable knack to make cases and earning praise from everyone in this department. You have the unbelievable ability to uncover major violations through your unique talent. Not many cops have this special gift, so keep up your good work. I hate to lose you!"

"Captain, I'm honored and thank you for supporting me. I won't let you down!"

I returned back to the squad and couldn't believe that this was actually happening! Sergeant was grinning and said, "Frenchy, I'm going to hate to lose you. There was never a dull moment when you were out there. Just remember that we are here to support you and help you anytime you need our help, Detective Charette!"

Choked up and almost on the verge of tears, I said, "Guys, I won't let you down. You are the best!"

"Frenchy?"

"Yeah, Sarge!"

"Lieutenant Stewart wants you to report Monday morning to the vice squad at 8:00 a.m. in civilian clothes, You're going to need to buy yourself a small snub nose gun. You're now a 'Dick!'" he said as he laughed!

"Got it!"

As I left the squad room, I looked around and thought as I left, *I plan to be the best in my field. Thank you, God, for always being there for me.*

I drove home that night with all kinds of thoughts flashing in my mind about this new assignment. I arrived home in Miramar and could tell that my parents were still up watching tv. When I walked in, my mom already had a cup of coffee waiting for me as always. Dad said,

"There's my boy! How was work?"

"Ok! Great night! Something happened tonight that I need to talk to you both about!"

"Oh my God, something happened. I knew that this job was too dangerous!" Mom said.

"Mom, no! You worry too much, this is good! I was promoted tonight to a vice detective!"

"What? Did you say detective?" Dad asked.

"Yes, it was a shock to me too. I report to work tomorrow."

Dad slowly got up and came over to me then he wrapped his arms around me and said,

"Pete, I'm so proud of you. I know you will be a great one!"

Mom jumped up, started crying and said, "Now, I will worry even more about you! Damn! I'm happy for you." She wrapped her arms around me and said, "Please promise me that you will be careful, and if you do things that are dangerous, I don't want to hear about them!"

"Mom, I promise I will be careful, and I'm sure that stuff we do will be in the paper, but I promise it will be all good!" I smiled to ease her worries!

I went to bed that night with the greatest high one could get from this news. I thanked God for keeping me safe so far and prayed that he would continue to keep me safe along with all my brothers in blue!

I realized then that the 'ride' was beginning to become even more exciting.

I woke up on Saturday morning and planned my day to go purchase a Detective Snub Nose .38 Caliber 2-inch S&W pistol. My parents were already up having coffee in the kitchen as I sat down for breakfast. I told them my plans for the day, and Dad asked if he could come along. I gladly agreed. We left the house and went to Hollywood Boulevard in town to purchase my weapon and detective I.D. wallet.

Once again, Dad purchased my weapon as a promotion gift as he was beaming proudly to tell the Salesman that his son just had been promoted to detective. This was a side of my dad that I never saw, and I enjoyed every minute of it.

When we got home, Dad and I had a beer by the pool and he said, "Pete, I need to say something, to tell you that vice work as I know from cops that I have met, can be dangerous and have a lot of opportunities for corruption. Like I told you when you became a police officer, don't ever give up your integrity, no matter what! I want you to be a great cop. Don't ever give in to corruption. That's all I ask of you!"

"Dad! I will keep my promise to you that this will never be!"

"I believe you and please be careful." I could see his eyes were watery, and he was holding back from showing his weak side!" I never forgot that moment, and I only wish that my dad could still be around!

Monday morning, I was up at 5:00 a.m., nervous as hell and put on a white shirt that Mom had gotten the night before, insisting that it had to be starched and ironed. As I got ready, I put my gun in its holster on my waist. Mom watched me then immediately left the room. I could hear her crying in her bedroom, but Dad told me, "Go ahead to work. She'll be fine."

One thing that my four brothers learned growing up was that Mom was overprotective of her five boys, and at times Dad had to step in to make her back off. What can I say? Motherly love doesn't diminish as we grow older.

I arrived at the Courthouse at 7:30 a.m., took the elevator to the eighth floor and walked down the hall of the Detective Division to a door that read Vice Squad. Upon entering, I was greeted by Lieutenant Cecil Stewart, who was speaking with the secretary. Stewart looked at me with a big smile and said as he reached out his hand to shake mine,

"Frenchy! Congratulations, Detective Charette. Welcome to the Crazy Squad. I told you I would be seeing you again." He laughed.

"Yes, Sir, lieutenant. Thank you for this honor and opportunity, Sir!"

"Frenchy, you earned it on your own, and it's Cecil off the job and lieutenant in the office. And dispense with sir."

"Ok, lieutenant!"

"Good, this is our secretary and mother to all of us. She covers for us, and we take good care of her. She's actually a pain in the ass, but we all love her," he said as he laughed out loud.

"You're a kid! Are you sure you're old enough for this!" she exclaimed with a broad smile.

"I hope so!" I answered.

"Frenchy, meet the rest of the wild bunch. This is Lieutenant Joe Pierce (*deceased*). And this is ex-NYPD Detective Jimmy Nugent (*deceased*). He works bookmakers and racetrack mob violators, and last but not least, Sergeant Joe Clark (*deceased*), head of the narcotics section. I think you two met recently?"

"I told you that I would see you soon. Glad to have you on board. We will be working closely together."

"Thank you so much for this opportunity, I'm proud to be here and be part of the Wild Bunch!"

"Ok, here's your desk. Let's go in my office and talk."

Joe Clark looked at me smiling, gave me a wink, and said, "Watch him. He's a softie. His bark is harmless!"

Stewart's reputation I learned was impeccable in the Sheriff's department, and his integrity was beyond reproach. He stood behind his team and took no crap from anyone. His leadership was simple –do your job to the best of your ability, don't lie to me, we don't talk about any case we work on, not even to the Sheriff or Chief of detectives. His reason for this was his belief that if he kept his investigations from management and the Sheriff, then no one could accuse him of covering up for anyone who might be connected illegally with suspects. He believed in the saying, "Let the chips fall where they may."

The best way to describe Lieutenant Stewart is to picture the movie actor Ernest Borgnine! He stood tall, about 6'1", big-chested with muscular arms and big hands. His voice was raspy, and he always smiled when he talked to you. The lieutenant never lost his cool, but you knew when he was ready to cut loose when his blue eyes looked at you with daggers! If he clenched his fist at suspects who gave him hell, you knew that this stupid idiot was going to be laid out with one punch! He had a sort of a dirty laugh that sounded a bit perverted at times, causing everyone to burst out laughing!

The lieutenant was very protective and loyal to his team, and we were the same with him. The one thing I learned quickly from this man was that honor and loyalty to your teammate was a must in law enforcement. If we discovered that someone was not preserving this moral code, then we had a duty to report any violation of the badge of honor that we wore and took an oath to support for the rest of our honorable career. I lived my entire 33 years in law enforcement and am proud to say that I never forgot this principle! Closing the door, he pointed to a seat which I took, and he began, "I want you to know that the first encounter with you, when I ordered you to arrest your shift lieutenant for being involved with that prostitution ring, I was impressed on what you did, and to keep it to yourself, that took guts! I had a gut feeling about you. I knew that I wanted you in our Wild Bunch." He continued, "And when Sergeant Clark told me about what you did to keep his cover, that reinforced my feelings. I did my homework discretely about you and was impressed with your patrol cases and your military background." I sat there listening to him continue to speak. "I spoke with the Sheriff about you, and he immediately approved my request to have you. We are going to teach you all aspects of vice work, and you will be assigned to work with these guys for a month at a time and do some undercover night club work at strip joints since you don't even look like a cop!"

"Lieutenant, I appreciate your confidence in me, and I'm ready to learn and go to work!"

"Great! See our den mother secretary. She will give you paperwork for your reimbursement of the use of your private car for work and get the tech unit to install an undercover radio in it."

Detectives in the sixties had to use their personal vehicles for work and were paid for mileage by the department! One can imagine the wear and tear this caused on one's POV (personally owned vehicle)! You accepted it and did your job. During my first week, I was assigned to be with Sergeant Fish, who was in charge of us as detectives.

The vice squad detectives specialized in gambling investigations, organized crime, prostitution and bars and striptease clubs. This involved doing undercover work in all these areas and in the development of confidential sources. You never knew what to expect when you went on duty. The hours were never scheduled, and most of the work was night work, with the exception of gambling cases.

Fish did not waste any time putting me to work in an undercover capacity, working the strip bars on US 1 Highway by the Ft. Lauderdale Airport in Dania. He pointed out to me three bars on the strip and told me that these strip joints had B (burlesque girls) working on commissions, encouraging the male clients to buy them drinks, which was a violation of Florida law called Solicitation!

He said, "Frenchy, we want you tonight to go in as a client and sit at the bar, buy a drink and enjoy the show. Usually, girls will be sitting at the end of the bar. Eventually, they will approach you and engage you in a conversation. They will begin by rubbing your knee and grabbing your privates and asking you to buy them a drink. If the bartender asks you if you are going to buy her a drink, go ahead and agree!"

"That sounds easy to me, no problem. I can string them along."

"The thing you have to watch out for, is that they will run their hands over your sides to see if you're carrying a gun or feel a badge! Don't wear a gun on your waist, strap your piece to your ankle. Once you buy her a drink, she will try to get you to buy a drink for another girlfriend. Just tell her that you always wanted a threesome! Once the other comes, buy her drink and if they suggest sitting in a booth, go ahead and agree! For every drink you buy them, that's separate counts of Solicitation!" I sat there, very intrigued. "We will give you 30 minutes and then come in and conduct a bar check. The girls will try to get you to say that they are with you, just having a good time! That's when you ID yourself as a detective! Any questions?" Understanding the procedure, he concluded, "I will give you $300 in marked bills for the drinks!"

"Got it! Sounds easy and I'm ready!"

"Oh, by the way, don't be surprised on your first time if you get a 'A tilt in your quilt' from the rubbing of 'little Frenchy'!" He laughed! Then he told me to go home and change into my stud gear, laughing! "we'll meet at 10:00 p.m. at the motor pool."

Fish was a big, strongly built man who spoke softly with authority and knowledge of his job. He had a great sense of humor and was always emphasizing for us not to discuss our business with others in the department. Unfortunately, the early sixties in law enforcement was divided at times by politics, corruption, and at times, questionable on its tactics and method of operation. It was not a custom to advise defendants of their Miranda Rights, which gave a lot a latitude to police officers. For the most part, law enforcement officers respected people's rights, except for some who didn't and, as a result, gave the rest of us a bad name. The ones who opposed Miranda were usually the ones who violated it. Eventually, Miranda Rights corrected this unfortunate violation of People's Rights.

I went home and changed into my 'stud gear' and when I told my dad of my assignment, he laughed and told me not to say anything to my mom; otherwise, she would insist on my going to confession on Friday!

10

My First Undercover Assignment

As I was walking out of the house to go to my first assignment, I could tell that my mother was worried when I walked over to say goodnight. She looked at me with tears in her eyes and said, "I'm telling you right now I don't like this one bit, and you better be careful, or so help me I will never speak to you again!"

"Mom! It's Ok. It's my work, and I would never do anything that would endanger me," fully knowing that I loved this crazy and dangerous life.

"I know you. You love it! And you're just trying to make me feel good! Damn you, I love you, and I can't help but worry! Just be careful. Now get out of here," she said as she kissed me goodbye!"

Dad said while smiling, "Go get them, Cowboy." He gave me a wink displaying a proud grin on his face.

I drove off in my Mustang and thanked God for having such great parents. All the way to the Sheriff's office, I kept going through various scenarios that could happen and going over what I needed to do once I entered the bar.

During the sixties, courses in undercover work as a police officer didn't exist. Officers were basically on their own, and they picked up techniques from seasoned officers as they went along in this type of highly dangerous job.

I learned quickly that undercover officers who worked in this specialized field had to be constantly vigilant and assess their surroundings and the subjects who are the targets. Any officer who claims he is not scared when dealing with criminals in an undercover capacity is a danger to himself and to his partners and team members working with him. I can say without hesitation that every time I worked undercover, I was scared and did my homework prior to meeting violators to ensure that I had planned an exit strategy along with making sure that my story, if confronted by the suspicious suspect, could be corroborated by the bad guys in order to maintain my undercover identity. I can't stress this enough because our lives depend on being able to make a quick decision to keep ourselves alive and to protect our back up officers.

As I arrived at the motor pool, I saw the vice squad team there, ready for this night's work. I was greeted by Lieutenant Stewart who said, "Frenchy, are you ready to have fun?"

"Yes, Sir, scared but ready."

"Good. Just be yourself when you go in and enjoy it. Remember, these broads will be feeling you to make sure you don't have a gun or wire on you! Just make sure your piece is on your ankle just in case you need it!"

"Yes, Sir."

"When we go in, act natural until I ask you for some ID, and that's when you say, 'I'm a cop' and place her under arrest! "The more the better it is. So, spend time chit-chatting with the ladies and let them ask you for a drink. If the bartender asks you if you're buying for the ladies just respond, 'Yeah why not!'"

"Got it."

"I want you to meet this guy here. This is our state beverage agent, and he's with the Florida Beverage Commission. He's going to be with us and will charge the owner and bartender for violating the beverage laws."

"Pleasure to meet you, Sir. Looking forward to working with you!"

"Same here. Heard good things about you. Welcome to the crazy world of ours."

Stewart broke into the conversation. "Ok everyone, let's head out and remember, we don't take no shit from anyone and let's keep it under control. And Frenchy, you're going to do just fine!"

We drove off and I took a deep breath. *Relax! Act natural and please, God, watch over all of us on this one!*

The strip club was located on US-1 in Dania, south of the Fort Lauderdale Airport. As I arrived, I noticed several cars in the front parking lot. Taking a deep breath, I entered the club to the sound of music playing. To my right was the bar and a couple of male clients enjoying the stripper who was performing a striptease dance, and two girls were enjoying drinks with them.

To my left along the wall were individual booths with clients watching the show and B-girls entertaining them. I could see one of the girls rubbing a client's crotch and caressing him around the neck.

I scanned around the club for a quick exit door and saw an exit sign in the back. Part of being an undercover agent is to know an escape route always before any meetings. Too many agents have gotten hurt by being too cocky or fearless.

The bartender greeted me and said, "What'll you have?"

"I'll have a gin and tonic," I answered as I sat down at the bar.

"Gin and tonic coming right up."

From out of nowhere, a beautiful blond wearing an evening gown walked up from a table, sat down and said, "Hey, handsome, care for some company?"

"Sure, where you from?"

"I'm just passing through and stopped by to see a friend of mine who works here! What about you?"

"I'm just vacationing here."

"Are you married? She asked.

"No, too young for that. Just a happy bachelor!" I answered, laughing.

"I can make you really happy if you buy me a drink?" her voice became sexier as she began to rub my leg close to my groin with a big smile.

"Sounds good to me. What can I buy you?"

The bartender worked his way back to me and asked, "Are you going to buy the lady a drink, kid?"

"Sure, why not?" *Gotcha both, you idiots.*

"What will you have, lady?"

"The usual. A glass of champagne."

"Give the lady champagne! You have expensive taste, eh?" she asked as she began to rub my side and back with her hands to check me over for a wire or gun.

"Just call me Frenchy I'm from Canada."

"Here's your drink! That will be $30.00 for two drinks."

"Here's $35.00."

"Thanks! Enjoy yourself."

My new friend said," Let's go sit in a booth and watch the show. It's more private there!"

"Sounds good to me." We got up and walked to a booth.

As we sat down, another female got up from a table where other showgirls were sitting, came over and sat down next to me also then said, "Who is this good-looking guy? She was rubbing my thigh too.

"This is Frenchy. He's a Canadian."

"Hi! You work here also?"

"Oh yeah, I'm on break. I sure could use a drink too."

"Give this lady here a drink!"

"The usual! coming up."

She asked, "How long are you here for?" She continued rubbing my inner thigh.

"At least a week. Just vacationing from work!"

"Here's one special drink! Champagne for the lady!"

Music was playing, and a young stripper was doing her slow grinding dance, stripping down to her G-string and topless breast! Before long, the door to the entrance opened and in came Lieutenant Stewart, the Sergeant and a couple of uniformed deputies and an unknown small-built man about 5'9" and wearing a suit and a badge holder over his outside coat breast pocket. He appeared to be in his early thirties.

Both girls said at the same time, "Damn! It's a raid!"

"What's going on?" I asked, acting nervous.

"Just say that we are together out for the night!"

"Ok. No problem."

"I'm from the Florida Beverage Department here with the Broward Sheriff's Department Vice Squad. Everybody remain still and calm!"

Once the premise was secured, Lieutenant Stewart and Sergeant Fish started to ask customers for IDs. They worked their way to where I was sitting and started asking for some IDs!

Stewart said, "Good evening, young man. You have any ID? You look too young to be in a bar."

"Yes, Sir. I'm 21, and I have some right here!" I Reached in my back wallet and continued, "These are friends of mine who are with me, right?"

Looking at each other, one of them spoke up smiling. "Yeah, that's right."

I slowly pulled out my ID credential and said, "Ladies, I'm Detective Charette with the Vice Squad, and you're both under arrest for soliciting drinks under Florida law!"

"You son of a bitch!"

"Thank you for the compliment," I said.

"Lieutenant, the bartender there also is under arrest for soliciting!"

"Pete!" the agent said, "one count or two counts?"

"Two counts in all!"

"Great! Officer, can you please go outside, get my boss and tell him to come in please."

"Yes, Sir!"

The agent's boss came in and Lieutenant Stewart asked the manager of the bar who had come out of his office to come over. "Sir! Let me introduce you to the Commissioner of the Florida State Beverage Department from Tallahassee."

The manager started to laugh and, in a sarcastic way, said, "Sure he is!"

The Commissioner began, "Let me assure you I am who they say I am." He reached for the Night Club License that was in a picture frame over the bar. He took it off the wall, pulled out his ID and showed it to the manager, pointing to the name on the license saying, "Now, any more doubt, because I'm closing you down, and you can come to

Tallahassee for your Revocation Hearing, Sir!" Turning to Stewart, he continued, "Lieutenant, close this establishment down now! Have a good night, Sir!"

Stewart told the deputies to transport the suspect to jail, and an agent placed a notice of closure on the door. We left and regrouped at the Fort Lauderdale Airport parking lot and continued our night's work at two other establishments. I posed as a customer again and two more establishments were closed that night.

When we finished work that night, we were all pleased, and Stewart said to me, "Frenchy, hell of a good job! You're going to do just fine. Sarge will help you with the paperwork and acquaint you to the solicitor's office tomorrow to file the charges and appear in court before the judge for a bond hearing on these people. Have a good night. See you at noon!"

"Thanks, Lieutenant! See you later!"

Everybody parted, and I headed home around 5:00 a.m. with a feeling of excitement knowing now more than ever that this was my calling.

11

Vice Investigation Training

As a new detective in the vice division, the numerous duties and procedures can only be learned from seasoned detectives in this line of work and by hands-on training with various tools used in this line of work. The vice squad duties were to investigate prostitution and gambling offenses such as bookmaking, lottery, illegal gambling, liquor violations and organized crime. Training in these areas can be complex and dangerous when working in an undercover role.

One of the most important parts of any investigation is the report writing of any cases. In report writing for any prosecution, all investigative actions must be reduced to writing. Along with the making of a case, is learning how to memorize the actual details of the case that will lead to a successful prosecution. If the details aren't properly organized in chronological order in a written report as they occurred, then those detectives are heading for failure to get a conviction in court. No serious law enforcement officer wants to be subject to criticism from the court and prosecution attorneys because his credibility will be constantly judged and questioned right from the start. In addition, this damaged credibility will linger later in his career because defense attorneys will ensure that his credibility will be passed on to other defense attorneys and will be used against him in future cases to discredit his testimony.

Every detail of time, conversation, observations, and actions must be memorized once the undercover meetings or arrests are completed. Then they must be recorded and reduced to writing everything that was said and done by all involved! If not documented while memory of the facts are fresh in mind, the delay may result in a lost case due to a simple omission of the facts!

In any UC investigations, one of the best tools to use when feasible is choosing the location for meetings so that surveillance teams can photograph the meetings and also have an electronic recording of the conversation. There are times when this is not possible or too risky for detection by the suspects. This is a decision that needs to be made by all involved, and after weighing all the options together, the final decision should always be the undercover agents' call.

I personally know this and have lived by this because I lost a friend and a great agent who was killed when acting in an undercover assignment. He did not like the arrangements made by the supervisor and made it known, but he was still ordered to do it. As a result, he lost his life!

Unfortunately, the supervisor had to live with this tragedy, and one hell of a lesson was learned by this bad call.

When deciding to be in this type of work, the risk of one's life or the life of a colleague is ever-present. Too many undercover agents have failed at this line of work because their egos got in the way resulting in a failed investigation or a co-worker getting injured or killed.

As soon as I got to work after my first UC operation that day, Sergeant sat me down and with our den mother, secretary and him, he basically debriefed me on my entire evening at these clubs ensuring all details were covered on paper and all conversations documented in a step-by-step chronological order which was corroborated with other surveillance officers' observations and supervisors' reports. By the time we had this completed, we spent close to five hours putting the case together.

From this debriefing, I learned to always make sure that I and the surveillance officers and agents didn't put erroneous information in reports that were not seen or done by me or them. This is called fraudulent reporting, and if testified under oath, it's called perjury. The reason I say this is because I have actually experienced hearing a fellow detective testify as a surveillance officer on one of my UC cases after I had been excused and allowed to sit in the courtroom.

I heard him give false surveillance testimony. I personally asked the prosecutor to speak with him, and the judge called for a recess. I advised the judge who was a friend that this person had committed perjury and requested that the case be dismissed. This was unheard of in those days. In the end, the prosecutor agreed, and the case was dismissed.

The detective admitted to his supervisor that he didn't think that by saying he had seen the suspect give the drug to me, it would cause an issue and would only strengthen the case. This individual was removed from his position and eventually resigned from the Sheriff's department. No case is worth prosecuting if facts are omitted or fabricated.

After doing our case preparation, Sergeant Fish took me to the solicitor's office in the Broward County Courthouse. I was introduced to Chief of the Solicitors Criminal Department, who at one time had been a Florida State Trooper and went on to law school to become a prosecuting attorney for Broward County.

The case was accepted for prosecution and all parties pled guilty to the offense. Learning how to prepare for a case with this type of training is extremely important and should be taken seriously.

12

Bookmakers/Gambling Investigation Training

After working the B-Clubs, I was assigned to be trained by Detective Jim Nugent, a retired NYPD Detective. Jimmy was in his late fifties, a silver-haired New Yorker with a deep voice and great New York accent! He always dressed casual like a retired Floridian: sport shirt, white slacks and white sandals. He could have played the part of a New York bookmaker or racetrack gambler anytime.

Fish called Jimmy in and asked him to take me under his wing for a month to learn about bookmaking, off-track betting, and gambling. Jimmy said, "Ok, Frenchy! You and I are heading out now. We're going to the Gulf Stream Horse Track to start!"

"Ready when you are."

"Frenchy, what I do is to go there and make sure you don't let the Racing Commission investigators know that you are there. First thing you need to learn is never alert these guys that you're working the track! We don't know who to trust. These guys do a half-ass job and allow known mobsters who have criminal records to be on the premise when state law prohibits convicted felons from being on any racing facility. The law is punishable by a two-year offense. They look the other way and are scared shitless of these guys.

"That's bullshit!"

"Oh, I can tell, you and I will do well together. That's what I like to hear! I was told that you were good and love the job!"

"Jimmy, I want to learn and was told you were the master at your job!"

"I see Cecil's been talking to you. He's one of my best fans!"

"Yeah, he speaks highly of you, I think the world of him, and he has guts and does not take any crap from anyone!"

"They don't come any better than him, that's for sure, kid!"

As we arrived, we parked in the front lot and Jimmy told me, "Never badge your way in! We'll go in like father and son and sit in the grandstand to the left of the finish line, four rows back near the fence line." He explained that the track undesirables will always sit or stand by the fence line and try not to be visible. Usually, the winter mob crowd of New York wise guys try to stay away from the center bleachers, so they don't get caught on tv.

We came in and sat four rows to the left. Jimmy, prior to going in, had handed me a pair of binoculars. He also had one. Jimmy said, "Ok, now look by the fence line and don't use your 'nocs,' just your eyes, and look for guys who look around intermittently, who are scanning their surroundings for cops!"

"Ok, got it." I started looking, and after a while saw two white guys who looked in their mid-forties wearing nice silk shirts. Jimmy was scanning the stands with his 'nocs' before the race started and said, "Jimmy! I got two Goombahs acting a little strange! One's wearing a black silk shirt and the other a white silk shirt, open collar, over by the fence!"

"Got them, Frenchy! Yep! Looking a little nervous, all right! We'll keep a sight on them. No need to act right now. Between races, I'll get my photo book from NYPD vice out of the car that I have on guys that come down for the winter and see if they are in our book! Ok, let's go make a Daily Double Bet so we look normal."

"Sounds good to me. I've never been to the track before."

"Wow, you are a virgin! Love it. Maybe we will be lucky!" He laughed.

Jimmy and I place bets on the Daily Double and returned to our seats to watch the races. He advised me that when the fourth race started, we would leave and go position ourselves by the front exit gate which faces U.S. 1 in Hallandale. Jimmy said to watch for any males coming out in a hurry and making a beeline toward the small motel across U.S. 1 to our left. Once we spotted a 'runner,' we needed to follow him and see if he goes to the payphone booth located on the side of the motel office.

The fourth race ended, and we spotted a young male hurrying out of the complex and making a beeline for the motel. Jimmy said, "Ok, Frenchy, go to the right and set up behind a vehicle and watch him with your nocs. Let me know if he gets in the phone booth and makes a call!"

"Ok, I'm on it."

I ran to the rear of a pickup truck where I positioned myself. Then I observed him open the door to the phone booth and immediately drop quarters into the phone to place a call, holding a sheet of paper in his hand. He appeared to be reading from the note as he spoke on the phone. This call lasted less than five minutes, after which the suspect hung up, looked around and casually walked back to the track. I signaled Jimmy a thumbs-up sign, and he leisurely started back to the track and observed him sitting to the left side in the back row near the front exit.

Jimmy said, "Ok, Frenchy, we got a spotter for bookmakers! Now here's where it gets fun. After the next race, this guy is going to repeat what he just did and call in the race result for the fifth race to the bookies and give the win, show and place dollar amount to his associates.

Race results can't be released immediately, and by doing this, it allows the bookies to lay off bets that are winners to offset their loss before the official call is made by the racetrack. I'm going to go and get in position, so when he goes back, you are going to be in the booth acting like you're on the phone, and he will be waiting to make a call! I will start across the highway, and when you see me coming across, hang up and slowly exit and let him in. Then walk around the corner by the office as if you're going into the motel court.

"Hopefully, he will be in a hurry to make his call, and I will stand outside the door like I'm waiting to make a call. He will have his back to me, and I will memorize the number being called and let him do his thing and listen to his conversation. Once he hangs up and starts to exit, you come around, and we will take him down to the ground immediately!"

"Ok! Got it, Jimmy."

"When the race starts, you head out when the horses are on the half-mile post. Got it?"

"Yep!"

When the fifth race started, I left when the riders were at the half-mile post and exited the park to go into the booth. I held the hand-phone as I watched the track parking lot for our guy! Within five minutes, I spotted the target walking fast in my direction. I turned sideways, leaning back and having a conversation with myself and laughing and when the target stood by the door, I looked at him, I smiled and saw Jimmy walking across coming toward the booth. I said loudly,

"Ok, I'll see you tomorrow" and pointed one finger up to the target to indicate 'in a second' and said, "I Love you!" I hung up and opened the door, saying, "It's all yours; have a good day!" Then I walked around to the office area of the motel.

I heard the target saying as I left, "I won't be long" to Jimmy, who was behind him waiting to make a call also!

Jimmy was heard to say, "No problem, pal. No hurry!"

I stood by the corner of the office and heard the sliding door of the phone booth open and the target said, "All yours, pal with a New York accent. I stared around the corner of the office and saw Jimmy flashing his badge saying, "Police! On the ground, now!"

"What the hell is going on, you mother fucker?"

"You're under arrest for off-track betting," I said as I helped handcuff the suspect!

"We're with the vice squad," said Jimmy as he removed from his clenched left fist the paper that had the race data and money post for the fifth race.

"I got him, Jimmy. Get up!"

"Frenchy, I got the number he called, and I'm calling my NYPD contacts to give them the info and PC (probable cause for a search warrant).” Search his pockets for papers with previous race results for the first, second, third, and fourth races. We'll give it to NYPD.”

“Got it, pal. I'm going into your pocket.” When I went in, I pulled out four slips with all the race result data on it!”

“Great, Frenchy! Let's call Hallandale PD and get Chief Emerich (*deceased*) on the phone to fill him in on this!

“Ok! You sit your buns on the ground now!” I made a call to HPD and within two to three minutes, a uniformed HPD Unit arrived as well as an unmarked car with blue light flashing.

“Hi, I'm Detective John. Hey, Jimmy.”

“Hi! On the phone with NYPD now. Be with you in a few! Meet Frenchy, new kid on the block,” he said as he pointed to me smiling.

“Hi. Pete Charette. Pleasure to meet you, sir!”

“Wait a minute. Did you say Charette?”

“Yes, Sir!”

“It's Frenchy. Is your Dad Phil Charette, Manager of the Moongate Motel on the beach?”

“Yeah, that's my dad.”

“He's a great friend of ours. We usually go there after work for a few brews at the bar!”

“Looks like we will be working together. I'm new in Vice for BSO!”

“You're a lucky guy to get that job! Stewart and his guys work closely with us. Jimmy is the best!”

“Yep! This guy was calling race results to New York. We nailed him and got his race results on paper. Jimmy's calling NYPD to give them PC for a search warrant.”

“Great! We depend on you guys because everybody knows us since we are so small. So, you have our support for anything!”

“Great! I'll be working with you closely; that's for sure and will come and see the Chief! He will remember me from my high school days! He was an influence on me for being a cop!”

“Ok, let's get this guy out of here. We'll take him in and book him and call your paddy wagon to transfer him over to your jail!”

“Sounds good.”

After all our administrative paperwork was completed, Jimmy and I returned back to the office and briefed Lieutenant Stewart of this arrest. Stewart said, "Great job, both of you! Jimmy is a human bloodhound when it comes to this type of work. You are being trained by the master of gambling investigations!"

"Thanks, I learned that firsthand and proud to be trained by him!"

"All right, the bullshit is getting deep enough!" We all laughed and went back into the squad car.

Jimmy and I learned from NYPD that our info paid off. They busted a major bookmaking operation from our info. My training showed me that cooperating with other agencies like we did today pays off if information is shared and not withheld from others.

The key to this is to contact one's counterparts and show a willingness to work jointly with them in their jurisdiction. It is important to make the case a joint operation to achieve success in eliminating criminal activity for the good of the community and not for the good of one's ego and self-recognition. Once the case is made, then an agreement can be made on a joint press release. This will lead to future trust and sharing of information. It is surprising how quickly requests for assistance and new cases arise as a result of this type of cooperation.

Federal, state, local officers, or detectives are no better than others in the same field of work. Those who carry this chip on their shoulders are to blame for creating a bad image for the rest of us. If I found out that one of my colleagues showed this lack of respect on the job, I immediately took action and knocked them down to size.

That is not to say, that if we encounter personalities who upon contact act arrogant, abrasive, demanding and controlling due to their level of authority or agency title, then we should have every right to politely decline their request to cooperate jointly with them or share information, or be like some us from the 'old school' to kindly tell them to "Fuck Off!"

I have to be the first to admit that I have encountered these individuals throughout my career in my own organization in DEA, FBI, customs, and state and local agencies. Those who think that they are better than others because of their agency title are destined to be labeled as assholes because they give a bad name to their colleagues who are not in the above category. I truly believe that this has been a great part of law enforcement problems when it comes to cooperation among agencies!

Working with Jimmy the next day was once again, a new adventure to watch the master at work. We met at the office at 9:00 a.m. where the team was having coffee. The mood, as always, was pleasant, and everyone went over what they were working on and shared information with one another.

Jimmy spoke up and began to brief all of the team, "Yesterday, Frenchy and I popped an asshole at the track and helped NYPD nail a nice bookmaking ring in New York! The kid did well and believe it or not, I was impressed!"

Stewart said, laughing, "The kid is more like a high school senior by the way he looks!" He looked over at me and continued. "Have you started to shave yet?" More laughs erupted from the others. "Bet you haven't been broken in yet!" He laughed again.

Betty responded and said, "Um, maybe I need to get to know you better. I never had a teenager!" Now the room exploded with more laughter!

I had to jump in after that one, "Den mother, all I can say is that once you go French, you'll never be the same!"

"Cecil responded, "Now there's a challenge!" With that, he got everyone back on task and said, "Everybody, back to work, and be careful out there. Would someone get me a pry bar from the raid cabinet? I think we are going to have to pry our den mother loose from her chair after Frenchy's comment to her." He then winked at me.

The whole squad roared with laughter, and she slowly blew me a kiss. Then Jimmy added, "Ok, Frog, let's go. We're heading back to Gulfstream for another day to get another collar!"

"Let's ride, I'm ready to learn from my master!"

Jimmy said, "Today, you're going to see how we develop informants in order to bust bookmakers. We are going to look for an undesirable target and flip him! Once we spot the target, we discretely badge him and tell him to walk out with us discreetly. Then we give him a choice— go to jail for two years or play the game and give us a bookmaker in the area. Simple as that! They will always know who the bookies are and will give them up in a minute because they don't want to do the time! We tell them that they will be processed and released to work with us, and once we make the case, then we will have the charges dismissed by the Solicitor's Office for his cooperation. That's how it basically goes Ba Da Bing Ba Da BOOM!"

We arrived at the Gulfstream Racetrack, got our binoculars and headed into the grandstand. It was a typical, beautiful, sunny Florida day. Nice large winter crowded the racetrack, and we got ourselves a couple of beers along with Jimmy's favorite, a large pretzel! *Can't take the New York out of him*!

We seated ourselves just like before to the left and up four rows from the field fence.

Looking around, I espied my guy from the previous day with his silk shirt, greasy black hair, and fitting the profile of a typical wise guy from New York. You would think these studs would change their identical look, but they love to stand out!

"Jimmy, my guy from yesterday is back!"

"I see him. Let's go and introduce ourselves to this fine American," he stated cynically. "Just let me handle it and learn."

We worked our way along the fence line, stopping to lean on the fence rail while watching the horses being paraded around like others on the fence line. Finally, Jimmy eased himself next to our new soon-to-be friend.

"Hey, Frog, according to the scratch sheet seven, odds look pretty good today. I made $500 off that one last week, and I'm going to play him to win!"

"I'm in. You always come through, master."

"Hey! How you doing, pal? Any lucky one you like?" Jimmy said in his New York accent!

"Hey, You from Jersey? You sound like it!"

"Yeah, Rockaway! Where you from?"

"Brooklyn. Here for the winter! What about you guys?"

"Funny you ask! Here, let me show you. Jimmy had already had his shield in his hand behind his open racing form, showed him the shield, and said, "Nice and quiet, not a word, asshole. Walk out with us, or you will be in jail for a long time! Let's walk and smile," he ordered as he put his left arm around the man's back waist, slowly patting him down for a piece. "Great. Nice and clean! We're walking out and to the right and to our car!"

"No problem, man, I didn't do anything."

We walked out all smiling and laughing, put our new-found friend in the back seat of the car and drove off for the Sheriff's office.

"Ok! Here's the news of the day. You been arrested before, right? Yeah, convicted, right? For a felony, right?"

"Yeah. How you know all this?"

"I do my homework before I act! So, here's the scoop. Florida law says that convicted felons aren't allowed to be at gambling establishments, and if caught, it's punishable up to two years in prison. It's plain and simple. That's the law. My partner and I are vice detectives for the Broward Sheriff's Department."

"Man, you're fucking with me. I wasn't doing anything wrong. Just going to the track for the first time today while I'm on vacation."

"Wrong! You were here yesterday. We got a photograph of you here, and we sent them to NYPD Intelligence Bureau. They said you are a convicted felon and have some interesting associates in the Italian community. "How am I doing so far?"

"Man, I swear I'm not doing anything. Yeah, I like the track. I'm sure we can make this straight, what can I do?"

"BINGO! You said the magical words of great intelligence to help yourself! This is your lucky day. We have to book you, and we will make it quick and fast, no publicity. Then we will bring you upstairs, have the prosecutor agree to dismiss the charges if you willingly decide to cooperate with us and give us information on bookies you know here! That, my friend, is how easy it is. Like you guys always say, 'You wash my back, and I will wash yours.' Understood?"

"Yeah, yeah! I can't go back to jail again. You got me!"

"Ok, pal! We're here! Once we process you, we will come get you, and I'll have the prosecutor come up and tell you what he can do. See you in a while."

When we left the booking desk, I looked at Jimmy, who was grinning from ear to ear and said, "That's unbelievable, Jimmy. You were awesome and made it look so easy. Did you really have info in your NYPD book on this guy?"

Laughing, he said, "No, I was just playing him. These guys will give up their mothers to stay out of jail. Let's stop and see and get him to come up and tell him how the deal works: Cooperate, and if you do, then pass go, collect $200, and you get a free out of jail card. Simple as that!" He laughed.

Just as Jimmy said, the solicitor got the Ok for the deal, and our newly acquired friend began to help us in our investigations of illegal gambling activity.

Jimmy and I briefed Lieutenant Stewart of our pinch, and he advised us that it was time for Frenchy to venture out on his own to settle in and check out the county. He made sure to inform me that if I develop a target to advise Sergeant, and he would assign someone to work with me in a week as a partner. The Sergeant also advised me he was working on getting a new body who would be assigned to work with me. He emphasized to be careful and said he wasn't worried about my work, that I was a 'natural' for this.

13

Never a Dull Moment

I met with my Sergeant, who gave me my marching assignment and said, "Pete, Cecil told me that you were ready to be on your own for a week until we get the new guy. Just go out there and get acclimated with the bars, strip joints, and check with the intelligence guys on any possible targets of interest they may have for you. If you pick up anything, just call I and we will back you up! Don't do anything foolish! There's no rush in making a case or trying to prove yourself. We know we got the right guy for this, and you have nothing to prove. You already did this on your own."

"Thanks, Sarge, I won't do anything stupid, and I appreciate your support! I'm going to start by visiting the PDs in the county and introducing myself!"

"We got some great relationship with a lot of departments in the county. I would suggest that you hit the South End first with Hallandale, Miramar, Pembroke Pines, Hollywood, and Davie PDs first. Then work North, Oakland Park, Pompano, Lauderhill, and Davie PDs. All of these are working closely with us and we trust them! I've already talked to most of them that you were on board and would be dropping by! I'm glad we are on the same page, Pete! "Hit the road, Frenchy, and give it hell!" he said, laughing.

"Thanks, Sarge, will do my best!"

I left the office and pulled into the Motor Pool to gas up. Gassing up his patrol car was my buddy Rebel coming on the 4-12 shift! He yelled out, "Come here, you son of a bitch! How in the hell are you, Frenchy?" He gave me a crushing bear hug!

"I'm still pinching myself, can't believe it, man! This is a dream, and I'm sorry I haven't been in touch yet. Been in a training mode. It's awesome!"

"Man, you are the talk of the road. Everybody is happy for you. Do you realize you're the youngest detective ever promoted in this area?"

"That's what they say! I couldn't have done it by myself without you guys showing me the ropes out there for the past eight months!"

"Hell! Pete, I saw that you had it from our first get-together. Hey, I need to get going. How 'bout meeting for supper at the diner at seven?"

"You're on. Be careful, and I'll see you then. I'm buying. I'm making big bucks now! Ha-ha."

"Yeah, right! See you later. Thumbs up!"

✦✦✦✦✦

Rebel was an ex-state trooper who kind of looked like the movie actor Dennis Farina. He had a southern accent and was used as a stunt driver in a movie, which was about moonshiners who drove loads of moonshine through the North Carolina mountains. He could drive a car like no one I had ever seen!

He could do a full 360 turn at 60 mph and come out of it in the opposite direction without ever losing speed. I can attest to this because he trained me to do this while on patrol one night.

I recalled one night when we had just finished supper at the diner and observed a car being driven at a high speed going East on Hallandale Beach Boulevard from State Road 7. He gave pursuit with his blue light. I dropped behind him as the suspect tried to outrun us.

He advised dispatch that he was in hot pursuit. The suspect turned north on the on-ramp to I-95. The chase was at speeds of 90-95 miles per hour. He was right on this sob's bumper and he advised the Lieutenant by radio that he needed permission to 'bump' in order to prevent someone from getting killed. He knew at that time that I-95 ended at State Road 84, and the suspect was going to take the off-ramp and exit right.

He got the go! As predicted, the suspect slowed down to get off and take a quick right. He knew how to do it and sped up to hit the suspect's right rear bumper as he turned fast and slammed on the brakes. I did also, knowing what was going to happen next. The suspect's car immediately flipped over on its left side, causing it to roll over several times. Luck had it that there was no oncoming traffic, and the only one banged up a bit was the suspect. We all came to a halt and the suspect, who was in a daze and banged up, was removed and placed under arrest. He looked at me laughing and said, "Damn, boy! That was great driving, Frenchy. You were right with me." I smiled as he patted me on the shoulder.

"I learned that from a crazy redneck son of a bitch."

"You nut case! Damn, that was fun!" Howled Frenchy.

"Ok! You know, I think both of you are nuts! And thank God you're Ok!" said the lieutenant who had arrived on the scene. Little did I realize that he and I would cross paths again.

⟡⟡⟡⟡⟡

I arrived at the Hallandale Police Department, walked to the front desk and asked to see Chief George Emrick (*deceased*). I gave my name and said it was a personal visit. The desk officer got up, knocked on the door and said, "Chief, a Pete Charette is here to see you and said it was personal. The Chief walked out and looked at me smiling, and said, "Come on back, Pete.

My God! The last time I saw you, was in this office when I gave you ten whacks on the ass with my paddle for drinking beer on the beach when you were in high school!"

"Yes, sir, and it still hurts. I never forgot it! Because of you and a few others who inspired me, I became a cop!" the Chief shook my hand as he hugged me.

"My lieutenant told me that you were now a new detective with BSO and working for that mad man Cecil Stewart!"

"Yes, Sir!"

"Pete, congratulations and it's George from here on! You look too damn young to be a cop. We sure are glad for you, and you know you got us anytime you need anything. I could use some help from you since you are here! By the way, how's your dad doing? I have not been at the Moongate lately. Please tell him hi for me!"

"He's great. I'll tell him!"

"Hold on. I'm going to get the lieutenant in here." He buzzed on the phone intercom, saying, "Get in here. Pete Charette is here!"

The lieutenant came in, smiling and said, "Pete, great to see you. I told the Chief you would be coming!"

"Pete," said the Chief closing the door, "the lieutenant and I got a tip this morning that we have a bookmaking operation going on at a restaurant on the corner of I-95 and Hallandale Beach Boulevard. Word is that the waitress and owner are taking bets from customers openly. We can't go in because they know all of us and our cops since we are a small department. Their clientele are mainly workers who usually can't go to the track because normally they only have an hour off, so they place their bets while at lunch. Could you help? Any suggestions?"

"No problem. The way you describe it, I got an idea on how I could help. What if I go in tomorrow at lunchtime as a construction worker with my work belt, T-shirt, a little bit of grease on the arms, bruised up pot helmet and work boots. I'll keep my eyes open and see how the action takes place. I'll schmooze the waitress and put on my playboy approach to her and see if she bites. What's her age and looks?"

"Man, that sounds great! I love it!" John said. "She's in her late thirties, redhead, nice rack on her, about 130, single, lives in a trailer park across I-95, no prior arrest. Don't have a last name. Been there a few years."

"Chief, what do you think?"

"Go with it!"

"I'll get Jimmy to go in since he looks like an old retired tourist from New York to sit in and corroborate my UC work."

"Sounds great, Pete. Just call me after your lunch. John and I will be waiting for your call!"

"Ok! I will brief Cecil and Howard! It's great to see you, Chief! And by the way, do you still have that damn paddle in your desk drawer?"

"Glad you asked." He reached in the drawer and pulled out the paddle while laughing! "Do you want to assume the position just for old time's sake?"

"Yeah, right, I wouldn't be able to sit down for a couple of days like the first time!

"I got a few more stops to make, so I will be there tomorrow at noon! I will call after I'm out of there."

"Let's hope we can close this down within the next few days! Glad to be working with you. Be safe!" said John.

"Thanks, Pete. We look forward to doing great things together, my friend!" the Chief added.

"Same here. See you Chief!" He waved and gave him the thumbs up.

• • • • • • •

I headed out to meet with my friend for dinner and made a call to my Sergeant and briefed him on what had happened. He was happy that I offered our help and said he would have Jimmy there tomorrow at noon as a lookout and brief Cecil. I told him I was going over to Miramar PD to do liaison and would be on the radio if needed. He liked my plan and was surprised that I came up with that scenario and ID on the spur of the moment.

Arriving at the diner in Miramar, I observed my friend had already arrived. I went in and seated myself in the booth with him. We ordered our food and got caught up as to what had been happening since we were separated. I told him about the guys in the squad and what a great team we had. He was envious and proud of my appointment. He was about 12 years older than I was and loved his work. I told him that I had heard that we were going to have an additional man coming to the squad and hopefully that he would soon be promoted to the DB (Detective Bureau) since he was a senior deputy on the road patrol. He wanted me to know that he would alert me on anything he observed or heard in regard to vice violations and refer informants to me whenever he came across any potentially good snitches. We had a great supper and parted ways agreeing to have supper together at least once a week. I admired him and knew that we were loyal friends, no matter what.

After leaving, I went to the Miramar Police Department to meet with the Chief of detectives who was on duty. I had made friends with him when I worked Zone 1 on patrol and let him know of my new status. He smiled widely as I walked into his office and said, "Well, look who's here, Detective Charette! Congratulations, Frenchy. The word got out fast about your promotion! You earned it, Kid!"

"Thanks. I'm still in a daze!" We both laughed.

"Frenchy, as you know, we are a small department and anything you need from us, you got it!"

"I know that! And the same from me. Call me anytime if you need us and tell the Chief I will stop in during the day to see him!"

"I'm on my way to the house and will stay in touch with you. Stay safe!"

With that, I left and went to my parents' home in Miramar, where I lived in order to check in on my mom and dad.

The remainder of my evening was spent checking on bars in the area and acting like a normal bachelor on a night out bar hopping! Prior to calling it a night, I drove by a construction site near Hollywood Boulevard, where a retired cop friend of mine was Chief of security. I told him I needed a favor; I needed a used carpenter's work tool belt and a used hardhat for an undercover job along with a pair of work boots. He advised me that I came to the right Sears Outlet jokingly and took me to the supply shed where his company kept these items for new workers. He outfitted me completely, even with a worn short sleeve work shirt with a company logo on it. I thanked him and said I would return them in a few days.

"I'll sign them out as loaned equipment to law enforcement," he advised.

"I owe you!"

"Just be safe, Frenchy. That's all I ask."

———————— ‹‹••••‹‹ ————————

And that's the reason why we call ourselves the Brotherhood. We are always there for each other!

14

Fun Time

Time to be a construction worker today, dressed and ready to play the part. I didn't sleep well because my mind was continually going over my scenario for this role. I went through a checklist of my cover and answers if asked to make sure I had all bases covered. I realized that I was missing one part, my vehicle was a two-door Ford Mustang, clean as a whistle and did not fit that of a laborer. After much thought, I came up with the solution. I left the house and went to a tow truck outfit that towed vehicles for BSO on Pembroke Road. The owner was a great friend to all of us. When I arrived, I pulled in, parked and went in to see Charlie. I told him I needed to use one of his pickup trucks for two hours. He handed the keys to me and said, "I don't know why, and I'm not asking. Good luck!"

"1-0-5 to 1-0-3."

"1-0-3, on my way. Should be there at 11:45 inside ordering a filet mignon with a glass of Merlot, a baked Alaska for dessert with a glass of your favorite Remy Martin XO, and a great Cuban cigar! How's that? Oh, I forgot. I'm putting it on your tab! Ha-ha!"

"1-0-5, where are you going, Paris for this?"

"No worries! Got your back, Frenchy!! Put $20 on the 5th, number 3. Later, dude!" Then with a deep breath, he finished, "My money's on you. out 10-7!"

"10-4."

The New York stud was in rare form and was glad to have him covering me. One thing about Jimmy was that he was not afraid to step in from what I heard about him. He was fast and allegedly had one hell of a knockout punch when needed!

I arrived at noon and walking in, observed the cash register was to my right with what appeared to be the owner behind the counter. I said, "Hey! Table for one!"

"Grab anyone, and she will be with you shortly."

"Ok." I walked to the left and grabbed a table for two, then sat with my back to the wall facing the front door. Jimmy was seated to my left against a large glass window facing toward me reading the menu. The place had about 15 workers scattered around some with four at tables and two at others. The waitress was as previously described and was starting to wait on three guys at the table next to me. She looked at me with a smile and said, "Be right with you, Hon!"

I kept looking at her up and down smiling, and she smiled and said to the clients, "Ok, you guys look hungry. who's first?"

"I'll have a cheeseburger with mayo, lettuce and tomato, Coke and fries, and I need a ticket, Sweets," one of them said.

"Got it, Joe," she affirmed as she ripped a blank order slip and handed it to him with a pencil to write.

"Who's next?" The second worker said, "Baby doll, I'll have a BLT and Coke. That's it."

"What's the matter? Not playing today?"

"Nah! Payday is tomorrow, so got to skip it today!"

"Got you! And what will you have, Tom?"

"I'll have the same and a slip!"

"Here you are! Handing him an order sheet and a pencil."

She turned around and said to me, "A newbie. Hey!"

"Hey! You got to be from good old Canada?"

"How in the hell did you know that?"

Laughing, I said, "Well, being from Canada originally, only Canadians say 'Hey' at the end of a sentence, hey."

"I'll be damned! I didn't realize I did that!" Laughing, she added, "That's rare for me! Your first time here? Where you working?"

"Off Hollywood Boulevard on 441. I'm a construction worker and on lunch break! I'll have a cheeseburger, coke and fries, hey!" I said with a smile.

"Ok! Be back, hey! Ha-ha," she answered with a wink!

She left for the kitchen, and I noticed that the guys had written on the blank check slips, and each had put a $20 on the slips that they had written on. She came back with their orders and took the slips and money, tearing the slips in half after initialing each one and returning the half to each playing customer at the table and saying good luck!

I noticed that a few other customers had purchased a racing form by the cash register. So, I got up and got one in order to look at the form for the day.

Before long, she brought my order and noticed I had a form open. She placed my meal in front of me and said, "Do you go to the racetrack?"

"Only when I'm off. Work has to take priority."

"Right. By the way, I'm Nancy, and you are?"

"If I said Pierre, would you laugh at me?"

"Pierre. Yeah, right?"

"Yep! I swear on it!"

"Prove it!"

"You're hard!" I pulled out my driver's license, and she gasped!

"My God, it's Pierre!" She exclaimed.

"I told you. Just call me Pete."

"You got it. Say, if you ever get a good tip and are working, come in for lunch and I'll place your bet for you, and if you win, I get 10% as a tip. It helps with the bills."

"That's funny because there's a horse in the 5th race, number 3, that looks good to me today!"

"Ok! Be right back. I got an order up. Here put it twice on the slip half and half with your name Pierre on each half with your bet amount, and I'll be back." She then blew me a kiss

I wrote down Jimmy's bet–5th Race, number 3, $20 to win. Pierre.

Nancy came back, and I handed her the slip. She placed her initials on both halves and tore it in half, giving me the bottom part. She said to come back for lunch tomorrow. if I won, we'd settle up! "Oh! Also, my phone number is on there. I see you're single like me. I'm always available for a drink any time after 6 p.m. Here's your bill!"

"Will see you tomorrow, same time, and I will be free Friday after work. Would love to have a drink!"

"Sounds great, Pierre. Don't overwork yourself!"

She walked away, turning to give me a wink! She then went up to the checkout, where I noticed that she placed the bet slip and money inside a cigar box with other slips.

I looked over at Jimmy, who was sipping his coffee and winked at me. This went better than expected in my estimation. Sometimes by improvising and reading body language, we can get lucky. I paid my bill at the cash register, took a ten spot, and walked over to give it to her, telling her I'd be back tomorrow for lunch! I gave her a quick kiss on the cheek and said, "I'm French, what can I say?"

She responded back, saying, "Bye, Pierre, you naughty boy! See you!"

I left and drove west towards State Road 7 and made a few fast turns into Carvers Ranch checking for any tails. I then drove to the gas station and picked my car and called Jimmy on the Radio. "1-0-5 to 1-0-3."

"Go ahead, you flirt!"

"Talk about wide open in public operation! That seemed too easy!"

"Yep, good job. I'm heading back. See you at the office!"

"Ok, I'm going to call John and the Chief to brief them."

"10-4."

I called the Chief and John and gave them the entire story! Needless to say, they were elated and couldn't believe I did it on the first meet. I advised them that I would go back one more time and place one more bet. On Friday, I would go in and do it one more time, and then they could move in for the bust. We all agreed, and I went to the office to brief the boss and Lieutenant Stewart.

Arriving at the office, I met with Howard and the lieutenant and gave them a blow by blow tale of the entire meeting. Cecil and Howard kept laughing until Cecil finally said,

"These people are totally operating in the open, as if there was nothing being done wrong here. Frenchy! You could probably take this broad to bed now! Or even ask her to marry you! Ha-ha! Good job! Bag the slip into evidence and go ahead and write it up for a case. Betty will get you a case number. Go ahead and dictate the report to her before the end of the business today!"

The den mother and I went to her office, and I dictated to her my activity. Fortunately for us, she was the best typist in the bureau, and we knocked out the report in 45 minutes. Jimmy knocked out his report, and when we finished, everybody went home. Sergeant Fish stopped me and said, "Frenchy, take the rest of the night off so you're fresh for tomorrow. Hell of a job, Pierre. Good night!" he said as he walked away!

"Night, Sarge!"

As I got into the elevator, Cecil yelled hold it and got in. We both walked out toward our cars and Cecil stopped and said, "Frenchy, keep up the good work, and not for publication till Monday of next week, but we got your new partner approved for Monday. I think you will get along great with this guy. For your info only and no one else, he's your friend, the ex-North Carolina trooper."

"You're putting me on, right?" I was shocked, yet feeling jubilant.

Laughing, he said, "No, he's your new partner. I know you guys worked well together, and I think you guys will make a great team!"

Cecil reached out, shook my hand and said, "I know you won't let me down. Enjoy your evening, and not a word to him or anyone!"

"Yes, Sir! Thanks, Lieutenant. You made my night. Good night, Sir!"

Walking away waving, he said, "Don't call me Sir!" He laughed.

On Friday, we all met at the Hallandale Police Department, and plans were made for the bust at noon. I departed to the restaurant and walked in and observed Jimmy sitting and having a cup of coffee and reading a racing form. Nancy, the waitress was waiting on a table and smiled. I gave her a wink and sat down near the front door.

"Hey! Hon! How are you?" she asked as she walked up to my table.

"Great, how about you?"

"Busy as usual. What will you have and are we still on for tonight?" she asked, smiling.

"For sure. I'll have a cheeseburger, fries and Coke, oh, and a slip!"

"Here you go." She handed me an order slip on which to place my bet, then walked away, placing my order and picking up two slips from a table and giving them to the owner behind the cash register who placed the slip and money in a large cigar box on a shelf.

She returned, and I handed her my slip. She signed it and gave me my half receipt. I gave her a $20 bill for the Daily Double with my favorite number 6-9. She smiled and said, "My favorite number also, you naughty boy!" Then she took the money and slip to the manager.

At exactly noon as planned, Chief Emerich and Lieutenant Cataldo, along with two uniformed officers, entered the restaurant. The Chief walked up to the owner behind the counter and said, "You're under arrest for bookmaking, illegal gambling, and conspiracy to violate Florida gambling laws. Jimmy got up and walked over to Nancy and told her she was under arrest the same.

The lieutenant immediately seized the cigar box, which was full of gambling slips and money. All the patrons were told they had to leave the restaurant, and Jimmy went over to three customers who had given her their bets and told them they were under arrest for illegal gambling. Jimmy searched them and seized their betting slips from their pockets.

I looked at her as I got up and walked out, acting stunned in order to keep my cover so that she'd never know that I was a cop! I left and met with the Chief at his office. He was smiling and thanking me for helping him in this bust! I advised him it was my pleasure and that he could count on me anytime.

The case was clean, and all parties involved all pled guilty to the charges. I never had to expose my cover and never ran into her again.

I drove back to the office feeling good about the results. Lieutenant Stewart and the Sarge congratulated me on this case and told me to keep up my liaison with the other departments in Broward County. They also reminded me to be ready to meet my new partner on Monday morning. I thanked them and sat down to do the paperwork on this case.

15

New Partner

I couldn't wait to get to work on Monday to see the look on my new partner's face. I got to work early, had my coffee and joked around with our team when Lieutenant Stewart walked in the squad bay with my new partner, who was grinning from ear to ear.

"All right, everyone, listen up!" said Stewart. "We have a new man assigned to this crazy bunch! Meet our new detective who was just sworn in and is assigned to partner with Frenchy. God help us all!" He laughed! "You know everybody here and welcome to the most elite group in this Sheriff's department! Sergeant will brief you and get you set up and show you the ropes. Just remember, we all work together as a team and watch out for each other at all times. What we do here and say here, stays here, and we do not disclose any investigations to anyone outside this room. That includes all of management in this department!"

"Yes, Sir," said Bob.

"Good. Proud to have you on board. I know you fit well with this crazy bunch!"

Everybody shook Bob's hand, welcoming him to this unit, and we both gave each other a bear hug. I said to him, "I knew about this last week when we had supper but couldn't say anything."

"Payback is hell, Frenchy," he said and gave me a hug.

"All right you two! Knock it off. You come with me, and you and he can kiss later!"

"Yes, Sir, Sarge!" I had learned a lot from Bob when we were on the road patrol and knew that he and I could kick ass and make a difference in this type of work.

In detective work, partnership is an art of its own. Managers who assign partners need to be able to recognize compatible traits that will work with this type of assignment. If both individuals are too opposite of each other, the assignment will be doomed for failure.

Partners must be able to read one another in order to react with whomever they are working undercover and be able to read each other's body language in any situation that they are confronted with. They need to establish signals that will alert possible imminent dangers and when to play the good guy/bad guy scenario with defendants and suspects. In short, having a mutually agreeable plan of action is vital. Loyalty is a must!

———————— ✦✦✦✦✦ ————————

He and I spent our first month together doing liaison with various police department detective squads and organized crime units in Broward County. We participated with numerous gambling investigations with other team members that involved bookmaking operations and illegal lottery investigations known as 'Bolita,' a numbers racket popular in minority neighborhoods and among motel workers, prostitution investigations and organized crime.

There are a few investigations that occurred during my vice work with my partner that were highly significant during that time. Some were humorous in nature and some were directly tied with organized crime in Broward and Dade Counties. One area of vice investigations involved racetrack violations, which were frequent in locations where horse racing and Greyhound dog racetracks existed. My partner and I were checking the Pompano Horse Sulky Racetrack with the Agent of The Florida Liquor Board and our Sergeant. We entered and sat in the bleachers midway between the top and front fence of the track, sat down with beers and looked around for any suspicious activities.

While looking around, we spotted a well-known madam who was sitting with two suspected prostitutes who worked for her. This was the same madam that was involved with my first night on the job where I had arrested the shift commander for being involved with her. We decided to watch them and observed her two girls get up and go down by the right side of the grandstand to the fence line as the Sulky jockeys were parading their horses in front of the grandstand. One of the jockeys was observed approaching the fence at a slow pace and appeared to say something to one of the girls.

Both girls immediately climbed the grandstand in a hurry, and we observed the madam rise to meet her girls. They then proceeded to the line of betting fans who were waiting to place bets at the betting windows. The state agent and I approached the windows and got behind the three ladies who we heard place $100 on Sulky Horse number 8 then returned to their seats. We watched the race begin, observing Sulky Driver 8 go through his pace. As the race rounded the far turn for the stretch, 8 was given an opening by a Sulky rider to take the lead and won the race.

All three ladies went to cash their tickets and made a bundle of money. At that point, we suspected that we had a possible touting violation, which is defined as offering racing tips for any resulting winnings or spying out the movement and conditions of a racehorse in training in order to gain information to be used when betting. We decided to observe again after we checked the racing form and saw that the same jockey who won was racing a different horse in two more races. We had the agent go and stand by the fence line for these races, and the girls again stood by the fence line away from Bob, but within earshot. The Sulky driver came by close to the fence and called out a number. Once again, they all met with the madam and placed their wagers twice again and cleaned up winnings for that night.

After the races, we left the track and followed them to Hollywood to the madam's house. Once we determined this was her new residence, we left and agreed to come back to the racetrack the next night to observe this jockey, her and her girls again and effect an arrest. We briefed Lieutenant Stewart, who was enchanted over the prospect of getting another chance to take down this madam.

The next night we went to the track, took our positions while Stewart went to the upper level to stay out of the madam's site. We looked around and found her and her girls sitting in the same area. Three races passed with the same results. After they cashed in on the third race, we moved in and arrested Betsy and her girls and the jockey. Needless to say, the racing commission was not pleased that we had not notified them.

This case turned out to be one of the biggest racetrack busts in Broward County at that time. No case had ever been made like this before in that county!

16

Mistaken Identity

My new partner and I worked on several clubs in those days in Broward County that had suspected ties to organized crime. We made nightly rounds to these clubs and were not well received by the bouncer doorman of these establishments. One, in particular, was a bar near the entrance of Port Everglades in the city of Fort Lauderdale. While riding around at 1:00 a.m., Bobby said, "Frenchy, why don't we pay a visit to the club and check on Big Jim Capatorto (*deceased*)?"

"Sounds good to me. That piece of crap just loves us so much. We can make his life a little bit more miserable. I'm in!"

Big Jim was in his middle thirties, weighed about 250 pounds, had greasy combed-back black hair, spoke with a New York City accent, and had a side job as a muscle man for the mob, which entailed collecting debts from people to whom the mob had given loans. We arrived at the busy club, parked, then walked around to the front door surprising Big Jim who was checking IDs at the door. Big Jim looked at us surprised and said, "Need to see ID" (fully knowing who we were) while blocking the door with his left arm stretched across the doorway.

My partner responded, smiling, "If I were you, you fat bastard, I'd move that arm now, or I'll do it for you, and I mean NOW!"

I said, "C'mon, let's see some ID?" as I put my hand on his shoulder.

Well! You Poor Stupid Idiot, you shouldn't say things like that to Bob.

In an instant, Bob grabbed Big Jim by the balls with his left hand crushing them like he was making grapefruit juice! Big Jim dropped to the ground screaming as Bob and I walked into the club. When the manager saw us, he approached us, surprised at our entry, and asked if Jim was at the door.

Bob calmly answered, "I think he's looking for his balls in the parking lot!"

"Frenchy, let's look around for a minute. Let's check to see who's in town." We observed a few of Santo Trafficante's (*deceased*) wise guys from Tampa at the club and some local punks and wannabees then exited. Outside the club, we observed Big Jim sitting on a stool, still rubbing his 'gems.' At the same time, we both looked at him and said, "Pussy."

After leaving the club, we pulled out and headed toward Lauderdale Beach when we were blue lighted by an unmarked police car and pulled over. It was LPD Organized Crime Detective Sergeant Charlie White (*deceased*). We got out of our vehicle to his laughing as he said, "You two, that was the best laugh I had this night. I was watching the place from across the street. You're going to teach me this new technique on busting balls!" That fat piece of shit an hour ago went to collect money from a guy on the beach and broke his arm with a baseball bat. The victim refused to press charges on Jim. I need to have you guys come to the office. Got a call to find you 'cause we need to talk."

"Our pleasure, Charlie. See you in ten!"

⁓ ✦✦✦✦✦ ⁓

Bob and I arrived at the Fort Lauderdale OCB (Organized Crime Bureau). Charlie and his detectives were sitting around when Charlie finally began, "We got a black janitor who works at a prominent attorney's office (*name withheld*), who claims he caught someone breaking into his office. The suspect ran out, and we were wondering if you guys may know anything about who this might be since this attorney represents several bad-asses in Broward County." Charlie paused, then continued.

"The janitor is being interviewed right now so we can get a description of this suspect."

Just at that moment, the janitor was brought out of the interview room and pointed immediately at me, saying, "That's the guy who broke into the office. That's him!"

Charlie said, "Hold up for a second." And he immediately walked up and asked, "Are you sure that this guy (pointing to me) is the guy that ran out of the office?"

"Yep, that's him!" the janitor replied.

"Ok, thank you. Go with this detective for now!"

Charlie, puzzled said, "No Fucking way it's you! You were at the club with your crazy partner massaging Big Jim's balls." He was laughing with everyone in the room.

I responded and said, "What the fuck is going on? Am I being set up? Maybe I got a twin I don't know about!"

My partner responded," Frenchy, you need to come clean. We all know he is a pain in the ass for you because of all his clients you have arrested."

"Look, this is not funny. You know damn well that this janitor will tell him that he ID me and all hell will break loose."

"Sarge, I just got a call from the attorney. He's on his way down here to see what has happened, and he's hot!"

"Ok, we got to figure this out guys!" Rebel exclaimed.

Everyone was trying to make sense of this when all of a sudden, one of the detectives blurted out," Holy shit, I know who did this!"

Charlie said, "What? Out with it now before that asshole comes here."

"Hold on, Sarge. I got to go to my desk. I have a picture of Frenchy's twin brother!" Charlie left, shaking his head.

We all stood there with questionable looks on our faces. Returning from his office, he continued. "Here's the proof." He held out a photo, putting the mug shot of a suspect next to my face. Everyone looked amazed and said, "Holy shit! You have an identical twin!"

Charlie said, "Jesus Christ, that's Dicky Morrison (*deceased*), the 'Babbling Burglar' from Chicago who ratted out on the Chicago cops, which was a major scandal in the Chicago PD for corruption years ago. He's been living here and has this attorney on retainer!"

I looked closely at the picture, started laughing and said, "Bring that janitor back in here and show him the picture, now!"

The janitor was told to look at the picture and see if he recognized that person. Upon looking at the picture and looking back at me, he said, "Mother fucker! That's the guy I saw! Not him!" He pointed at me.

Everybody laughed and the janitor said to me, "Man, are you guys brothers? I'm sorry for mistaking you for him." He reached out to shake my hand.

The Attorney arrived at the police department and was escorted to the OCB Office where we were all sitting around. Charlie told the attorney that a positive ID had been made. The Attorney responded immediately, saying, "Whoever it is, I want that SOB charged and prosecuted."

Charlie said, "We will do that, but you may want to rethink that because this guy is a client of yours." He showed him Morrison's photo. The look on the Attorney's face was priceless as we all held back from laughing. The attorney nervously said immediately, "I'm not pressing charges and will handle this myself!" He thanked all of us and left abruptly.

Relieved by all of this, we thank everyone, but we all had some good laughs. I was glad that I had great friends who immediately dealt with this in order to clear my name.

17

Informants

I learned very quickly during my early years in my work as a detective and as a patrolman that law enforcement is helpless without having confidential sources of information as its most valuable tool in protecting the public we serve and apprehending criminals worldwide. Sources of information or confidential informants are basically categorized by the following categories:

Informants

Persons who give information on another person are called informants. Various motives control those who fall into this category. They can include money, retaliation, patriotism, professional sources, cop-want-to-be citizens, or planted infiltrators who are attempting to gather information for criminal intelligence by infiltration of police agencies.

Regardless of the motives of individuals who come forward to assist, we know never to let our guards down and assume that we are fortunate to have their cooperation and accept them as being fully trustworthy. All of us have learned that sooner or later, we will be blindsided by an informant and can pay a heavy price for being too trusting and eager to make a case without corroborating their information. Many officers have lost their jobs for becoming too friendly and trusting of their sources.

Professional Sources

These are in a class of their own and are to be judged as persons who want to do the right thing and, in most instances, can be trusted. Once we learn what their motives are for cooperating, we will normally realize that they are sincere in assisting law enforcement. I say this from professional experience, and to this day, I still get calls from them and consider them friends who have served their country in an honorable way, not looking for any recognition or glory. They are made up of various professions, such as private investigators, lawyers, doctors, business professionals, private citizens, security guards, motel employees, and can be a tremendous help if handled properly.

Sources are valuable to this line of work and must be protected at all times and not disclosed unless they understand that they may have to be identified as a result of their cooperation. It is important for them to understand upon their first debriefing and willingness to cooperate.

I have had in my career numerous professional sources. One source who introduced himself to me at the office in the sixties was Miami Eddy/ Fast Eddy (PN). His profession was in private security as a private investigator and was one hell of a pool shark. Being a bachelor and traveling a lot, he had a natural knack to work undercover and had been in Fort Lauderdale vacationing and running across dope dealers in the area who offered him drugs at various bars. He immediately made contact with us and agreed to make buys and introduce us to the lower-class dealers.

Eddie made numerous cases for the Broward County Sheriff's Department, Oakland Park Police Department, and Palm Beach Sheriff's Department, where he helped dismantle the largest theft ring in Palm Beach and Broward Counties. His cases are too many to list, but I referred him to DEA offices all over the country when he came across information that impacted their jurisdiction. He would call me, and I would reach out for a contact for him to meet. From the sixties to the present, he's been a Chief investigator for a law firm and has owned his own investigative business. Professional Sources like him are rare and extremely valuable assets to law enforcement. Eddie remains a dear friend, and we have stayed in contact for the past 45 years.

Two of my best professional sources in DEA, whose code names were Dr. Mike and The Shadow were responsible as a team for the seizure of hundreds of kilos of cocaine and millions of dollars from the Ochoa/ Escobar Colombian Cartel. They were responsible for locating and proving to us that the Colombian Cartel was growing opium poppies for heroin production to sell in the United States. This will be covered in detail in a future book!

Criminal Sources

Every investigator has had to develop SOI (Sources of Information) on his own. Usually, whenever we make an arrest, we have to judge if one of the arrestees can be approached to cooperate in order to receive leniency on his charges. Usually, instinct will kick in since many defendants display a typical body language at the time of their arrest.

Normally we see either an arrogance of masochism by some who act like this is no big deal and showing a F.U. cop attitude. This type of asshole usually will not even want to talk and will advise he wants his attorney. With them, we don't push the issue; however, once he understands that he is facing jail time, his attorney may approach us for assistance. Some will roll over, and some will eventually get convicted at sentencing.

On the other side is the defendant who displays fear at his arrest, gets a case of the shakes and shows dismay at facing jail time! This person is, most of the time, a target for cooperation and should be shown that we care about their situation and slowly gain his trust that things can be worked out because we are willing to help.

We never promise those persons who are defendants that we will get their charges reduced if they cooperate. Only one person can give that guarantee and that is the prosecutor. We will make sure to convey their willingness to cooperate and work with the prosecutor on this from the start. It's always good to get this in writing. If the defendant doesn't live up to this agreement, and double deals, then we will certainly dump him and wish him luck in his stay in the joint. Yeah, we do have some sense of humor in our work.

All I can say is that without sources of information, our careers and chances for advancement in our organization can be limited. Bob and I worked together as partners throughout Broward County, and one of our routine functions was to ensure that we developed sources that were connected to organized crime in Florida.

When I arrived at the office, Bob was already looking over some intelligence bulletin and said, "Frenchy, take a look at this. Some people have called in that they got ripped off on bar tabs at the club in Dania."

"Well, let's pay a visit to Mr. Jerry Springer's (*deceased*) strip joint and have a 'come to me, Jesus' talk with Jerry."

In those days, the Dania Police Department was a small one, and we had a great patrol enforcement relationship with them, but our unit had some concerns about some of their officers who were questionable about turning a blind eye to underworld crime figures in their area. So, we never involved them with us until arrests were made and notifications were made as a matter of courtesy once we had secured the scene.

"Ok, partner! let's go and do our patriotic duty in ensuring that Mr. Springer is put on notice to ensure that their clients are properly treated or else it's 'Don't pass go; go directly to Jail without collecting $200.'"

"Hey, you two wankers, be careful out there and give Springer my best regards," said Lieutenant Stewart, laughing and shaking his head.

"Yes, Sir!" I said and waited for his response.

"I don't have bars on my collar, and the name is Cecil," he responded with a wink of his left eye.

Within 20 minutes, we arrived at the club and parked our car in the valet lot. The valet/doorman/ bouncer saw us arriving and immediately went inside to alert the owner Jerry that vice was here.

As we approached the door, I said to the bouncer, "Good job! We always like to be announced, and soon we will do the same for you at the booking desk." Then I smiled and bowed as we walked in.

Greeting us at the door as we walked in was Jerry who said, "Gentlemen, how are we doing this evening?"

"We're doing great," I answered. "How's business tonight? Any issues or problems with the clientele or your beautiful ladies?"

"No, Pete, business is always good. To what honor is your visit here tonight?"

My partner interjected, "We have a complaint and need to see you in private, Jerry!"

As we walked into his office, Jerry said, "This isn't good, is it? What have we done now?"

"Jerry, It has come to our attention that clients are being overcharged on their bills and credit cards. You know the law, and if we get one more complaint, it's a fraud investigation, and the DB (Detective Bureau) will get a court order to subpoena all your records for the past six months and close you down," I explained.

"Look, guys, I will look into this and find out if the bartenders are jacking up the charges and if so, asses will be fired! I don't need this shit!" He turned and called for the manager to come join them, then continued. "You guys have always been straight with me since your appointment, and I respect your honesty, not like those crooked fucking cops in this city."

"Ok, we will take you at your word, Jerry, and it stops now! Are we clear on this?"

He responded while pointing to the manager, "And you! Pass the word out to the girls, no private shows in the back bar. The law is strict to total nudity, and I hear rumors that there are private shows going on after closing hours by that piece of shit doorman of yours!"

Springer's face went into a rage, and he said, "Get that fat son of a bitch into my office now! And if you had any knowledge of this, your ass is grass, you fuck! I don't need this kind of heat!"

We both enjoyed this show of affection by these two gentlemen, and we were amused as they both parted our presence. We went to the bar where the bartender had two cokes waiting for us. Eight girls were sitting around tables and two were stripping on the runway bar. The bartender softly said to my partner, "Call me at home late after closing."

"Roger that."

A shapely stripper dressed in a beautiful nightgown walked over, greeted us and asked how we were doing. A brief conversation took place, then she went back to sit down, and as she did, gave me a wink and smile. My partner said, "You got it?"

I said, "Yep, will call her later and see what's new." After we finished our soft drinks, we went by Springer's office, leaned in and said, "See you at the diner in one hour," and we left.

⁜

We drove off feeling that our message was loud and clear, and that people would be arrested if they didn't comply. We had been working for three months to develop people at the club as confidential sources on organized crime. Our efforts paid off having developed four sources, all who had no idea that they were supplying info to us. This was so sensitive that only Lieutenant Stewart and the Sergeant were aware of this.

We then headed out for breakfast at the diner. When we arrived, Jerry Springer sat in a booth waiting for us. He said, "I just want you to know that there will be no more complaints on fudging on bills and credit cards. My bartender got his ass handed to him by me." He continued, "I got to make this quick, but you should know that something big is coming down, and I will know in a few days as to where and when. I have been contacted to meet next week with a representative of Santos Trafficante of Tampa. That's all I know for now."

"Ok, call us when you get the word." Springer left, but we finished our coffees then continued to check several bars around the county for the rest of the night. Driving home, I stopped at a phone booth in Pembroke Pines to make a call to my female source at another phone booth near her house at exactly 4:30 a.m. When she answered, I said, "What's up?"

"I picked up some info that our doorman is doing some burglaries in Lauderdale with some low life wannabees! Mob guys! He has a small blow torch in the trunk of his car and was showing it off to customers he drinks with. I think Lauderdale PD might be interested in this!"

"Thanks, I'll pass it on. Oh, and did your manager get his ass handed to him by Springer tonight?"

"Yep, it wasn't pretty. We could hear the screaming. Jerry told everyone that he doesn't need the heat, and everybody walks the line from now on. He hates you guys!"

"I guess we're doing something right. Well, take care and behave yourself!"

"Yeah! right!"

"Keep me posted later!" I said as I hung up!

Based on what we had learned, I passed the information on the doorman to OCB Lauderdale PD Sergeant White, who advised us that they have had several burglaries with blowtorch MO (modus operandi) to get into warehouses lately. We appreciated the info.

··◆◆◆◆··

After my partner called the bartender when the bar had closed, he called me to report that the bartender had confirmed that the doorman was having private shows in the back after closing and doing it without Springer's knowledge and that the manager knew about it but was just looking the other way because he feared the doorman since he is also connected. He advised us that we needed to look into the doorman's background closer. We both agreed that our work was paying off, and he would brief Cecil tomorrow.

All three CIs (confidential informants) were developed by us by gaining their respect and confidence over a period of several months of on-site visitations and by being able to determine who could be approached for cooperation. The manner we used was to surveil them before and after work and see where they went after work and at what eating establishments they ate and what bars they frequented on their off-duty time. Once we knew their routines, we planned on dropping in at these locations to engage them in social conversation and slowly recruit them to supply us with information. The club was a perfect example of the proper use of informants by having multiple sources, who may be working in a group environment. Developing sources in a place like a nightclub allowed investigators to verify the accuracy being given by the CIs. When encountering these individuals, we learned never to give the appearance that we were giving them special treatment because this would arouse suspicion and compromise them with their associates.

A few days later, we were contacted by Springer, who had received a call to meet Trafficante's associate at a motel on US-1 in Dania. Springer advised us that he and, to his surprise, his doorman had been requested to attend. They were told that the state attorney in Dade County in Miami, Richard Gerstein (*deceased*), was creating a lot of problems for them and that they needed to have him 'taken out.'

The plan would be to have him involved in an accident during Memorial Day weekend. He and the doorman were asked to see which one of them would take the contract and, if accepted, be paid $50K for the job. Springer advised us that he refused because this was not something that he had experience in and that the doorman immediately accepted. The meeting was short and sweet, and everyone left.

"Frenchy, we need to meet with Cecil and the Sergeant now and agree on how we want to handle this."

"I'm on my way now, and I'll be there in one hour. We got to handle this in the right way in order to protect Springer since they are the only ones who attended this meeting. It wouldn't be hard to identify the snitch in this case."

"I agree, Frenchy. See you in an hour!"

We arrived at the same time and headed up to the office. As we walked in, den mother said jokingly, "Well, if it isn't the Bobbsey Twins. If I had to guess by the looks on your faces, trouble is about to happen. The brass are waiting for you in Cecil's office!"

"Thanks, beautiful," I said, blowing a kiss and asking her if we were having our regular Friday night drinks at her place after work?

She responded, "Bar will be open at 5:30 p.m. as usual for you boys!"

"Got you. I'll pick up the vodka and tonic since I'm the single guy!" I offered, laughing.

As we walked in, Cecil said, "Why is it that I got a feeling you two are going to drop a bomb on us? There's no telling what you two maniacs have got this time?"

I responded by saying, "Your Royal Highness, I yield the floor to my redneck partner."

Bob went through his entire conversation without leaving out any details. At the end of his presentation, Both Cecil and Howard looked at each other and said at the same time, "HOLY SHIT!!!"

Cecil added, "This is big, and we're only a week from Memorial Day holiday! We got to go see the Sheriff and the Chief of detectives to brief them. Let's go now!"

As we walked out, Cecil ordered, "Den Mother, Get the Chief of Detectives Captain DeBlois (*deceased*) now and tell him to meet us in the old man's office. NOW! I turned around and blew her another kiss and winked, and she blew one back, shaking her head and laughing as I skipped behind the guys.

When we walked into the Sheriff's office, Mrs. Michell, the Sheriff's secretary, looked up and said, "He's in, and this looks like big problems." We all entered the office and saw Deblois already sitting down on the big red couch as we closed the door.

Sheriff Michell began, "Cecil, looks like you brought some muscle with you. Let's get to it!"

Cecil briefed the Sheriff and, once done, said, "Well, looks like Gerstein's got a problem that we have to address. I really don't have any love for this guy! Word is that he may have ties with Joe Sunken (*deceased*) who owns The Steakhouse on A1A on Hollywood Beach and plays both sides of the law. With that said, what's the plan of action on this?"

Cecil replied, "Frenchy and his redneck partner have a plan that sounds good in order to protect their source, so I'll let them explain it!"

Bob explained, "We both feel that if this was to be investigated and arrests were made for charges of conspiracy for murder, our source would be dead within 24 hours. We feel that we need to meet with Gerstein to tell him that this must be kept quiet and for him to leave town with his family for a Memorial Day weekend vacation somewhere. This can be done with no fanfare or publicity. This way, we avoid issues with our source. This would give us time to work with Dade Metro OC (Organized Crime) Bureau on this conspiracy and try to make a federal case against those involved in this!"

"I agree, and I like this plan," the Chief said, "and I'll call Gerstein's office to tell them that Frenchy and Bob need to meet with him because we can't discuss this issue on the phone as to why."

The Sheriff said, "Ok, sounds good. Good work! You guys are making Cecil's and your Sergeant's hair get grey fast! Keep up the good work!" He shook our hands as we walked out.

Back at the office, Cecil said, "Well, that went well. You two head out to Dade and see Mr. Gerstein and give him my love! When you're done, we will meet you at the mom's bar for our Happy Hour!"

Got it, Cecil!" We left the office and were at the state attorney's office an hour later by blue Lighting it all the way to Dade County.

We walked into Gerstein's building and were escorted into his office. After exchanging greetings, we sat down to begin our advisement on this assassination plot. I never met this man before now. He stood approximately 6'1", about 200 pounds, muscular and a sharp dresser, a very distinct one-eyed person, blinded in his mid-fifties but very arrogant. I could tell now why the Sheriff had no love for this man.

My partner took the lead and began his briefing. When he learned of the contract on him by the mob, he went flush white, and his body language totally changed from relaxed to very nervous and shocked. He said," Are you guys sure that this is for real?"

"Do you think that we would drive all the way from Broward if this wasn't serious?" I replied. "We have people on the inside of Santos Trafficante Organization who trust us. This is real! We are here to save you from getting killed! It doesn't get more real than that, Sir!

My partner is not finished. We have a plan to avoid this from happening. He will explain it, and you will have to do exactly what we want you to do in order to save your life. Go ahead, Bobby!"

Gerstein shot me a stern look that was saying, "How dare you talk to me that way!" But being politically correct, I smiled even though I really would've loved to tell him to fuck off!

My partner meticulously laid out what we wanted done, and he and I both asked him for his cooperation on this life-saving plan, to which he agreed. We stressed the importance of total secrecy about this since people's lives were at stake should this be made public. He thanked us and said he would make plans to be out of town and asked us to keep him informed on this matter to which we agreed.

Once we drove off, my partner humorously commented, "What an arrogant SOB!"

"Yeah, I noticed at one point when he was talking to you, that your left eyebrow started to cock up, and I said to myself, 'Please, God, don't let him knock him on his ass!'

"Frenchy, I came close, trust me!"

◦ ◦ ◦ ◦ ◦ ◦

We drove to mom's house for happy hour and had some good laughs with the Wild Bunch! That's when we found out that she was secretly dating a deputy Sheriff. Needless to say, we had some digs to throw at her! Doing this Happy Hour was our way of letting out stress from the job and showed how close we were as a family on this job!

After some time passed, I left and went home to spend time with my parents and cleaned up after a crazy day. Then I got dressed to go out. As usual, my Mother Teresa, aka mom, inquired as to where I was going, and as usual, my dad started laughing, holding up the palms of his hands and shaking his head. I said to her, "Mom! I'm going to meet a lady whom I met at work for a few drinks. She is 30 years old, stunning, and looking for a young stud Frenchman. She wants to make mad passionate love to me. I agreed, and so I'll see you tomorrow!"

She blurted out by looking at my dad saying, "See, I told you this job is no good for him!" She made the sign of the cross and continued, "I can't take this anymore! My God! That's sinful! Are you crazy?"

I said, laughing, "Mom, I'm joking," and kissed her goodnight. "I lied, she is only 28 and has a kid! Goodnight, Ma!" And I left laughing.

Even from outside, I could hear her saying, "I can't make out whether he is lying or telling the truth anymore. God help me!"

18

Disaster

I was at home a few days after our meeting with Gerstein when my partner called me and said, "Frenchy, turn on the tv news channel and call me back." Then he hung up. Bob sounded hot, and I asked my dad to turn on the news channel right away. There it was—a news flash stating that State Attorney Richard Gerstein was the target of a mob contract on his life. Television cameras were running while Gerstein told the media that his office had received credible information that a contract had been taken on his life for the Memorial Day weekend and that he had been asked to leave town but decided that he would not run from any threats. He added that security measures had been taken to protect him until a full investigation was conducted on this matter.

I immediately left the house and called Bob, who was fuming. I said, "I'm on my way to pick you up and did you call Jerry?"

"Yeah, and he is fucking hot! And he is laying low! I'll be waiting, and I called Cecil. He's with the Sheriff and is waiting for us at the Sheriff's office."

"Ok, coming around the corner now!"

He got in the car, and we headed to the office. On the way, he said, "Frenchy, I'm so fucking pissed at that son of a bitch who deserves to be fired from his job!" He slammed the dashboard with his fist.

"We're going to ask Cecil and the Sheriff for the go-ahead for us to go and confront that idiot. This is bad for Jerry!"

As we walked in the Sheriff's office, already there were Cecil, Howard and The Chief of Detectives Captain DeBlois (*deceased*).

The Sheriff began, "I can't believe that this man screwed us and you're CI. It's your call, you two. Make it right!"

Bobby spoke up and said," Right now, boss, it's a good thing he is not in front of me because I probably would put him right through your window and watch him drop nine floors! But I will be calm. Me and Frenchy are going to pay this man a visit and inquire as to why he screwed us and wish him luck."

I said, "We will let him know that any information pertaining to this matter will remain with us, and he will not ever see us again. With your permission. Please don't advise him of us coming. I want this to be an unannounced surprise!"

"That sounds good to me. Go, and please don't lose your cool over this man!"

"Roger that!" I added as we all walked out.

Cecil warned, "Watch what you say and make sure that it's only you two and him. No one else in the room, and make him sit on the couch, not behind his desk in case he tries to record the conversation. I don't trust this man!"

"Yes, Sir!"

My partner said, "I'm driving, Frenchy. Give me your keys!" I handed him my car keys, and off we went. He took off like he was back in North Carolina as a state trooper chasing a moonshiner in the hills.

To make some humor out of it, I started singing the ballad song, "Thunder Road." Bob started laughing, and I kept on singing.

When we arrived at the State Attorney's Office, we walked past the secretary. Bobby said, looking at her, "Don't bother calling him. He's expecting us, and we walked in and shut the door.

Gerstein said, "Excuse me, what do you think you're doing, coming here without an appointment?"

As he got up and walked around his desk, Bob said," I think you know why we are here, Sir! Have a seat here with us. We just want a couple of minutes with you to advise you on the latest developments in your case."

"Ok, speak up and make it quick!"

"Oh, I will. Trust me!" I was enjoying every minute of this and only wished I had a camera to film this wonderful encounter and demeanor of Gerstein, who was actually trembling and most likely shitting in his pants. Bob began, "On behalf of the Sheriff of Broward County and our boss Cecil Stewart, Pete and I both appreciated your wonderful press release on the failed attempt to be killed by the mob!" Bob continued, "Because of your disregard for this investigation and endangering the life and safety of our confidential source, who may end up dead because of your negligence in not disclosing this attempted hit, from this point on, we feel that any new information our department gets on this matter will not be released outside our agency and will remain confidential. We will proceed solo on this case without further contact with you. Sir! You have a great day and good luck and stay vigilant."

Bob and I got up and left him standing there as he was saying, "How dare you come in my office and insult me!" We both waved him good-bye!

He and I had a great laugh all the way back to the car then headed back to the office.

I said, "I never saw this beautiful, sophisticated side of your charming personality, and I am proud that you didn't drop him right there on the spot!"

"Frenchy, you have no idea how bad I wanted to!"

"The problem is Jerry. I don't see any help we can give him unless he would agree to be put in the Witness Protection Program. Knowing him, he will not accept it, so let's hope that we don't get a call that they did him in."

"Frenchy, I don't know what to say! Let's keep our fingers crossed."

◆◆◆◆◆◆

As we arrived at the office, we briefed Cecil, Howard and the Sheriff. We were told that Gerstein had already called the Sheriff and filed his complaint about us busting into his office and all. The Sheriff wished him luck and told him we were acting on his order.

Within 24 hours from the news flash, we received a call from Dade Metro Homicide Bureau that someone had reported seeing a body in a canal at the Dade/Broward County line on US-27 by the Everglades. The body was on the Dade side. It was reported that a male had been shot, bullet-riddled to death, and the body was identified as that of Jerry Springer. Our worst fear came to a reality, but we never mentioned that he had been a source for our department at that time.

———— ·✦✦✦✦· ————

Months later, I happened to do a drive-thru at Joe Sunken's place on Hollywood Beach to see if any of our local bad guys were there. I observed as I pulled in that State Attorney Richard Gerstein was entering the restaurant.

I waited about five minutes until I couldn't pass up the opportunity to go in and show myself to him. I entered and sitting in a booth by the large window facing the Inter-coastal Waterway was Gerstein and Joe Sunken engaged in a conversation.

I approached the table, and Joe said, "Detective Charette! How are you, son?"

"Doing well, Joe! Just making the rounds. Do you know Mr. Gerstein?"

"Yes, I do! We have crossed paths in regard to the Jerry Springer matter."

"Nice seeing you, Sir. Have a great evening, Sir, and hope you're in good health." I left with Gerstein's mouth open as he was staring me down.

"Damn! That felt good!" I said as I walked away, smiling.

That was my first loss of a CI in the death of a source that was totally unnecessary because of an official who disregarded the safety of a confidential source who was trying to save his own life! Unfortunately, that is something that he will have to live with for the rest of his life! The Dade Metro Sheriff Investigation much later arrested the doorman at the club for the murder of Springer, but the defendant was acquitted on lack of evidence to prove his guilt.

19

Surprise Career Change

My work with the vice squad was exciting. We had the best team in BSO. I will never regret this experience. It had ups and downs along the way, but it was one hell of a ride for someone of my age. One piece of advice that I cannot emphasize more is that staying alert and being always prepared for the worst can actually protect you from being hurt or killed.

I had been working with my partner checking various bars in the county and suspected gambling establishments. My partner advised me that we would call it a night. I told him I would head south and stop in at the Hallandale PD to see the lieutenant.

I arrived at the police department at around 3:00 a.m. and greeted everyone. The lieutenant was drinking coffee with some of the cops. He said, "Frenchy, what's up, pal?"

I responded, "Lieutenant, I just stopped by to see if you guys are staying out of trouble. Want a cup of coffee?"

"Sure, how're things going?"

As he was pouring me a cup, he said, "Well, we've been having a crazy situation that we are trying to figure out! We have some broad, who for the past several weeks, has been robbing motorists late at night by hitchhiking on Hallandale Beach Boulevard. She gets in and begins having a conversation, then pulls out a switchblade knife that she holds to their necks and demands their wallets, gets them to stop, then jumps out and takes off running."

"Wow, ballsy bitch! Do you have a description of her?"

"Well, she is about 5'3", slim build, long blond hair, jeans, silky shirt open, low cut in the front and about mid-20s."

Well, I will keep my eyes out for her. I usually go home to Miramar up Hallandale Beach Boulevard at night."

"Sounds good. We're always here for you if you need us!"

"Thanks! Got to go and you guys, be safe!"

I got in my car and placed my .38 revolver tucked under my left thigh, figuring that if she is out there, I'll pick up this gutsy bitch and put an end to her game. I drove up Hallandale Beach Boulevard and was just passing under I-95, heading west approaching the rock quarry lake when I observed a young female hitchhiking on the side of the road. I slowed down and pulled over. It was around 4:00 a.m. and figured this was luck that it had to be her. She opened the passenger's door and sat down, closed the door and placed her open purse on her right side of the seat, then slid closer to me and said, "Hi! Thanks for the lift. I just got off work and am heading to State Road 41!"

"No problem. I'm heading to Miramar. Late hours at work?"

"Yeah, I work on the beach. My car is in the shop, so hitching is the only way for me right now." As she started to sneeze and reach into her purse, I reached for my gun and pulled over at the same time that she started to pull out an open switchblade knife.

The quick stop jerked her forward against the dashboard, and I immediately pointed my gun at her saying, "Drop the knife, bitch. Police!" She immediately complied, and I said, "Slowly, hands behind your back and face toward the door, now! I locked the doors, reached for my handcuffs and put them on her. Once this was completed, I pulled back on the road and made a U-turn to head back to the Hallandale Police Department, then radioed the dispatcher, advising that I had one female in custody, reported mileage and advised her to dispatch the paddy wagon to HPD for a pickup.

While traveling to the police department, I advised her of her rights. She was crying and pleading to me to give her a break. I advised her that she was being arrested for several counts of aggravated assault with a weapon, armed robbery, attempted aggravated assault, and robbery on a police officer. She remained silent as we arrived at the PD. Waiting outside after receiving a call from BSO dispatcher was the lieutenant and two uniformed officers who were smiling.

I said, getting out of the car, "Lieutenant, are you still looking for a female suspect?" Laughing, I continued. "I got a gift for you. She's right here in the front seat. How's that for quick service?"

He said, "Frenchy, how in the hell do you do it! Do you want a job with a promotion with us? I'm sure the Chief would love to have you with us!"

"Thanks, but I like the wide-open territory. A small department would curtail my fun! I'm going to process her and call in the victims and see if we can get IDs of her to fully charge this lady!"

Once the BSO wagon picked up my client and I called in the charges to our booking desk, I told them, "Time for me to go home and get some beauty sleep. I'll see you guys later. I'll file my two charges with the solicitor's office tomorrow and call you to confirm it. Thanks for the tip! Best to the Chief, and you guys owe me a drink!"

"You got it, Frenchy! See you soon, and we owe you!"

"Nah! Anytime, pal!" I left feeling good by having been so lucky to nail her and to help my good friends! "God, I love this job!"

By the time I got home, it was 6:30, and Dad was up drinking coffee before going to work. We chatted about this crazy night, and he said, "Pete, I don't know how you do it. I am amazed at all the stuff that you get into, and I really think that God has given you a special gift to do what you do. He's watching out for you!"

"Dad, I am amazed on how I get so fortunate to make these cases. Thank you and Mom for your support! I just keep falling into all this stuff, and it seems that there's never a dull moment. Just remember, I can't take all the credit. I have great partners, and we do this together. The credit is all ours together!"

"You make me proud when I hear you say that. Some cops that I have known will try to claim all the credit for themselves. Don't ever change."

Dad left for work and Mom came into the kitchen asking why I was up so early. I told her I had to be at work early today and left it at that. God forbid if I told her what had happened. She would have flipped out about me being in a dangerous job. She had a cross to bear with two sons in law enforcement and little did she know that a third son was also going to be following in our footsteps in 10 years. This would be my kid brother Bernard. I guess three out of five boys is not too bad! We sure made life interesting for her!

I left for work without getting any sleep, in order to knock out my arrest report on this young lady and meet with the prosecutor and appear for a bond hearing. When I arrived at the office, our den mother looked up and said, "Yes! I was waiting for you. Dispatch gave me a heads up about your encounter last night while you were out prowling around. Let's knock out the report before Cecil gets in. I responded, "Yes, Mom! I love you too! You're just jealous because the dispatcher has a crush on me?"

"Watch it, Frenchy, or I will call your mom! Ha-ha."

"You got me, let's do it!"

We finished the report in one hour and another two hours with the prosecutor and the bond hearing and I were done. Bond was set at $10,000, and our client was remanded in custody since she could not make bond.

Back upstairs, my partner was already in doing reports. When he saw me, he said, "You can't stay out of shit, can you?"

"It was a fluke collar. There she was hitchhiking, wanting to be arrested, and I politely accommodated her request!" I laughed as I sat at my desk.

"Ok, Frenchy, we got to do a stakeout tonight. We got a tip from our strip club sources that there are a couple of guys who are bragging to the ladies that they are boosting parking meters at Dania Beach parking lot on Saturday nights when they are loaded with quarters from weekend parking."

"Sounds good to me, your call, partner!"

"Ok, I got a great idea. The lot is big and hard to surveil, so we are going to get there just after dark and come in from the south side from Hollywood Beach. We will walk in from the ocean side and dig ourselves in with small Army shovels that I picked up at the Army store. Then we will cover ourselves up with a big Camouflage tarp and nail them after they cleaned out several rows of meters."

"Sounds like a plan. We need to get some binoculars and extra cuffs just in case we have more than two. I'll get the cuffs and nocs!"

"This will be a fun one." We proceeded to brief Cecil and our Sergeant. They laughed and loved our plans. We asked them to assist us in having a couple of unmarked cars stationed, one south of A1-A of the Dania Bridge and one west of the bridge staging at the Dania Jai Alai in order to block the road once we give the signal in case they try to flee. Cecil agreed, and everybody had portable radios to communicate with each other, with us being the point men.

We had a briefing at the vice office and made sure Dania PD was not notified for obvious reasons. As an old police saying goes, "Burn once, never twice!" We left the office around eight. Bob and I went south on A1-A and parked near the Hollywood line at a roadside parking area near a trail to the beach from A1-A. We got our tarp and digging tools, then proceeded to the beach and began walking by the water north for one mile.

By the time we got there, it was 10:00 p.m., and we notified everyone that we were on location and could see a few cars parked facing the ocean on the first row. Everyone was told to hold their position for at least two hours. A quick look at the occupants of the cars with our nocs revealed the occupants to be teenagers smooching and caressing.

This brought back memories from my South Broward High School Days as a senior in 1963 when a bunch of us used to come here and park and make out. It was always funny when guys used to bet on who would be the first to yell out "Periscope Up," at which time we would all start sounding our horns and check to see who was running up their radio antenna with a pair of ladies' panties. It was better than nowadays where the fun is getting whacked out on drugs.

Finally, around midnight, after all the cars had left, Bobby and I gave the word that we were coming in to dig in. We had one lookout inside the bridge tender's hut watching for cars coming south on A-1-A to the beach exit and east to alert us. Luckily nothing came, and within 40 minutes, we had dug in and covered up within 20 yards from the sidewalk and close to the meters. We waited patiently until we were alerted that a vehicle with two males was turning in the lot. The car made a pass through the lot slowly, after which the two males then drove down the road that led to the Coast Guard station, turned around, made a pass by the south side of A1-A, returned and parked on the south side of the lot by the first row. The passenger got out with a mop pail and walked quickly to the north end of the first row, where he began opening all the first-row meters with a key, dumping all the coins in the pail and putting the first-row pail in the car.

When he was done, he repeated the process again with a new pail. Each row had approximately 20 meters and 10 rows. We waited until the subject started the third row then we gave the signal to go ahead and block the two roads within one block of the area.

We slowly slipped out from underneath our tarp, and Bob slowly went by the south side of the lot and came up slowly from behind the lookout car while I had worked my way to the north side down toward the fifth row and worked my way back up quickly. My partner grabbed the driver, and I gave the signal to move in. I was within ten feet of this asshole and yelled, "Police! Down on the ground now, or I'll blow your head off!" The suspect immediately dropped the bucket and went face down on the ground. The guys came in, blue lights blaring. Everyone was safe, and the two dirt-bags were in custody.

While we were securing the area and getting our info on the meters and such, a Dania PD car pulled up, and an officer asked what was going on? We advised him and IDed ourselves as BSO Vice Squad then told him we caught two guys breaking into meters. He thanked us and left quickly. I'm sure Cecil was going to get a call from the Dania Chief on this one. We all went back to the office. Our tip was good, and these two defendants later pled out. Our hunch was right! Cecil got a call from the Chief whom he set straight, saying that our source had informed us that these guys had some cops on the force who looked the other way for them. The Chief thanked Cecil and said he would investigate this. Case closed.

---- ✦✦✦✦✦✦ ----

The time I spent in vice was truly a great law enforcement education, and we all made many cases and always supported one another as a family of trusted members with one another. I chose some cases that were unique for that era in law enforcement, and the support I received from Cecil, our unit, and Sheriff Michell was above and beyond what one would expect as a detective. These individuals, along with my crazy bunch of partners, will never be forgotten. They were, in my opinion, the pioneers of the Broward Sheriff's Department, and I am proud to say that I was chosen by them to be part of this history. Once again, I was not prepared to be asked to serve in another truly unique and specialized field of law enforcement that few get the opportunity to experience.

20

Transfer of Assignment
Special Squad – June 7, 1968

Lieutenant Stewart had called an all-hands meeting for Monday morning to go over cases that were active and to get input from us on what more we could do to keep up with changing times. It was becoming obvious to all of us that Broward County was experiencing a population growth along with an increase in organized criminal activity by the Florida Mob and the rise in narcotic activity with the use and sale of heroin, methamphetamine, LSD, marijuana, barbiturates and some cocaine. Also, on the increase were a rise of illegal gambling and bookmaking activity.

Our small vice and narcotics unit consisted of only seven detectives, only two of whom were in narcotics, Sergeant Joe Clark and one detective. We all agreed that we needed additional manpower, and Cecil advised us that it was time for him and Clark to have a meeting with the Chief of Detective Captain Joseph DeBlois and the Sheriff. In the one year that I had been on board, arrests in our unit had tripled from previous years.

Cecil said, "Ok, since we all agree that we need a change, I knew already that this was going to be the feeling of ya'll! The Chief and I are due upstairs in five minutes. Wish me luck! Anyone of you want to bet on the outcome? Twenty-five bucks says we get what we want! Who's in?" To his surprise, all 8 of us took the bet. "Damn! If you guys win, I'm out $200! That's 50% of my salary!" he said, laughing on his way out!

Two hours later, he returned with a drained look on his face, and we all waited for him to speak. "Well, it's good news and bad news! First, the good news. The old man agreed to our request, and we will be increasing our manpower!"

"Yes!" Everyone yelled out and smiled, looking extremely pleased.

"Now the bad news! Narcotics is going to be separate with Joe and his partner Sergeant Chuck. You guy's got your job cut for you because he's approved one new position, and we all agreed that Frenchy is our choice since he looks young and has shown a unique talent to work undercover, a talent that we all have admired. And Joe, he was your original choice to come on board."

Everyone was cheering and saying things like, "You're the boy!" and some chanting,

"Frenchy!" I was stunned and speechless for a minute, trying to fathom what had just happened.

"Cecil and all of you, I can't believe this has actually happened. From the first time I saw Joe lying in a gutter and posing as a drunk, I knew that this is what I wanted to do, and you guys helped me get there. I will always be there, and Joe and Sarge, I'm ready to give it all I got. I won't let you down, trust me. Thanks guys! Oh, Cecil, with that $25 that you owe me, the drinks are on me at Betty's bar tonight."

"You little punk, you're on," he shot back, laughing and shaking my hand. "Frenchy, you go out there and give them hell and enjoy the ride." He continued laughing as he usually did when he was with his crazy bunch!"

Joe said, "Frenchy, enjoy the weekend off, and on Monday, come to our hole in the wall office where we are going to start kicking ass and put dopers in jail."

We all went to Our den mother's bar, and I brought

some vodka and beer. We celebrated our victory and left after midnight! It was quite an evening. Surprisingly, no one got drunk, but all had a slight buzz!

I drove home and ran several scenarios in my mind as to how to break the news to Mom. She will really flip out when she sees her son transformed from a clean-cut detective to a hippy!! God help me! I pulled in the driveway and could see that they were still up, snuggled together on the living room couch watching a movie. "Well, caught you lovebirds!"

Laughing, Dad said, "What are you doing home so early? Are you Ok?"

"Oh yeah! Let me get a glass of wine. Be right back." I removed my gun and placed it in a locked drawer next to my bed, poured myself a nice Beaujolais Nouveau and sat down with Mom and Dad. Then I continued, "Ok, quite a day today. We made some new changes in vice and narcotics by getting the Ok to increase our resources because this county is growing too fast, and we need to adjust. Things are changing for the better, and I'm part of this change. To my surprise, the Sheriff, Cecil Stewart and the Chief of detectives reassigned me to the Narcotics Bureau to work undercover on drug users and drug traffickers."

"Oh! My God!! Are you crazy?" Mom exclaimed. "That's dangerous, worse than what you were doing! My God, Pete, think this over, please!"

"Mom, I wanted this type of career in undercover work ever since I joined BSO. I've been praying for this, and it finally happened. This is what I believe my role is in law enforcement, and nothing anyone says will change my mind on this."

"Kitty!" Dad said, "Pete is his own man, and I'm with him on this. He's found his purpose in life, and he's always cautious and knows better than anyone how to do this work! Pete, I'm proud of you! Keep going and follow your heart, son!"

Mom said, "Ok! You made your point. Pete, I never thought I'd say this, but it's time for me to stand with you and not against you. You are so special to me, as are all my boys. I want what you want, and from here on, I will always be worried in a good way for you." Mom gave me a hug and held me.

Finally, I said, "All right, let's have one more drink together and celebrate." And that we did until 3:00 a.m., just laughing and going over how my life has changed over the years. I went to bed not being able to sleep and going over in my mind various scenarios of being a 'narc.'

* * * * * *

Monday morning, I reported to the narcotics office bright and early. As I walked down the hallway, I was greeted with cheers by the detective bureau team and given a thumbs up and handshakes by my friends. It was hard to hold the emotions that I was feeling and to stop smiling. By far, this was the best day of my life.

I opened the door to the office and sat. At the secretary's desk was our den mother who was grinning when she saw me and got up to give me a big hug and kiss and said, "Surprise! I'm also part of the package!"

Then entered the Sergeant who said, "Well, we finally got you. Joe and I will show you a completely different world than what you have been involved in. Let's get you settled in and get your desk set up by the window."

"Great! I'm anxious to learn the ropes and start this crazy ride!"

Joe chimed in, saying," Oh, don't worry! You might as well learn very fast that this is a dangerous job, and the assholes we deal with are crazy and suspicious of every person they meet and will not hesitate to kill you if they suspect you're the man. Frenchy, I'm not exaggerating one bit. As of right now, let this sink in and never forget it. If you learn one thing about this work, remember to never let your guard down. If you do, it can cost you your life."

Joe was looking at me with a look to kill, and I could tell that he was very serious. He of all people, from what I had heard about him, was the best that the state of Florida had in this line of work. He was a legend, and I was so fortunate to learn from the best in this profession.

At the back of the office, the Sergeant and Joe had set up a table with an assortment of drugs laid out for me to see and recognize for this job. The assortment consisted of packages of heroin, marijuana, cocaine, barbiturates, amphetamines, LSD, hashish, and opium, in various modes of packaging for sale. They both took their time to make me memorize and feel these drugs until I did so numerous times to ensure I knew what it looked like and how it smelled or felt.

Joe than sat with me for a couple of hours, teaching me the street lingo and slang of the drug culture world. This was something that the Police Academy didn't teach you in a classroom setting. Narcotic trafficking was just beginning to flourish in 1966 with the hippy culture. I was also told that my entire appearance had to blend in to fit inside this crazy world.

"Frenchy, you need to start growing your hair long and grow a beard or goatee and dress in bell-bottom pants and a colorful hippy shirt to fit in with these assholes," Joe said. "Tomorrow, we are going to take you around the county where the drugs are being sold and to bars in order to hang out and introduce you to informants who will set up buys for you. The problem we have had that held us back, is that Chuck is fat and older, and although I can blend in with the older crowd, I can't among those of your age! That's why we chose you because you have surprised us with how quickly you made cases. You had a special talent, and we knew you were going to fit right in.

"Wow! I just hope I won't let you guys down! I'm ready once you think I'm good to go!"

⋅ ⋅ ◆ ◆ ◆ ⋅ ⋅

I was given a day to review prior narcotic case files that had been worked on by both of them. I quickly learned that undercover work is highly complicated and requires quick thinking and alertness at all times when playing this role. The first thing I discovered is that once I have a target, I need to learn as much as I can about him. This involves researching criminal records to determine if the target has one, the number of arrests, photographs, and to verify if any of our law enforcement agencies have any active cases on the target. Joe taught me to be sure that the agencies I check with are those with whom I have established a contact within that department who are trustworthy. This is a must because I can ruin my entire case from the get-go.

Once I have done my homework, then I need to do loose surveillance on the target and determine his daily activities, associates, driving patterns, and get his cell phone numbers, house phone numbers and subpoena his phone records for three months to gather intelligence on his contacts. This can lead me, according to Joe, to known drug suspects and possible sources for his drug network. Reviewing case files is a great tool to learn from those who have worked in this unique job!

After reviewing files for several days, we learned that Joe had been recruited to work for the newly formed Florida Department of Law Enforcement (FDLE). He was hired by them as a supervisory agent, and even though we were elated for him, we were disappointed in losing the best narcotic agent in the state of Florida, in our opinion.

This meant that we needed to get a replacement and do so as soon as possible. The Sergeant said, "Frenchy, you and I are going to be out for the rest of the week, for me to introduce to you to our narcotics counterparts in Broward County, Metro Dade County Sheriff's Department, Miami P.D. and our Federal Bureau of Narcotics agents in Miami. These people are it for south Florida, and we have worked together using each other for undercover resources when we can't do the UC role because we are known by the targets. These detectives and agents are part of our special family, and you will be part of a unique and trusted group of narcos that are legends since drugs started to flourish in Florida the past several years."

"Sounds like a plan. How many are doing this work?"

He replied, "You won't believe this. Right now, there are three with Hollywood PD, five with Dade Metro, three with Miami PD, five with FBN, four with Ft. Lauderdale PD, and you and I. That makes 22 in total."

"That's crazy. I can see why we need each other's help!"

"Just a heads up. These guys are the best you can have the honor to work with, but they are also wild and crazy in a way that makes for some great fun and exciting work at the same time. The one thing you will never have to worry about is that if any of us get in a jam or in a bad situation, these guys will always be there for you regardless of the danger, and they will kick ass big time! They expect the same from each other. Just remember, we work together, fight together, and play together!"

"Got it. I wouldn't want any other way, but I got to ask this and hope I'm not speaking out of line by what I'm going to say. I have one thing since I went into law enforcement work that I live by and will never surrender!"

"Shoot. Let me have it!"

"That's my integrity! I will never accept a bribe, ask to perjure myself for anyone's benefit, and will always be ready to back my partner and fellow officers no matter what the cost is!"

Cecil, Joe and I saw this in you, Frenchie, and that is why we brought you in, and we all feel the same about our integrity."

"I am honored to hear this from you, so let's go and kick ass!"

"Now, you're talking!" The Sergeant shot back, laughing.

"I love this job!"

"Ok. Turning to the secretary, the sarge said, "Hey, Mom, it's time to close down the fort! Is the bar open? Frenchy and I sure could use a drink before heading out for home!"

"You bet it is! I thought you two were on the verge of crying, listening to the two of you!" She smiled and continued, Let's go, my boys. See you at the house!"

We all left the shop and ran into Cecil, who said, "By the smile on all your faces, count me in. See you at Mom's bar!" He blew her a kiss, which she sent right back, laughing.

We all met at her place and had a few drinks and laughed and took swipes at each other. It was then that I realized I was fulfilling my dreams and that I was part of this special family few can ever experience in their lifetimes.

21

Meeting the Narcs

Sarge and I met at the office and headed out for my introduction to the best narcotics agents in south Florida. Our first stop was at the Hollywood Police Department Narcotics office. The department had three detectives. The head of the unit was a Sergeant who was in his late twenties, approximately 175 pounds, 5'10" who was highly trusted along with his right-hand partner, a black-haired Italian in his late twenties, 5'10" who had a great sense of humor and was highly regarded as an expert in this field of work. The third member was a detective in his late twenties, about 6 feet, 180 pounds, soft-spoken, and liked by everyone. I was given a briefing about the rising drug problem in this city and welcomed graciously into the family.

"Pete, we heard about you, and you can be assured that we have a solid relationship with BSO and look forward to work hand in hand with you."

"I assure you that you have my full support and help anytime you want. I know that I'm up to the challenge anytime you need me."

"Don't worry, we will be calling on you to help us in surveillance and undercover cases because when it comes to this work, we don't have any boundaries."

My boss responded by saying, "I think that Frenchy is what we need. He has displayed a skill for being great, working in undercover investigations when he was in the vice squad."

We left after talking about various ongoing investigations, and I felt extremely good and honored to be a part of this great team.

We next stopped at the Oakland Park Police Department Detective Bureau. This unit had three detectives who worked all aspects of crime. The Chief of the unit was Pierre Pelletier (*deceased*). Pierre was in his forties, with a jovial personality, short in stature, and very well respected by all. His narcotics detective was Rick Riggio *(deceased),* who was approximately 5'10" and 175 pounds who became a close friend and, in later years, joined the BSO Narcotics Unit under the command of Nick Navarro (*deceased*) who later became the Sheriff of Broward County. Our meeting was very informative, and our relationship was one of the best in Broward County.

I realized that the drug problem, according to law enforcement in south Florida, was beginning to escalate and that the most prevalent drugs being used and sold were heroin, marijuana, LSD, barbiturates, amphetamine and the introduction of cocaine. Luckily, law enforcement was getting fantastic support from the judicial system and prosecutors. Drug defendants were given maximum sentences, and this made an impact and had a deterrent effect in our favor.

Unfortunately, around the late 1970s, we began to see a change with liberal judges releasing defendants with low bonds, lower jail sentences, which resulted in a rise in repeated offenders that should have been given stiffer sentences. I firmly believe that this contributed to the rise of narcotic trafficking in the United States and has been one of the major contributors to our escalating drug problem.

<hr />

My Sergeant made sure that I met our counterparts in Dade County, which bordered Broward County. We met with the Metro Dade County Sheriff's narcotics unit Chief, who was a short man about 5'8", soft-spoken and highly respected by his team, which consisted of two detectives. This unit had a reputation of being feared by the dopers because of their ability to infiltrate the narcotics underworld and were very effective in arresting traffickers in Dade County. They were the best and craziest narcs I ever had the pleasure to work with. One was around 6 feet, approximately 25 years old with long blond hair who dressed like a hippy. He wore bell-bottom pants, hippy shirts and rode a motorcycle chopper. (He was a clone of the star of Easy Rider.) The other was the calmer of the two who stood at 5'10", black hair, 165 pounds, dressed casually and was soft-spoken and an extremely good narc!

Our meeting was once again amazing to see their enthusiasm to work in this field, and I felt once again that I was part of an unbelievable brotherhood of narcs into which very few law enforcement officers have the opportunity to be inducted.

Heading back to the office, Sarge said, "Frenchy, you only have one more group to meet, and that's the Federal Bureau of Narcotic Agents of the Miami office. They are a small group of great guys, some of whom you will meet when they come to the office usually on Friday afternoon. We usually all get together on Fridays at one of the watering holes at a pool bar on Fort Lauderdale Beach. These guys are great to work with, but be prepared to be evaluated by them before they accept you. They have high integrity and expectations and expect those who they work with are also up to their standards. The boss of the office is Joe Reed (*deceased*), who has five agents."

"I hope I will pass this test. Sounds like they are on guard with who they work with."

"That's for sure! FBN (Federal Bureau of Narcotics) works all over the world in undercover scenarios to infiltrate the suppliers of narcotics into the United States to the U.S. mob. They combat the major organizations at the highest level of narcotics trafficking worldwide, but they have to be careful with whom they work, since there is a lot of police corruption involved with drug trafficking. They can't afford to be compromised because that could result in the endangerment and murder of UC agents."

"That makes sense, wow! These guys must be good. I never heard of them before. I hope that they will trust me."

"They will. Best advice is not to try to act like you're a hotshot. Just listen and be yourself. If you're arrogant and try to impress them, you're done with them. Sloopy is extremely suspicious at first, but once he accepts you, you are solid with him for life! You will do fine. That's why we picked you, so don't worry!"

"Got it. This has been quite a day. I'm still amazed that I am actually one of you all, and trust me, I won't let you all down!"

"Ok, let's head in and call it a good day!"

<hr />

Working with the Sheriff's Department in the state of Florida was always a challenge because Sheriffs were elected to their positions and had the right to fire deputies at will. This caused deputies to be fired once a new Sheriff was sworn into office. In 1966 Sheriff Michell was indicted for "knowingly, willfully or corruptly," allowing gambling in Broward County. An interim Sheriff was appointed by the Florida governor.

Elected was a prominent county politician named Edward Stack (*deceased*) from Pompano Beach. He was sworn in after the election results were announced, and an all-hands meeting of employees was ordered at midnight in the courthouse meeting room. This is where I saw firsthand that if you became involved in the political race by taking sides with a candidate, the price for sure was being fired!

Sheriff Stack entered the room with his new entourage of loyal supporters and introduced himself to all. The room was silent, and he wasted no time asking that the names which he called out to stand up. He went through a list of about ten names, all deputies, detectives and line officers. Once he finished reading the names, those of us remaining seated were told to stay in the room. He continued, "Those of you standing, please leave the room and turn in your property. Your service is no longer required by this department." I couldn't believe what I was seeing and quickly learned that if we wanted to keep our jobs, we shouldn't get involved in politics when employed in a Sheriff's department. The Sheriff addressed all of us, thanking us for being excellent members of this department then dismissed all of us. Fortunately for us, the Vice and Narcotics Bureau remained intact, and we all went to the vice office to meet with Lieutenant Stewart.

Stewart said, "Ok, anyone shit themselves after that meeting? All I got to say is that we are solid and that's because we don't play politics–ever! Just remember that we maintain our integrity and honesty, and I'll handle the heat if we get called on the carpet! There's going to be some changes in the detective bureau, so I heard, and he is bringing in some Ex-New York cops to be put in charge of units. So, watch what you say and do as your told. As long as it's legal, go with the flow. If it's an illegal order, then see me right away, and we will go for the jugular fast! Let's go have a drink at the watering hole because I sure could use one right now, and if you're wondering if I shit myself, I came very close to it like some of you." He was laughing as we walked out.

Once at Betty's bar, we all discussed this night and felt sorry for some of those who had a family to feed and were now looking for work. Thank God that they all got hired by various police departments in the county.

Coming back to work was, needless to say, a bit uneasy, but Sarge and I were told that the new administration had authorized seven new positions to our special squad. We had a sit down with Lieutenant Stewart to discuss a list of names given to him for consideration for the new detectives' positions. After several hours of discussing these individuals, it was agreed that we needed a variety of males and females who would blend in with the drug culture we were facing. The good thing was that Stewart and Sarge made it very clear that the call for those chosen would be our choice. In the end, our selections were approved without any objection. It turned out that the new hires turned out to be the right choices.

Sarge told me that we had been requested to meet with Chief of Detective Pierre Pelletier of the Oakland Park Police Department, who needed me to work undercover for them with one of their detectives, Rick Riggio (*deceased*). Upon meeting with Detective Pelletier, he advised that their department had received information from an informant that there were two females who were working as prostitutes out of a local bar. The informant had been advised to tell them that he had two friends from out of town staying at a nearby motel who wanted to party with them.

Arrangements had been made for Rick and me to meet with them at 7:00 p.m. Before our arrival, the motel room had been wired for sound to be monitored by OPD Detective Pelletier and Sarge.

Rick was in his early twenties, tall and weighed approximately 175lbs. We spent some time together getting our story straight as to where we were from, along with our work background and other pertinent information.

Rick and I became close friends throughout my career. He had two wonderful daughters Jennifer and Shari, who are still close to him. He eventually became a BSO detective in narcotics under Sheriff Nick Navarro and was one of the finest narcotics agents in Broward County.

Detective Pelletier gave each of us $100 of previously recorded serial numbers for payment to the hookers. The room was already prepared with travel suitcases with clothes out in the open and half a bottle of vodka with glasses, tonic and ice bucket out in view. The beds were made to appear used and ruffled.

Rick and I picked up a pizza and took it to the room to await their arrival. The two ladies arrived as expected and were invited in. Rick said, "Welcome, girls. I'm Rick and that's Pete."

"Nice of you to come and party with us. You two look great!"

"Thanks," said the blond, whose name was Cindy, "nice to meet you both. Where you from?"

"I'm from Quebec, Canada, and Rick is from Jersey, and we're here on vacation for a week!" I said.

The other female, whose name was Anne remarked, "Yeah, I noticed a Canadian tag on that Mustang in front of this room. Nice ride!"

"You ladies like a drink? Or shall we get down to party?"

"First, I guess you were told that our price is $100 each for two hours of fun together, and we'd like it first!"

"No problem! Business is business first. Then the fun begins." Rick reached out with his wallet and gave her $200.

"Thanks!" Then both girls started to undress, and Cindy turned around and stuffed the money in her underwear as I watched her. The girls stripped down to their underwear as I said the code words– "Wow, you look great!"–for our guys to hear and come in to make the arrest. Expecting them to come in the door with the spare key, we waited, but nothing happened! I could hear laughing on the other side of the wall.

Then Anne said, "Well, come on! It's your turn to undress," as she and her friend sat on the edge of the two beds.

"Wow, you both look great!" I repeated, hoping that our backups would once again come in. Nothing happened, but more laughter.

"Ok, let's do it, Rick. Let's give them what we all want." I started to take off my shirt while Rick looked at me in a puzzled manner. Anne was becoming impatient and said, "What's the matter, Rick, are you a queer who likes to watch? Come on, take it off." Rick began undressing while I continued by taking my shoes off slowly, once again saying in a louder voice, "WOW! You two sure look good! I'm ready! Come on, let's do it!" I could hear our back up moving and within 30 seconds, they burst through the door and said, "Police. You're under arrest."

The girls looked at both of us who were partially naked, and Cindy said, looking at me, "You son of a bitch."

I looked at her and said, "Let's have the money."

"Fuck you. I don't know what you're talking about."

"The money in your crotch, either you produce it, or I will do a cavity search, bitch! What's it going to be?" I threatened as I started to reach for her underwear.

"No, I'll get it." She reached in her underwear and pulled out two marked bills.

"Good girl. Let's take a picture for court. Smile pretty." Rick and I held them.

Laughing, Detective Pelletier said to Rick, "Now that I see you like this, you do look kind of queer!"

"Sarge, why didn't you guys come in right away?"

"We wanted to see how far you two would go for laughs! Good job!"

The two girls were booked and pled guilty to soliciting for prostitution and were fined and given a sentence.

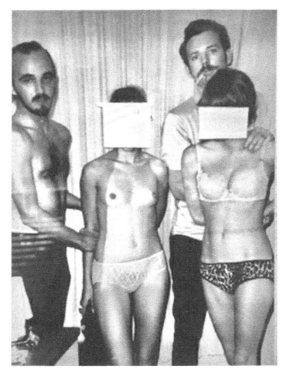

Arresting the Ladies

Returning to the office, Sarge told me that we would have the visit of our federal narcotics friends tomorrow, which was on the last Friday of the month. He explained that they had called and would be at our office to get us on-board for a heroin buy with one of our confidential informants.

The CI would take me to the A&W Drive Inn on Broward Boulevard to meet a black heroin dealer. The CI would introduce me as a new client looking to buy five dime ($10) bags. The feds would fund the purchase, and additional buys by me would be made for their federal case. Sarge advised that we help them with heroin cases every month so that they can then arrest the seller in order to go further up the chain of major suppliers. Doing so would allow us to testify in federal court for them and would usually lead to arrests of significant traffickers and larger seizure of drugs. The heroin purchases are also analyzed for intelligence on strength and purity of heroin being sold in locations throughout the U. S.

This type of case was new for me and sounded exciting and fascinating on how the feds worked their way up the echelon of the narcotics underworld. State and local departments did not have the financial resources to work large cases. Our narcotics budget was around $5000 for the year, so we relied on the state and federal purchases to make arrests of narcotic traffickers worldwide.

On Friday, we met the informant and spent the time going over our stories about how long we had been dealing with each other, where I lived and about our search for a new weekly source. We discussed that I would do the talking once we met with the suspect. If things went wrong, my signal to move in would be my removing my baseball cap and rubbing my hair. I advised the CI that I would be there at 4:40 p.m. in my white Mustang and park facing Broward Boulevard in front of a burger drive-in.

Returning to the office, we waited for the feds to arrive. Sitting at my desk doing some initial report for this case, I saw two individuals walk in dressed in sport coats, one being about 6 feet tall, about 190 pounds and wearing a smile. The other, about 5'7", short and stocky build, had black hair and looked suspiciously at me without a smile on his face. Laughing, Sarge said, "What a surprise!"

Sarge first spoke to Sloopy, AKA Agent Gerhardt (PN), and asked, "Why are you hanging around with such bad company!"

Gerhardt answered, "Yeah, you know me, always with Mr. good-looking. Someone's got to keep him straight and out of trouble, especially if he is around Mom here!" While he said this, he already made a beeline for her, embraced her, gave her a big kiss and hug, saying, "You are more beautiful than the last time! How about we leave these guys and go for a drink alone?" he said, laughing.

"Miller, you talk big, but never produce! GOTCHA!" Laughing.

"Oh yeah! You don't know what you're missing." He put his arm around her neck and hugged her.

Sarge broke in. "Ok, lover boy, meet our new addition to this group. This is Pierre 'Pete' Charette, who I told you guys about. I guess he already knows who the two of you are!"

"Agent Sloopy (PN) continued, "Yeah, heard a lot about you, guy! Pleasure to meet you and hope we can get to know each other, but I got to warn you about my partner. He will get you in trouble if you believe his BS!" We have been working together for many years, and I still wonder what he is all about. We try to live with him and protect him as best as we can!"

"Don't believe a word of what they say about me. I'm just a nice guy trying his best not to laugh," Agent Miller chimed in.

"Ok," Sarge said, "We got the buy set up, and Pete will buy $50 of smack with your money and arrange additional buys for you! We got to go. The meet is at 3:30 p.m. at the A&W."

Pete, here's five marked $10 bills. Let's do it! I like your dress code. You fit right in with this drug culture." Miller was referring to my hippy clothes, bell-bottom pants, flowered Hawaiian shirt, Goatee, and long, shoulder-length hair.

"Thanks. I'm ready. Let's do it!"

We left the office, and I got into my car and checked my ankle holster to ensure that my Snub Nose .38 S&W was secured. I arrived at the A&W, parked facing Broward Boulevard and leaned back on the rear of my Mustang, waiting with my ball cap on my head. A few minutes passed by before the CI arrived in his car, parked next to me, and got out, then we high fived each other. He advised me that the source should be here any minute that he only lives a few blocks from here.

The source arrived in a white Cadillac, pulled in next to the CI's car, got out and walked over to greet the CI and said, "My man, how's go, bro! Who's your friend?"

"This is Pete, and I'm good, dude. We've been doing business for a long time. He works on the strip near the Holiday Inn on the beach."

"Yeah! That's cool. He tells me that you looking to do some weight!

If that's what you're looking for, then I'm your man and can handle loads with no problem."

"Yeah, I got a good group of people, and I'm always looking for folks in case I lose a connection. That's just good business!"

"How long have you two known each other, and where did you all meet at first?"

"We ran into each other about eight months ago on the beach, had drinks, chatted and eventually started talking about stuff. And that started a close friendship. He began getting me stuff, and we been friends ever since."

"He told me that he could get me some flour if I needed it, and I got into it, slowly building up a clientele. But now I need bigger weight. He said you could hook me up and here we are. I hope we can do business. I trust him. Can you help me?"

"I can! If he says you good, then let's do it! He told me you wanted to buy five hits for $10 a bag, right?"

"Yep! Just need to start with that and see how good it is. Then I can go for a full load right away!"

"That's cool, it's about 2% and can get higher if you can handle it?"

"That's what I like. I got $50 and hope you got five here now!" I said as I reached in my pocket and handed him $50.

"That's cool," he said, removing his right hand from his pocket with his fist clenched and shoving his hand forward as I opened my right hand, receiving small glassine packets wrapped by a rubber band. Glancing at the packets quickly, I could see small amounts of white powder in the packs as I put them in my pocket.

"I like the way you do business, quick and to the point, and definitely will get back to you on Monday through the CI."

"Cool! Let's put it this way. If something was to happen, I know who to see!"

"Same here. We think alike! Be cool man. I got to go but will be in touch." We shook hands, then I departed. The CI remained with him to get feedback for us.

I drove back to the office where we all met to check out the heroin, which turned out to be real, and I briefed everyone, including our agent friends who were very pleased.

I glanced over at Sarge, who said, "See you at the bar in an hour. Great job, Frenchy!"

"Thanks! See you soon."

I suddenly realized that I had just stepped into a new world with these guys, and it would be exciting for some reason! Little did I know that this would be a lifetime friendship with Agent Gerard Miller, one which still exists after 50 years!

After completing my report on this buy, we headed out of the office and went to the bar on Fort Lauderdale beach. The bar was at poolside. Our friends waved us over, and we had several drinks discussing anything but business. While we were enjoying ourselves, Sloopy was eyeing a big, well-built gentleman sitting across the bar from us. He got off his stool and went over to talk with this individual.

Miller said, "Aw shit! Here he goes again!" He smiled.

"What's he up to?" I asked.

"Just watch!"

Sloopy was pointing at Sarge with the stranger, then came back and sat down on his stool and said, "Sarge, that guy keeps looking at you. what's up?"

Sarge looked over at him in a serious manner and stared him down. The stranger got up from his stool and came around the bar and said, "Your friend tells me that you wanted to kick my ass? Is that right?"

"Hey, pal. I'm enjoying myself and don't need any problems, got it?"

"If you think you can take me, come on, give it a try." He stepped back with his fist clenched.

"Look, pal. I don't know what he's pulling, and I have no beef with you. So, enjoy a drink on me! This little prick likes to see if he can get people agitated. Trust me, there's no problem here. Enjoy your drink!"

The stranger said, "Cool!" and as he walked by Sloopy, he looked at him and said, "Asshole!"

Miller burst out laughing as did I when I realized that Sloopy was just trying to get people riled up!

"Pete, you just saw this little shit's crazy side. He does this all the time, and a few times we ended up in a brawl because of him!" We all broke out laughing.

Sloopy said, "Sarge, I know you could have taken him. I was just hoping we could stir up some action to end the night." He laughed.

We ended our get-together several hours later, and we all left sober, thank God!

Sloopy said to me, "Frenchy, welcome to our private group. You did well today!"

"Thanks!" I replied as we all walked away.

Sarge said, "Congratulations! They liked your demeanor and getting his stamp of approval that quickly is a hell of a compliment! I had no doubt that you would pass the test. Let's go home. Monday, we need to be at the office for 9:00 am for a meeting with a Detective Phil McCann (*deceased*) from Lighthouse Point PD who wants to give us some info."

"You got it. Thanks for a great week. See you Monday! I got a rendezvous with a dispatcher for a few drinks in an hour. Nice to be single! You married guys don't know how sweet it is," I said, laughing.

He replied, "Bite me, Frenchy!" He laughed as he got in his car and drove off.

22

New Members of the Special Squad

S arge and I made numerous drug cases and assisted many police departments in doing undercover buys with their informants. We made it known to Lieutenant Stewart that we needed to get more deputies as detectives for our unit because our cases were getting more complicated and more complex, which required a lot more man-hours doing buys and conducting surveillances. The results would show that drug sales and use were on the increase at a rapid pace. Stewart came through and asked us for some recommendations requiring a mix of personalities and ages.

It took us approximately two years to grow. Once put together, the unit consisted of the following persons who deserved recognition for their bravery and courage to work long hours and make cases of magnitude that the Broward County Sheriff's Department had never seen before. Our unit was made up of deputies who were proven to be aggressive, loyal, and with integrity beyond reproach, along with having a clean record.

Our new unit consisted of a lieutenant, Sergeant, and nine detectives. For their personal safety, some of their names can't be disclosed. The two female detectives were the first to be appointed as detectives in the department. They both worked in dual capacity as vice and narcotics detectives. I was honored and proud to have worked with every one of these individuals from 1968 to 1972.

To list cases that we worked would take forever. Some that were highly significant and dangerous deserve recognition. These are examples of what we faced together. Our work and effort helped pave the way for new methods, techniques, and safety to be used by future narcotics agents in working narcotics cases. I firmly believed that our generation of narcs in Florida from the sixties to the seventies were the pioneers in this line of work, along with the small group of federal narcotics agents in Miami.

Sergeant and I trained the new members, and we all began making cases with many informants. We all depended on each other for surveillance and backups when buys were made along with physically being involved in the arrests and seizure of drugs.

These are accounts of some of the major cases that were highly significant in my years with BSO:

On September 26, 1969, Oakland Park Detective Rick Riggio came to our office with an informant who advised us that the son of the mayor of Wilton Manors, Florida, was involved in the sale of hashish and that his son could introduce one of us to buy ounces of hashish from him. An undercover call was made to him. The suspect was identified as a white male, 18 years of age, who advised the CI that he could sell ounces with no problem. The subject agreed to meet us at a gas station on the northwest side of Sterling Road and I-95 in Hollywood.

It was decided that since the subject knew some of us, that one of our detectives, ex- Middle Weight Boxing Champ of the Bahamas, who had joined BSO would meet and make his first undercover purchase. Then we would arrest this individual. This was his first undercover assignment. He was briefed and told that once he gave us the signal to move in for the arrest, we would come in and block the exit of the gas station and arrest him. The surveillance unit went ahead to surveil the location and remained out of sight until the signal was given.

The subject drove up to the meeting point and met with the UC agent. The exchange took place during which the subject gave two ounces of hashish to the UC, who paid the subject $145. Suddenly, the subject got nervous, and the UC advised the suspect that he was under arrest, not giving the signal. The subject subsequently jumped into his vehicle with a minor 14-year-old boy in the car.

Surveillance agents observed the subject fleeing. So, one officer shot out one of his tires as we gave chase heading east on Sterling Road into the Davie municipality and pursued him for a half mile, after which the subject pulled over and jumped out of his car. He then ran across Sterling Road into a golf course and was chased on foot. The subject ran to a heavily wooded creek, running north paralleling the golf course.

Detective McCann and I yelled at the subject to come out, after which McCann spotted the subject and ordered him out. The subject who had a Mohican haircut charged at McCann with a Bowie knife prompting McCann to fire a warning shot in the air; however, the subject kept coming at him, so McCann shot the subject in the leg. He dropped to the ground screaming.

"Phil, are you Ok?" I yelled As I drew nearer.

"Yeah, the crazy bastard wouldn't stop. He had a Bowie knife and was coming straight at me like he was going to stab me. I told him to drop it, but he still kept coming. I took quick aim and dropped him on the spot with a bullet in the leg."

"Ok! We got an ambulance coming. Everyone is Ok! We got the dope, and our UC is a little shaken up for his first buy to go wrong!"

"Well, like you always say, don't ever think things will go by the book! Be prepared for the worst!"

"Well, you can be damn well sure the media will be waiting for us. Sarge is dealing with the old man on the phone since his daddy is the mayor. Mum is the word! The subject was charged with the sale of hashish, fleeing a police officer, carrying a concealed weapon, aggravated assault and two counts of resisting arrest.

When we returned to the office, the group met upstairs. Chuck began, "Ok! Listen up and pay close attention. First, thank God everyone is safe, and no one died! Second, those of you who are married, get on

the phone and call your spouses and family to let them know you are
Ok! It's all over the radio, and I don't want to be swarmed with family
calls. Third, get together and write your surveillance report. No one
leaves while it's still fresh in your mind. Fourth, Our UC did good out
there. He bolted on you, but don't be ashamed about not remembering
to give the signal. It's normal to get nervous on your first incident. I
know that we all learned from these crazy incidents. Great job, all of
you! Now call Mommy! NOW!"

I can't stress enough that preparation is mandatory on every UC
deal. The meeting place needs to be checked out in advance. The
suspect should not choose the location for the meet, no exceptions. A
bar or restaurant that is in a comfortable setting with a lot of movement
and is easily open for visual surveillance is strongly preferred. Closed
areas are harder to surveil and make it easier to be noticed by suspects,
especially since the subject will attempt to have his associates canvas
for counterintelligence.

Speaking from personal experience, I never let my opponents get
the upper hand. If it didn't feel right, I didn't do it but backed off. If
a supervisor refused to go along with our final plan, then we would
professionally advise him that we preferred not to do it. Should he
decide to order you to do it, we nicely told him to fuck off!

23

Close Call

Detective Phil McCann and I were paired up as partners and rode around the Fort Lauderdale area beaches in his blue Corvette. Phil was muscular, bearded, 5'11", 25 years of age, wore long hair, and was single like me. Phil was very aggressive and hyped up in this type of work. I had to keep him on a slower pace and train him to be more alert of his surroundings and to follow my lead as his trainer.

As we were driving around on the beach, a red Corvette pulled up to us, and the driver started revving his engine as if he wanted to race while we were stopped on red. Phil said, "Looks like we have a challenge."

So, I looked at the driver and watching the light, I held up three fingers, then two, then one, and like in a race, we took off like a bat out of hell, beating him to the next red light two blocks south of Oakland Park Boulevard on A-1A. The driver rolled down his window and said, "Pull over. You got me!" He was Italian looking with jet black hair, in his middle twenties and wore a silk colored shirt.

"Ok," I said. "Phil, gut instinct tells me that he's looking to either score from us or he's got shit to sell! Let's have him bring up the subject and play with him that we are looking for action for our friends."

"Totally agree! If he asks our names, I'm Phil the Phantom and your Pete the Shadow!"

"Love it!"

"Where in the hell did you come up with those? I like it!"

"I've been watching tv too much!" he answered, laughing.

We parked on a side street off A-1A. We all got out of our cars and greeted each other.

"Hey guys, that's some ride you got there. Love it!" he said as he reached out to Phil to shake his hand.

Phil said, "Hi! I'm Phil, the Phantom! And this is Pete the Shadow!"

Laughing, he said, "You're putting me on, right?"

"No! Our friends came up with that name because we are together all the time, and you never know where or when we will show up. It's kind of our ID ever since they nicknamed us."

"Man, love your ride! You guys cruising?"

"Yeah, we're looking to score some shit for a big party we are having tomorrow!"

Might as well come right to the point and see if he bites. "Know anyone who can handle weight?" I asked.

"Man, you don't waste any time, do you? First time I have had anyone come out asking right off the bat!"

Phil responded, "The Shadow never holds back. He's a good judge of people and got brass balls. We're in the business to supply friends with stuff, if you get my drift!"

"That's cool. I do that on the side also! If you ever need any weight, I'm always looking for new clients!"

"Really? Prove it! Can you handle a K of smoke? I'm getting short, and my man is out of town this week."

"That's no problem. That would be $2K!"

I looked at Phil, winked and said, "Talk is cheap! Sounds a little high. How do we know you can handle that much weight?"

He reacted to this challenge, quickly laughing and said as if we had questioned his integrity, "Oh! I can!" He played right into our trap. "Come here and let me show you that I'm straight up." He walked to the rear of his car and opened up the trunk, where he then opened up a suitcase and said, "I don't bullshit." He then proceeded to lift up a blanket that was on top of several pounds of marijuana in plastic bags.

"Man, we owe you an apology. I will also prove to you that we are straight up!"

I quickly reached for my gun, which was concealed behind my back shirt. Phil also whipped out his gun and said, "Police! You're under arrest for the sale of narcotics. Hands on the car now!" I handcuffed him while advising him of his rights. He was in shock and disbelief that we were cops! We called for a paddy wagon for transporting our prisoner and a tow truck for his seized Corvette.

"Frenchy, you're unbelievable. You went straight for the jugular vein and caught him off guard right off!"

"Phil, I found out in this game you can't be a wimp. You size up the person by his body language and demeanor. If your gut feeling tells you to move in and catch him off guard, then do it and see the response and deal with it. Why fuck around and waste time?"

"Yes, Sir! You the man!" he answered, laughing.

We went to the office where he was booked for the sale and distribution of narcotics. All the evidence was processed, and it ended up that we had over 2 pounds of marijuana.

This arrest was, at that time, considered a significant one due to the quantity of drugs. While at the office, Betty answered a phone call, directing it to me. "Frenchy, Attorney Joe Varon (*deceased*) from Hollywood is on the line for you!"

"This ought to be good," Sarge said.

⋅⋅◆◆◆◆⋅⋅

Mr. Varon was one of the best defense attorneys in Broward County, highly respected, and his clients were from all sorts of backgrounds. I had testified before some of his clients and had beaten him on several occasions with my cases. On one occasion, when working a vice case, I had arrested a bookmaker, whom he represented in court. The arrest of his client was made with the execution of a search warrant on the suspect's residence.

During my testimony in court, Mr. Varon challenged my affidavit for the search warrant and questioned the wording and format of it.

The question was done in order to establish that I wrongly prepared this affidavit, even questioning where I had learned to write such a deplorable affidavit. The whole time he held it up to the jury and making fun of my lack of expertise and training on this matter.

Mr. Varon said, "Mr. Charette, did you prepare this affidavit?"

"Yes, Sir, I did."

"Where did you learn how to write a search warrant affidavit? Was it at the Police Academy?

"Yes, sir. We were given the basics on how to prepare one."

"You never received formal training, isn't that correct?"

"Yes, Sir."

Have you ever taken any courses on search warrants?"

"No," I responded.

"Then, this was prepared by you without any prior training, isn't that correct?"

I was waiting at this time for him to open the door and this question did it! "No, that's not correct!"

"Not correct?"

"You just testified you had no prior training, isn't that right?"

"Yes."

"Mr. Charette, kindly explain to the court why it's not correct?" he asked with a smirk on his face looking at the jury.

"Gladly! I never had prior formal training, but when I became a detective, I knew that our work in vice and narcotics involved utilizing search warrants, so I went to the library and got a book written by one of the best experts on this matter and has been used for teaching this subject. The book was written by Mr. Varon himself, and I copied his format for my affidavits on this search warrant, feeling that sooner or later, this issue would come up, and I must give him full credit for this."

Mr. Varon's face turned red and stood out with his silver-grey hair. Then he said, "Your Honor, I have no further questions for this witness, and he may be excused." Some of the jurors were trying very hard not to laugh, and the solicitor smiled, thanked me then excused me.

The judge called for a recess, and Mr. Varon approached me and said, "You outsmarted me, and I admire you for that. It's a pleasure to know such a great detective like you!"

"Mr. Varon, I have the utmost respect for you, and thank you. I hope to work with you again!" I said as we shook hands.

I never forgot the above incident and wondered why he was calling me?

"Mr. Varon, how are you, Sir?"

"Great, Pete, I see you've been busy with one of my clients whom I represent."

"Who are we talking about?"

"A young male who was arrested by you for the sale of hashish!"

"Ok!"

"Pete, can I meet with you Monday morning, say around 10:00 a.m. and see what we can work out?"

"That would be fine. Please run this through the solicitor's office so they can be present."

"No problem. Will do. See you at your office at 10:00 a.m. You have a great weekend!"

"Will do and same to you, Mr. Varon. "Ok, see you then."

After the call, Chuck said, "Pete, I heard what you said and fully agree. Looks like our boy wants to roll over. This may be good, and our deal will be that he has to take us up the ladder to bigger fish than him! Agree?"

"Phil, are you in agreement?"

"Totally. This could be good!"

Phil and I got to work doing all our paperwork. Solicitor Dan Futch (*deceased*) was contacted, and he confirmed that Mr. Varon had already called and agreed that we called the shots together to see if we could get bigger fish behind his client's connections.

Whenever contacted by a defendant's attorney for a meet, that's a sign that the defense wants to cut a deal with his client. Experience taught me not to agree on my own to meet without first clearing it with everyone who must agree together first, or it could lead to grounds for dismissal later on, which has happened in many cases. Ground rules must be established and signed for any request for assistance by any defendant.

———————— ✦✦✦✦✦✦ ————————

Monday morning at 10:00 a.m. Joe Varon and his client came to our office as expected. Sarge, Phil and I told them that the Solicitor Dan Futch was waiting for us, so we all went to his office and met in the solicitor's conference room.

Dan was waiting and greetings were exchanged. Dan spoke first, saying, "Joe, your client was arrested on two charges, possession of narcotics and sale of narcotics. Both are felony charges and carry a total of 15 years if convicted. Your willingness to cooperate is in your best interest. With that said, since you have no prior conviction, my office is willing to accept your offer to help yourself. We understand from your Attorney, Mr. Varon, that you could take us to major suppliers of heroin in this county and will testify if need be. Is that correct?"

"Yes, Sir. I'm ready to assist Pete and Phil with several cases to help myself in doing the right thing, Sir!"

"Your attorney can draft up an agreement for my office to sign which will stipulate that if at any time we determine that you have lied to us on any matter, or jeopardize the safety of any of these detectives intentionally, then the agreement is canceled, and I guarantee you that you will be prosecuted to the full extent of the law. Do you understand and agree to this?"

"Yes, Sir!"

"Just remember, we call the shots, and if you fail to do what you agree to, I promise you that you will be sent to prison for 15 years! Are we clear on this?"

"Mr. Futch, I'm a man of my word and will cooperate fully. I have to because I also promised my dad that I would. I think you probably have heard of him and his reputation!"

Mr. Varon immediately spoke up, saying, "Let's not go there. We are not concerned about your dad!" (Mr. Varon's comment was in regard to the boy's dad who was alleged to be involved with the mob in Florida.)

"Ok, Joe, get me the agreement by tomorrow and let your client go with Pete and Phil and the Sergeant so they can proceed on this as fast as possible. We need to protect the people of this county from heroin!"

"Dan, I agree, and I will have it for you in person tomorrow with my client to sign. Thanks for agreeing to his cooperation, and I assure you and Pete and his associates that he will honor his commitment or else he will have to face and answer to his dad! I don't think he wants that to happen. I think you know what I mean." He turned to him with a smile.

"Yes, Sir, I do."

Leaving the office, Mr. Varon said to us, "Guys, he's in your care, and I would appreciate you letting me know if there is any problem. I know that he is in good hands. Pete, don't hesitate to call me if you have any concerns."

"Will do, Mr. Varon. Let's go up to the office and get to work!"

"Yes, Sir!"

"Drop the Sir and it's Pete, Sargent and Phil from here on. Understand?"

"Yes, Sir! I mean, Pete."

I gave him a wink of an eye and smiled. "As long as you play the game and shoot straight with us, we will kick ass and take names starting tomorrow. Now we will pick your brain for details as to who are your connections and get you to introduce us to them for buys."

We debriefed him for several hours, outlining a plan to start making buys from his sources. We got names, phone numbers, cars they drove, addresses, physical descriptions, weapons they carry, their demeanor, and any paranoia when dealing with them.

The information had to be checked, and Sarge detailed surveillances to start on the first target by members of our group with a briefing to the group on this operation. Photographs were obtained from the Florida

Driver's License Bureau, which had never been done before and paid off extremely well! Within 24 hours, we had all of our targets' photo IDs.

The next morning Mr. Varon and his client, now referred to as CI, arrived and the written agreement had been reviewed by Dan Futch, who made some corrections and signed the Cooperation Agreement.

The CI came to the office and advised that he had made contact with a black male supplier of heroin last evening, and his source was willing to do a load of heroin for today for $300. The source lived off Sistrunk Boulevard and NW 14th Terrace, in the black area of Fort Lauderdale in a single duplex one-story apartment. The meet was set for 8:00 p.m., and he could only take one person with him. We agreed, and it was decided that I go undercover with the CI while the rest of the team would cover the area.

"Ok, let's you and I go to the interview room. We need to get our story straight on how we hooked up and how long we have known each other. After we finish up, give me your cell phone number and home number in case they ask me if I know your numbers."

The CI briefed the surveillance team as to the layout of the single-story duplex. He described the source's vehicle, which was a white Cadillac De Ville sedan, which he parked directly in front of his door. Furthermore, this man, known as Charles, was a very nervous character when doing a sale and had lookouts outside looking for cops in the area. This area of Fort Lauderdale was well known for some rough characters, and everyone needed to be alert.

I briefed the team, advising them that I would be no longer than 15 to 20 minutes, and if I didn't come out after that time, then be prepared to move in and hit the place fast. The CI was instructed to meet us at 7:00 p.m. at the Publix Supermarket on Sunrise Boulevard.

At 7:00 p.m., after being advised that the team had the location under visual observations, The CI and I proceeded to the suspect's apartment in the CI's Corvette.

"Ok, last-minute instruction. You make the introduction and advise Charles that we want a load, and we got people waiting for us to supply them, and I will be doing business with him on my own, got it? I'll then take over, and you just support and back me up, got it? If anything goes wrong, all I ask is that you back me up. Got it?"

"You're the boss. I got your back, don't worry. This guy and I been doing business for a long time, and he knows better than to fuck with me because he knows who my old man is, and this mother fucker would be gator bait!" He laughed.

"Sounds good to me!"

As we approached the duplex apartment, I could see several black males looking nervous while someone was peering at us behind a partially closed curtain window. Instantly I said to the CI, "Watch out. Something's got these guys spooked, so be ready if we're being set up!"

We got out of the car, the CI knocked on the door, and someone said, "Who is it?"

"Charles, it's me!"

The door opened, and Charles let us in. Two black males were sitting at the kitchen table eating spareribs, waving hello.

"Charles, This is Frenchy, the guy I told you about."

"Hey, man!" he said as he reached out to shake my hand. "He told me about you. So, you're looking for some shit for your people? What's up? Your man run dry?"

"He's out of town, and I got people waiting for their stuff. He told me you could help me!"

"He told you the price for a load?"

"Yep, $300 is cool. I need it and hoping that you got more because I got three drops to do tonight. If you can, I can be back in an hour and do two more with $100 for your helping me out."

He said, "You're cool. That's good enough for me!"

"You're the man and look forward to working with you."

"Ok, hold on." He turned around, went to the refrigerator and opened the door, then reached into the crisper box and came out holding a clear bag which of small plastic glassine packs, which contained white powder in the small packets. Charlie handed the bag to me to inspect the merchandise.

"Check it out if you care too. I'm a man of my word, right?"

"Without a doubt."

"No need to. Your word is good enough. Just remember, if we are straight up with each other, this could turn out to be a great business partnership for the both of us!"

"Cool, man. You forgot one thing before you leave. How about the three bills before you leave?" he gave a muted laugh.

"Oh shit. I forgot," I said, handing him three bills and letting out a tempered laugh. "Hate to cut this meeting short, but I got people waiting, and can you get me two more say in two hours around 10:30. I'll be back with my ride, a blue Vette, along with my right-hand man Bob!"

"You got it. See you then. My boys and I got to step out for a bit and will be here waiting for you!"

"Cool, see you soon, man."

We left and regrouped with the team at Publix. A subsequent check of the heroin load with a test ampule showed that the white powder was heroin of high grade by the look and feel of it.

<hr />

Going back to the office, I noticed several police cars at Andrews Avenue and 4th Avenue with blue lights at a gas station. I observed several narcotics detectives who were with the Fort Lauderdale Police Department. When I pulled in, Detective Art McCullum (*deceased*), a narc friend, advised me that the gas station had been robbed by three black males. The description matched that of Charlie and his boys. I briefed them quickly, and they asked if I was returning so that the perps could be arrested. Sarge had arrived, and we agreed to do it. Then we met at the office to turn in the drugs to the evidence locker.

The next step was to secure the heroin and prepare for the buy and bust. Sarge advised me that he had made a call to the FDLE (Florida Department of Law Enforcement), specifically to their south Florida agent Nick Navarro (*deceased*). Nick assisted us on the financing side in large cases when we had a major source of supply buys because our budget could not handle it.

I heard of Nick when he had been a federal narcotics agent under the original Federal Bureau of Narcotics (FBN). Nick was a legend as one of the best in the U.S. as an undercover fed and had joined the newly established FDL in Florida. He was born in Cuba and came to the U.S. and eventually was hired by FBN as an undercover agent in Miami then sent to New York to work on organized crime.

Nick arrived at the office neatly dressed, 5'10",185 pounds, silver-gray hair, dark tan and spoke with a definite Cuban accent.

"Pete," Sarge said, "meet Nick Navarro, our close friend and best narc you ever want on your side."

"Mr. Navarro, pleasure to meet you, Sir! Heard a lot of great things about you."

"Stop! The name is Nick! Heard about you already from my best friend Miller and Sloopy. They filled me in about the frog," he began laughing. "Sarge tells me that you have a good snitch that has set up some heroin buys?"

"Yeah, going back for two more loads in an hour!"

"Great! We got the money to help you guys on this, so let's do it!"

Little did I realized that Nick Navarro and Miller would end up being two of my best friends for close to 52 years. They were my mentors in getting me into the world of undercover work and eventually becoming a federal narcotics agent.

It was quickly the time to head out and do this buy from Charles. Sarge assigned our biggest bulldog looking detective to accompany me as my bodyguard/ right-hand man. He was 5'11", 200 pounds, muscular and not one to mess with. I told him to keep alert because the two guys in the apartment are really on edge. Once inside, the signal that we had taken the suspects down would be pulling up the window curtains. Surveillance was ready on point. As we drove up in front of the apartment, we noticed two males looking around nervously, and someone was looking out from behind a pulled curtain of a window. Suddenly the curtain closed.

"Something doesn't look right. These two assholes are nervous as hell, and the guy peeping out looked like he's in a fucking panic mode!

"Yeah, I saw it too. Let's be on guard, and if anything goes down,

I'll wink at you, and that's when we draw down on the sons of bitches. Got it?"

"I intend on us going home tonight, just like you! If these guys suspect anything about us and make a move to draw down on us, let's not give them a chance. If they don't do as we say and start to point guns at us, blow their asses away and put them down permanently!"

"Roger that! Let's do it!"

I approached the door, focused. *Relax, breathe in, and be cool!* I knocked and a voice responded, "Who's there?" It was Charlie.

"It's me. Frenchy!"

"Just a minute!" as the door opened, Charles said, "Man, get in, quick, both of you!"

We entered quickly as Charles shut the door and locked it. A quick look around as we entered directly into a small kitchen area revealed a black male approximately 25 years of age holding a black Smith & Wesson 3-inch gun on our right, just staring at both of us. A second black male with a 357 Magnum in one hand had the refrigerator freezer door open and was placing in it, a clear plastic freezer bag which contained a large sum of loose money.

I said to Charles, "What the fuck is going down, pal?"

"It's cool, Frenchy! Get in quick. We think that the cops may be around the area looking for us. I got two guys outside just in case."

"Man, what the fuck is up? We didn't come here to get busted. I just want to get my shit and we are out of here! Sorry, this is my man!"

"Cool, man. Sorry about us freaking right now. We just robbed a gas station a while ago off Andrews Avenue."

"Are you shitting me, Charles? Look, you got the shit? If not, we are not waiting around. We'll come back tomorrow if that's all right?"

"Man, no one leaves until its cool. If the cops come here, we're ready for them, and they will go down, trust me!"

"Charles, come on, man. Relax! If the cops knew where you guys were, they would have swarmed this place by now! We are going to leave, and we will check and drive around to see if cops are around the neighborhood. If the coast is clear, I'll call you and tell you we're coming back."

We looked at each other and now, all three had their weapons out. Bob and I moved towards the living room, which was small and faced toward the three who now were looking out the window and crouched down. Bob looked at me and did a quick nod and wink. Then we slowly started to go for our guns concealed behind the back of our shirts, rapidly drew them, pointing at them back and forth yelling, **"POLICE! DROP THE GUNS NOW, ASSHOLES, OR YOU DIE! GET DOWN NOW! MOVE AND YOU'RE DEAD!"**

As arranged, we raised the curtains, which was the signal to move in. Before you could say "Praise the Lord," Sarge, Nick and FPD detectives were in, and everybody was arrested, the money recovered, and the dope seized. Fortunately, we prevented police officers from being shot. Looking back, God was on our side and protected us from having a tragedy that night.

———— ✦✦✦✦✦ ————

This case illustrates to anyone that is interested in this profession to expect the unexpected when working undercover. I learned quickly from this case how important it is to familiarize myself with the area I would be working and to always evaluate my opponents' body language. In this case, we instantly noticed that things were different from the first rendezvous, and suspects were on their guards, which was a red flag that something was not right. Subsequently, we needed to make each other aware of it and adjust for a possible confrontation. When in doubt, I learned to take quick actions to either withdraw or confront the suspects in order to diffuse a surprise confrontation.

———— ✦✦✦✦✦ ————

Back at the office, Sarge and Nick addressed the group. Sarge spoke first. "Ok! Good job, everyone! Things could have gone bad on this one, but you all did exactly what needed to be done, and everyone had each other's backs like we should at all times. Since we started this unit, our goals were to get the best of the best in this department, and tonight proved that without any doubt!

"You two had the worst part of this, and you did exactly what was needed to be done in order to prevent any of us from being shot tonight. Your quick assessment of what was going on with these assholes shows to all of us that you acted as one as it should be. This is a lesson that all of us need to remember when being in a UC partnership and meeting suspects. Nick! It's all yours!"

"Like Sarge said, this could have turned out bad. Thank God it did not! These two knew what to do. I have worked in this business for several years, and you all performed like we all have been trained to do on this one. I'm glad that Pete didn't get confused and start to speak French to them!" he laughed loudly! "And you, big guy, I sure wouldn't want to be on your bad side, that's for sure! Damn, look at him. He's an animal! This guy could wipe them out single-handed!" This last remark caused everyone to break out in laughter. "Just remember, we are a brotherhood, and we always look out for each other. Thanks all. We won and these assholes lost!"

Nick Navarro, with his broken Cuban accent, knew how to make us feel good about how we performed, and he always knew how to cheer up cops after working a case. This made an impression on me always, and later in my career as a supervisor/ manager, I used his fabulous way of dealing with tight situations.

Nick and Gerard were the best when it came to dealing with narcs. I will always feel honored that I had the privilege to have these two as my mentors and personal best friends!"

Nick eventually became the best Sheriff that Broward County ever had. Nick passed away when he became terminally ill with cancer. There isn't a day in my life that I still think of him and always will! Rest in peace, my friend.

With our paperwork done, the team all agreed that we needed to meet at our watering hole at Betty's place and wind down for a couple of hours. Sarge called her and told her we needed to wind down in large part because of our close call. Sarge said, "Betty's bar is open! Let's get the hell out of here."

Upon arriving at Betty's place, we found that she already had our bottles out on the counter with appetizers. When we talked about what had happened, I saw Betty tear up. Then she said, "Damn! I love you all and thank God you are all here with me."

I worked my way to her and hugged her, saying, "Mom, we love you!"

"Pete, you guys are my boys, and I can't help to worry about all of you every day!"

"I know, and that's why this Frenchman loves you along with the rest of this crazy gang!" We all had a great time before we left. This was one hell of a ride on this day, another one I will never forget.

———— ✦✦✦✦✦ ————

When I got home, Dad and Mom were watching a movie and asked about my night. I responded by saying, "Pretty boring night. Things were quiet for a change!" I was not about to tell my mom anything, or she would have gone into a frenzy.

24

Forgot My Gun

There are so many cases that I could go on, but some need to be written about because I feel that we learn from our mistakes, and if we become negligent and we don't ensure that we always double-check ourselves before going out to make a bust, we may not survive.

LSD was becoming a popular drug for the hippies of the 60s in Broward County. Several cases at the Broward General Hospital were the result of users being brought in for not being able to handle its hallucinogenic trip. This caused major concerns, so we had to get a handle on this quickly before we ended up with deaths from this crazy drug.

My partner Phil and I went out to work the hot spots on Lauderdale Beach and Hollywood Beach to see if we could get some buys on LSD and work on getting to the heavy suppliers. We also passed the word to all of our information sources that we needed to hook up with some LSD buys; the sooner the better.

Phil said, "Frenchy, let's pop in at the music nightclub and see what we can drum up?"

"Sounds good to me, my man! If we get an offer, fuck the small shit. Let's tell them we need some weight and were looking for 25 kilos of blotter acid."

"You're nuts! No idiot around here got that kind of shit, and they will laugh at us big time."

"Exactly, look at us hippies! You with a beard, long brown hair, bell-bottom pants, boots, deerskin jacket and always act like your half stoned on weed! DUDE! I'm just as bad with a bearded goatee hippie, bell-bottom pants, flowered shirt, and always got a wad of money to put the money where our mouth is! A perfect match if I do say so. I have a gut feeling it may work. So, let the ride begin! Mother fucker!" he said, laughing.

Shaking his head and also laughing, Phil said, "Hey, you're the senior man, but I will prove you wrong, my man! Let's do it!" We drove up to Lenny's parking lot. The music was loud for a Friday night, as usual. The place was crowded with great rock 'n' roll music blaring and everybody dancing and enjoying the party. We made our way to the main bar, where we made a quick scan of the clientele.

Phil whispered, "End of the bar, right side, long bleach blond hair dude in his mid-twenties. Let's join him for a drink?"

"Got him! Here we go." We both high five one another.

We sat down next to this handsome love child, and I said, "Hey, dude? What's happening, my man?"

"Hey, man! How you guys doing?"

"Great, man. I'm Frenchy," I said, reaching out to shake his hand, "This here is my asshole buddy Phil!"

Phil responded, laughing, "He's a bigger asshole than me, but we make a good team together." He reached out and shook his hand.

The waiter interrupted and said, "I take it you two assholes want your regular vodka tonic?"

"Yep," I responded, "and give our friend here whatever he is drinking then another of the same!"

"Thanks, guys. Are you always that friendly with people you just met?"

Phil chimed in and said, "Me and Frenchy are easy going and enjoy life for all that it's worth."

"Yeah, the reason he is saying that is because we make people happy.

We don't have to work anymore since Phil's parents left him a ton of money, and we are having a blast while it lasts!

"By the way, we didn't give you a chance to introduce yourself."

"Oh, I'm Tom! You guys from around here?"

Phil responded, "Yeah, Lauderdale is our town!"

"Cool. I'm from L.A. down here to drum up some business for a week! My partner should be here shortly. He's a bit hungover from last night!"

"L.A.!" I said. "Never been there. I hear it's wild and crazy there. Plenty of shit out there and some cool blotter."

"You got that right. Blotter is all over the place and best there is! How's the market around here for that?"

Phil responded, "Wide open. We made pretty good money from the interest that's growing here for it. Just can't get enough of it fast!"

"Oh! You two are in the business?" he said with a grin.

"Well, let's put it this way," I said, "we provide a service to the community and it's appreciated by some."

"My partner and I do the same, and I know what you mean," he responded.

He and Phil engaged in a conversation about the single action here at the club. I was in deep thought. *This is unbelievable, either we are being slowly set up or this guy is really from the land of the fruits.*

Tom's partner arrived and was introduced as Bob. He had long brown hair, 6'1", weighed 195 pounds and did appear hungover. General talk about LA and Florida went on for an hour or so, and we all enjoyed the music and dance with the ladies. As the night went on, the bar was going to close and at 4:00 a.m. last call for drinks was made. We left the bar, but Tom excused himself to go to the men's room then met us outside. They advised us that they were staying at the Holiday Inn on A-1A on Lauderdale Beach. Tom reached in his pocket and handing me a folded paper towel said, "Frenchy, tomorrow night we will be here at 10:00 p.m. See you then and we can talk. Have a good one. Ciao!"

"Got it, putting the paper towel in my pocket, I said, "Looking forward to tomorrow."

We all left and got into the Vette! And as we drove out, we waved and got their LA tag number. "Phil, I don't believe this has happened so fast. Let's see what our new friend gave us." I had an idea what it was as I opened it. "Yeah, baby. Bingo! Houston, we have a lift-off! There in plain sight were two hits of blotter acid, Each the size of a postage stamp with a blot mark on the paper, suspected to be LSD!

"Holy shit! Are you fucking kidding me? That's insane! These guys are from la la land!" I blurted out laughing.

"We are in, and now it's our move tomorrow. We will run their tags and see if we have a hit on it! Game is on, my brother!"

The next day arriving at the office, I immediately got out a blue light and held it over the LSD tabs and Bingo! Two white spots glowed on the paper stamps indicative of what's called blotter acid. We briefed everyone on this encounter, and it was decided that we needed to get financial assistance for a flash roll from FDLE Supervisor Nick Navarro. Nick agreed and was at the office the next morning with a $25K sum to be used as proof that we were serious buyers. Arrangements were made for surveillance on these two characters whose criminal checks came back negative on the registered owner of the car.

٠٠٠٠٠٠٠

As we entered the bar at 10 p.m., Tom and Bob were sitting at a table outside drinking beer. Greetings were made, then Phil and I ordered a couple of beers while addressing Tom!

"Hope you guys had a good night. We had business to attend to, and your stamps are quite valuable. We are interested in purchasing 25 kilos of your product if you can deliver."

"That's not a problem. The stamps come in sheets of 100 @ $10 per stamp!"

"The price sounds good. When can we do it?"

"How about 4:00 p.m. today at our hotel room down by the beach, room 200! We'll need to see cash before we do it!"

"Deal! We will come, and Bob can see the cash. I can tell him where he can go to meet Phil downstairs when I see that everything is ok on your end!" Just want you guys to know that, like you, we are cautious. Also, and if there is any intention of ripping us off for the money, I guarantee you that no one will walk away from this place without paying a heavy price. Are we clear?"

"I respect your guys' way of dealing. And same goes with us!"

"We're cool. We can do business on a monthly basis if all goes well, and I will also want to see the stamps so we can examine the sheets for quality."

"Ok, see you guys at 4:00 p.m. Hope you got some drinks on hand once we are done to celebrate a hopefully long-lasting business association." Then they shook on it.

"Already there. See you soon!"

Phil and I departed while surveillance remained stationary to watch their movements. We regrouped at the office, and Chuck called the Fort Lauderdale PD Narcotics Bureau and asked them to assist on this case since it was in their jurisdiction. A briefing was held at the office at 1:00 p.m., and the plan was for this arrest was discussed.

Phil and I were to go to the hotel to go up and check out the room. Once we agreed that everything was Ok, Phil would leave with Bob and go to the pool bar, while one of our guys would come out of the hotel carrying a beach bag with a towel covering the bag and sit with us. Bob would be told to lift the towel in order to see wrapped 25 wrapped $1000 bundles of $100 bills. Once Bob was satisfied, Phil and Bob would come back to the room, and after we were shown the LSD sheets and tested the pages with an ultra-violet blue light, we then would close the hotel room curtains which would be the signal for the team to move in and come up to the room and arrest the suspects.

Once everybody agreed and understood their assignments, we departed the office for the meet. Betty looked at all of us and said, "Please, you all be careful!" I could tell by her watery eyes that she was worried for her family!

I told her, "We'll let you know once we were Ok. Piece of cake! Love you, kid!"

Once everyone was in position, surveillance advised that another male had joined our friends. Phil and I proceeded to room 200.

"Phil, let's be on our guard on this as usual, and if it smells, no waiting. We take them down, quick and fast by surprise. A wink is the code!"

"Got it, Frenchy! You nervous?"

"Always. Let's do it!"

We knocked on room 200. Tom opened the door and said, "Right on time. Come on in." He looked down the hallway on both sides and shut the door.

He said, "This is Steve. He's down here with us and has your stamps once we see cash!"

"Hey man, glad to meet you, I'm Pete and this is Phil."

"Hey, nice to meet you!"

"Ok. Tom, Phil, and Bob can go down, and Phil will take Bob by the pool bar where the money will be shown. Once this is done, they will come back, and we want to see the stamps to check them. Once we're satisfied, then our guy will come up and bring the cash! Wham, bam, thank you, Ma'am! and everybody is happy, and we will see you at the bar across the street around 8:00 p.m. to celebrate and party!"

"Sounds like a plan!"

"Before Phil goes, I like to be safe, if you don't mind? I want to look behind the closed closet door and bathroom door. It's a force of habit, and safety comes first!" I said.

"Have at it. We're cool, no issues."

I proceeded to check the room, noticing that they were staying in this room by the clothes in the closet and bathroom accessories on the sink scattered with razors, etc.

Once satisfied, I gave Phil the nod and he and Bob left to see the flash roll as discussed.

Phil was gone for approximately ten minutes, which seemed like an hour to me. Tom and Steve appeared somewhat at ease as we held a general conversation about living here. A knock on the door sounded, and I observed Tom, who was wearing a flowered colored shirt, start to reach behind his back, followed by Bob's voice saying, "It's cool. It's us. Open up!" Tom slowly stopped and brought his hand forward to open the door.

Bob said to Tom, "We're in the money," It's all there. It's a go!"

"Cool, Steve! Go get the stamps, and let's get this over and done."

"Be right back." He left the room while we all waited. After two to three minutes, he was back with a large brown manila envelope which he handed to Tom. I gave Steve a quick look and observed that his shirt was now out from being tucked inside his pants and also noticed a slight bulge on his back-right hip. Phil was sitting on the bed by the window, and I was standing by Tom. Slightly turning my back to him, I put my right hand behind and pointed my thumb and finger like a gun while looking at Steve. Then I turned back and saw Phil smile, relieved that he got the message.

Tom pulled out a stack of sheets and put them on the dresser against the wall and said, "Ok! Check them out. Phil got up and pulled out of his pant pocket a small battery-operated blue light and started moving across the stamped sheets, which highlighted a white dot on the stamps verifying that dried drops of LSD liquid had been put on the sheets.

"Bingo! We are in the money also!"

I said, "Ok! Our man will come up. Phil, close the curtains so he can see it's Ok to bring the money!"

Tom said, "You guys have your act together. I like that."

"He should be here in about five minutes! Looks like we will be doing business together for sure!"

Phil sat down in the edge of the bed and casually brought his leg across the other so he could reach for his gun once we heard the knock on the door and the door was opened. Everybody was somewhat relaxed and still no knock. I could see them looking a bit edgy. I realized the team was not here as we had planned. I looked at Phil and winked, giving the signal that we had to take them down fast and to the floor.

Phil pulled his gun out from his ankle holster and jumped up and yelled, "Police! Down on the ground NOW!" as he pointed at Bob and Steve.

I immediately pointed at Tom and said loudly, "Police! Down on the ground now or I'll blow your fucking head off! Now! Tom immediately dropped to the floor. I continued, "Everybody keep your face down and hands behind your head and don't move or we'll blow you heads off. Is that clear?"

All three responded, "Yes Sir!"

Suddenly we heard the knock at the door, and Nick yelled, "Police! open up now!"

Phil, still pointing his gun, opened the door while I was hovering over Tom with my gun. Nick came over while the team started handcuffing the suspects and said, "Frenchy! It's Ok! You can put your fingers away now. We got it!" He reached toward my hand, where I did not have a gun but was only pointing my finger and thumb like a gun! "Oh, fuck! I don't have my gun! Shit, I could have been blown away!" I shook my head in disbelief. "Nick, I can't believe I left my gun at the office. God was looking out for me. One hell of a lesson learned for sure! Where in the hell were you all? We had to take them down because they were getting nervous."

"Frenchy, when we got to the elevator, it was not working, so we had to use the stairwell to get here!"

Phil said, laughing, "Frenchy, I didn't notice you didn't have your gun. You had me convinced that you did and were ready to blow somebody's fucking head off if they didn't!"

"Damn! I was so pumped up, I actually felt I had my gun in my hand. Just goes to show that we shouldn't ever assume we got our guns. From then on, I always remembered to check before I'd go out in these situations."

We took the prisoners to lock up, and when we got back to the office, we got applause from the detective bureau guys and ladies for having made the largest LSD arrest in Broward County. Needless to say, the word had gotten out about my taking down an armed suspect with my new 'gun fingers,' and it took a while to live that down. Word travels fast among the law enforcement community.

There are times when suspects will ask if we are carrying weapons or check for a hidden wire. Prior to meeting suspects, a criminal history check would be a good idea in order to determine whether the person is known to have a weapon or to carry one. It is also a good idea to ask them if they are carrying a weapon. It would be a reasonable excuse to say that being armed in these types of situations is prudent because this is a serious business, and they are fools if they didn't. It is also reasonable to have them patted down. If they refuse, then it is wise to thank them and walk away from the meeting.

Nowadays, it's easy to check with the ATF Gun Permit Directory as a matter of safety and do a name check to determine if they own guns. I learned never to jump into a UC operation too quickly without first checking on the targets. Our teammates' lives are always more important than theirs!

25

Solicitor's Office Refusal to File First Conspiracy Case

As we grew as a unit, Sarge and I were advised by Agent Miller that BNDD was going to put on a two-week Federal Narcotics State class for state and local narcotics officers in Clearwater, Florida. Miller told us this school was offered to selected individuals only, who are nominated by BNDD only. We were honored to be asked, and it was immediately approved by BSO.

I had heard about this school from Sarge, who said that this was the best narcotics training and, if asked and pass the course, the certificate of completion was equivalent to having completed BNDD AGENT SCHOOL. We learned that the Miami BNDD office had also chosen the narcotics detectives from the Metro Dade Sheriff's Department and Hollywood PD detectives.

The school was the best I ever attended. The instructors were field agents from all over the U. S. Dept. of Justice, U.S. attorneys and experts in the field of heroin, marijuana, cocaine, etc. One instructor, in particular, was Dr. Carlton Turner, who was conducting marijuana research for the U.S. government. Dr. Turner later became the U.S. drug czar for President Ronald Reagan and remains a close friend.

Later in my career, I had the honor and privilege to be a guest instructor for this type of school with Dr. Carlton Turner, Gerard Miller,

FDLE Agent Nick Navarro, BNDD head of training for the Miami field division. I can only say that these individuals were the best in their fields and remain to this day, great friends. The only one of this group who has passed away is Nick. Rest in peace. While attending this school, I immediately realized that I wanted to be a federal narcotics agent and make it my life's career to work undercover to fight the biggest drug traffickers in the world.

One of the main topics presented to us was the lack of use by prosecutors at the state and local levels to charge drug traffickers with conspiracy to distribute narcotics. We learned that it was a simple way of indicting violators who agreed to conspire with two or more persons. The mere agreement and doing one overt act to put in motion the plan constituted a conspiracy. This immediately caught my full attention and made me realize that some of our cases that we were working were, in fact, conspiracy and could have a major impact in Broward County against traffickers.

We all completed the course and returned back to work. I immediately researched the Florida State Statute on conspiracy and discovered that this law was already in the books and not being utilized for narcotics prosecutions. I discussed this with Chuck and told him that one of our current heroin cases was an ideal example of this, and we needed to meet with the Solicitor Mrs. Angie Weir (*deceased*) to get approval to pursue this case as a conspiracy.

We scheduled our meeting with Angie and her assistant Dan Futch (*deceased*), an ex-Florida state trooper who then became a lawyer. Once we presented our request and cited the Statute and Overt Acts that supported our case for a conspiracy indictment, Mrs. Weir advised us that conspiracy cases are time-consuming, and her position was not to prosecute these types of cases. I looked at Dan and Sarge, who appeared amazed at her position and immediately made her aware that this was a violation of the law and that we wanted to proceed with a conspiracy prosecution on this.

Angie said, "Mr. Charette, I decide on what is approved for prosecution. I'm sorry, but my decision stands. This meeting is over."

"Angie, I understand, but I disagree. We have to use every tool available to us to stop the growing drug problem in this county, so please reconsider your decision."

"Sorry, I made myself perfectly clear. There is no need for any further discussion! Have a good day!" she said as she walked out of the meeting.

"Dan, I can't believe that she refused this! Is there anything we can do to change her mind?"

"Pete, my hands are tied. I agree with you fully, but she is the boss, and unless you can make her change her mind, we are not able to use this law. I hate to say this. I'm on your side. I fully agree with you and your research on this is 100% on this law!"

"Dan, I'm not blaming you. You know me. I have one more avenue to check, and hopefully, it will work!"

Sarge shot me a puzzled look and said, "Frenchy, I'm with you on this. What the hell are you up too?" He was shaking his head.

"I'm hoping that I have the law on my side. Let's go!"

"Dan, thanks for supporting us. You always have, my friend. I promise you that Broward County will be prosecuting conspiracies soon!" I smiled and winked at him.

✦✦✦✦✦

Sarge and I went back to the office where we sat down while I told him that in my research of the law, I also looked up, just in case we were denied, the Statute of Malfeasance and Misfeasance of Office by an Elected Official. "Here's a copy of that statute. When Angie was elected and took the oath of office, she swore to 'Uphold the laws of the state of Florida.' By refusing, she can be charged with this statute. I'm asking for your permission to go and speak with the State Attorney Phil Shealer (*deceased*) to get his opinion on this. He has always been there for us, and I think that if we ask him to confront Angie on this, we will definitely get her attention!"

"Frenchy, I hope you're right on this! You're sticking your neck out on this one. Are you sure about this?"

"One hundred percent sure, and I promise you if I get heat, it's my idea and you didn't have anything to do with this!"

"I know that and appreciate it. Damn, you never fail to amaze me on your determination to take on anyone who is wrong!"

"Thanks, I will be back."

Phil Shealer was, in my opinion, a great state attorney for Broward County, and when I met with him and explained my concern and case, he agreed that Broward County was becoming a major drug abuse county in Florida, and that BSO's drug unit was the best in the state.

He fully agreed that Angie needed to move forward in this area, and that my assessment of her oath of office struck a sharp warning, one of which he had never before heard taking on a solicitor with that statute.

Phil said, "Frenchy, I will immediately go and talk to her. She will not be happy about your position, but I will try to soften the blow by explaining to her that you are requesting this in order to put all of us in a better position to fight drug trafficking in this county, and that this will bring praises and a high visibility to her and her office by the voters of this county."

"Phil, let her know that I have always respected her and that this is about putting criminals in jail for 15 years in order to strike a blow and send a strong message to drug traffickers that Broward County is a place where you don't want to sell drugs!"

Phil was gone for over an hour and returned with a smile and said, "Well, at first I expressed my concerns and then told her your feelings and BSO's position on this law. I then told her that you felt that the law concerning her oath of office backed her up to prosecute traffickers, and that I fully agreed and that it would be a real detriment to her by not upholding her oath of office. She was taken aback by this, but I explained to her the positive side to this by her reconsidering the options. She told me to advise you to come and see her right away and said, 'He's got guts and I respect him.'"

"Phil, thank you so much for your support and advice. I won't let you down, my friend!"

"Frenchy, be careful out there and give them hell!"

"You know I will!" I answered with a smile.

———————— ◆◆◆◆◆◆ ————————

I returned to the office and briefed Sarge, then both went to Angie's office.

"Close the door and have a seat, both of you! Mr. Shealer came to my office, and after we had a talk, I have decided that conspiracy cases need to be prosecuted in this county! We need to use this law to our advantage! With that said, I wanted to let both of you know that I respect your determination to do the right thing. I overreacted with my first decision and want you to know that your unit is the best we have, so let's move on and keep these cases coming. One more thing, Pete, you should be an attorney. You did a good job on your law research! Be safe and give them hell!" she said.

"Angie, I'm sure I speak for Sarge also. I'm proud to be working with you and your solicitors, and we will make sure that the cases that come up will bring recognition to all of us who are putting criminals behind bars! Thank you!"

"You guys have a great day. Dan has been briefed by me and will be working on this conspiracy case with you!"

Sarge and I went back to the office and briefed everyone on the implementation of this new tool we can now use for our cases. This was a great success and was well received by the judges and prosecutors, thanks to our BNDD training.

Because of our decision to do this, we ended up indicting over 15 individuals in a major heroin case that included several municipalities in Broward County.

———————— ◆◆◆◆◆◆ ————————

There are times in law enforcement work where officers encounter resistance from politicians or prosecutors. When incidents occur such as these, a decision has to be made as to whether to stand up for what is right as long as you have the law and the facts in hand. I have never backed down because of politics as long as I had my facts correct to support my actions.

There many avenues available to achieve goals, such as media contacts, judicial contacts, and diplomacy in arguing a case.

Had the solicitor not changed her position, however, I would have followed through with the state attorney. I had already discussed with him the issuance of an arrest warrant for violation of her oath of office and was prepared to follow through with my decision with his support.

26

Facing Death at Gunpoint

One of my most dangerous moments with BSO occurred while working undercover in Fort Lauderdale. The case involved my confidential source or CI who had arranged for me to buy ounces of cocaine from a source of his. After making several purchases from this source with the help from Agent Nick Navarro, who help fund the buys, I asked the source if he could get me a half pound of coke that I needed. The source agreed and arranged from his supplier from New York to come to Lauderdale and introduce me to him for future dealings of large amounts.

The CI contacted me and advised me that Fred, his source, had called him to say that the New York connection was in town and needed to know when a meet could be made. I advised the CI to arrange the meet with the middleman from whom I had previously made purchases and his source for 1:00 p.m. at the Publix parking lot at on West Sunrise Boulevard and NW 27th Avenue in Fort Lauderdale and to park near the road on the southeast corner away from the store. I instructed him to tell the suspects that he would not be there because he had no one to run his store for him and to ask the middleman if he was coming in his car.

The source was given strict information to be prepared to answer should the suspect from New York decide to speak with him and ask him specific questions about our association. We discussed how we met, the length of friendship, the make of the car I drove, where I resided, if I had ever been arrested, my physical description, and if I used drugs. I repeated these questions several times to ensure that our stories matched. We both felt comfortable about it. The CI was advised to tell Fred that I would be driving my blue Buick sedan. The CI said he would call me back within five minutes. Five minutes later, the CI called and stated that he would be bringing the suspect in his car and would be there at 1:00 p.m.

A briefing was held with our team, and Nick furnished me with $7500 of 100 and 50 dollar marked bills. Nick sent Sarge with detectives from the vice unit and our special squad to set up in the area. Nick remained behind with the rest of the team to follow me for the meet.

The plan was to buy the drug and leave while the surveillance team followed the suspects to see where the New York connection was staying for the night. Once we established his location for the night, a search warrant/arrest would be obtained immediately, and the surveillance team would maintain a watch on the location until Nick and the team made the raid on the location.

At 12:30 p.m., I departed the office to go meet the suspect as planned. Nick told me that the suspects were there when the team arrived, driving around the neighborhood and parking lot checking for surveillance units. An undercover van with curtain windows and carrying two team members had the eyeball on the suspects and kept everyone apprised of their status. As I came into the busy parking lot, I observed the car parked sideways by the road, but the middleman was not driving. Instead, an unknown male in his late twenties was behind the wheel.

I parked behind the car and after I got out, the driver said, "Hey, how's it going, man. I'm George (PN). The middleman is with his old lady and his kid so she could do grocery shopping, He gave us his car keys, and Eduardo (PN)) and I are here!" He looked at me in a questionable way, making me feel as if he was nervous about me.

The passenger in his mid-thirties, dark brown skin, 5'10", 180 pounds, got out of the car and approached me smiling, saying, "Hey,

Man! I'm Eduardo. Sorry about our friend not being here. He told me about you and said you're a straight-up dude, and there was nothing to worry about!" He reached to shake my hand, and I did the same.

"That's too bad, but I know what it's like for someone to be henpecked by the old lady," I said, laughing.

Right then, George said, "Eduardo, we need to talk for a second," and he went toward their car with Eduardo following.

George had his back toward me, leaned over, and began whispering something to Eduardo. I was only able to hear Eduardo saying, "Man! You sure?"

George replied, "Positive!"

"Frenchy! Come over here for a second. I want to ask you something?"

"Yeah sure," I said, smiling, "what's up?"

Like lightning, Eduardo reached behind his back under his loose flowered Hawaiian shirt, whipped out a 9mm Beretta that he planted against my head, and pushed me against the right side of the car, saying, "You mother fucker, you're a cop! Aren't you? My friend George said he saw you today at the courthouse outside a courtroom as he was leaving the probation office, you piece of shit!"

"Whoa! Whoa!" You're fucking crazy, man? I'm no fucking cop!"

"You son of a bitch, I'm facing life if I'm taken down for a third time, and I'm not going back to jail again! I will kill you before I go down this time."

"Look, George is right! I was at the courthouse today. I'm on probation too, and I was reporting to my parole officer who was in that courtroom speaking to the judge about my status. He told me to wait outside the courtroom for him. Man, if he was there, how come you don't ask him if he's a cop or snitch?" I leaned into his face with a look to kill and added, "And how do I know that you're not a fucking cop?"

I must have struck gold with my rage because I could feel Eduardo's gun slowly pull away from my skull and could see him look around quickly to check for something to happen.

"Look, man, I don't need to work with two fucking wackos like you two, and trust me, George is going for a ride in the Everglades for this fuck up!" he said as he put the gun behind his back. "I'm calling CI to check you out now!"

Eduardo reached for his phone and got CI on the line. I was close enough to him to hear the CI on the line. "Hey! It's me. I got a small problem with your friend. Answer me some quick questions! How long have you known him?"

"Ok! Frenchy? Four years!"

"Where did you meet him?"

"At his store!"

"Did he tell you where he was this morning?"

"At the courthouse, at the probation office."

"Good enough, sorry to bother you!"

"Eduardo, listen to me real good. You know my old man is family. Anything happens to Frenchy, you better start making funeral arrangements. Fast! Later!"

Eduardo said, "Frenchy, I had to be sure, sorry!"

"You mother fucker! If you ever pull this shit on me again, you won't have time. You'll get one right between the eyes! Are we clear?" I shot back when he finished his interrogation of CI.

"Yep!"

"Now it's my turn. No money until I see some shit!"

"It's right there in the high grass by the light pole behind you," he directed as he pointed down with his finger.

There was a closed paper bag, and when I reached and picked it up, I saw inside clear sealed ounce plastic bags containing a white substance in every bag. I could tell by the look of the substance that this was the real stuff, so I went to my car and pulled out a small overnight bag with the money and gave it to Eduardo! He counted the money and placed it in the car. Then he said, "We're good. Let me know when you need more. All I need is 24 hours heads up!"

Shaking his hand, I responded, saying, "We will be seeing a lot of each other real soon! Ciao!" I got in my car and drove away, riding around several neighborhoods to ensure I was not being followed. Once all cleared, I headed for the office with part of the team and Nick following me.

Needless to say, this was one close call, and it could have gone the other way! God was watching out for me!

The surveillance team stayed with Eduardo, who was driven to his ex-wife's home in near Oakland Park. A quick check on the registered owner's home revealed that it was in Eduardo's full name. A NCIC (National Criminal Information Center) record check indicated that he had a long arrest record, for attempted murder, aggravated assault, narcotics trafficking and other offenses.

A search warrant was obtained along with an arrest warrant for sale of a narcotic.

The team, led by Nick Navarro executed the warrants. As we came up to the door in the evening, through the louvered glass jalousies, we observed Eduardo sitting with his back to the door.

Nick said with his Cuban accent, "Police! We have a search warrant for this residence. Open up!"

Eduardo turned and started to rush up from the sectional couch, and before I could do anything else, Nick clenched his right fist and came down on all glass window slats like a karate chop, crashing through the screen on the door running in yelling, "Eduardo! Stop!" as he dove over the couch tackling him, as he struggled to get free!" Nick was yelling in a broken accent, "You're under arrest, you son of beech, Tchou tried to keel my friend!" He continued as he punched him to make him stop resisting, "thees is my friend you tried to kill. I got you now!"

We grabbed Eduardo and handcuffed him, and I was laughing about what I had just observed from my crazy Cuban best friend! We recovered our money and more narcotics in the residence. Eduardo was able to make bond and returned to his ex-wife a few months later. Word got back to me from Nick that he had gotten into a domestic disturbance with his ex-wife and ended up killing her.

This case turned out to be the largest seizure of cocaine in Broward County in the sixties. I have never forgotten this incident, and we learned later on from Eduardo that if I had not answered the questions like the CI, he would have killed me right there on the spot.

I also learned later on that the backup unit was ready to move in to assist. However, Nick ordered them to hold their positions because he believed that if they moved in, Eduardo would have shot me AND him. Nick told me later, "I knew you'd talk him out of it!"

From that moment on, I learned that Nick's cool demeanor and quick action prevented me from being executed. He will always remain my best friend, and I know that God has a special place in Heaven for him.

———————— ✦✦✦✦✦✦ ————————

On December 3, 1968, Lieutenant Stewart held a meeting in the vice special squad office with the Sarge. He read the Merit Award from BSO included below to all of us. It took me by total surprise. I was embarrassed and did not know what to say. This was work that I had done but could not have made these cases without the backup and support of Chuck and Gordon and the vice squad. They deserved the credit along with me. This was a great honor to be recognized by the best in BSO.

PRC
Employee's Initials

BROWARD COUNTY SHERIFF DEPARTMENT

MERIT/DEMERIT RECOMMENDATION

Endorsements

Date December 3, 1968

Name   PIERRE A. CHARETTE

Rank & Unit DEPUTY SHERIFF - SPECIAL SQUAD

Recommendation: Approved/Disapproved or _____
Signature _____

Recommendation: Approved/Disapproved or _____
Signature _____

| 5 | Merits | | Demerits | |

Reason _____

SEE BACK ----------

(Details on other side or attached)

Recommendation: Approved/Disapproved or _____
Signature _____

Recommendation: Approved/Disapproved or ____ ____
Signature _____

Review Board   Date 1-6-69

Recommended by

Sheriff   Final   1-6-69

BSO A.- P #7   500   8/65

Copy To: Board / Personnel File / Employee

.1.   Worked 315 hours per man for the month of November, 1968
2.   Made 33 arrests for drug and narcotic violations - 31 adults, 2 juveniles
3.   Made 6 selling arrests
4.   Made 2 narcotics buys
5.   Conducted 82 investigations
6.   Conducted 48 follow-up investigations
7.   72 assists - other police agencies
8.   Cleared the following cases:
            68-11-697 -- 16 arrests
            68-11-847 and 68-7-1433 -- 3 arrests
            68-11-999 -- 2 arrests
            68-11-1344 -- marijuana field
            68-11-1613 -- 3 arrests (also 68-11-1670)
            68-11-1426 -- 1 arrest
            68-11-1784 -- 1 arrest
            68-10-1928 -- 1 arrest
    68-1   68-11-2399 -- 3 arrests
            68-11-2492 and 68-11-2513 -- 3 arrests
    6   68-11-2288 -- 2 arrests

In addition to the above, in July the first heroin arrest in Broward County was made at
the Harris House. Also went to Dade County to the source of the heroin and made an arrest
68-11-2073.

Participated in above activities with Sgt. Peart and Detective Sanderson

Merit Award for Pierre A. Charette - Broward
County Sheriff Department

27

New Sheriff – January 1968

The narcotics unit became very effective and changes in the Broward County Sheriff's Department began to occur drastically. The existing Sheriff Alan B. Michell, who was elected in 1960 until 1968, informed me that I was being considered for promotion to detective Sergeant as a result of my work accomplishments as cited by a Merit Award recommended by Lieutenant Cecil Stewart on December 3, 1968. I was told to take the Sergeant's Exam, which I did and passed it, and was advised that I would go before an Oral Panel Board. Unfortunately, the Sheriff was indicted and charged with "knowingly, willfully or corruptly," allowing gambling in Broward County. Governor Hayden Burns suspended the Sheriff while criminal proceedings were being conducted. The governor appointed an interim Sheriff named Thomas Walker until 1968 when a new Sheriff was elected named Edward Stack.

Needless to say, we were all shocked, but we remained focused on our priorities, which were to suppress narcotic activity in Broward County. The one thing that we did not get involved in was the politics. All of our investigations were conducted in total secrecy from the Sheriff's Administration. "The less they knew, the safer we were" was our motto!

While we continued to make cases, changes started immediately at midnight when Sheriff Ed Stack was sworn in on January 1969. It was customary once a Sheriff was sworn in for all personnel to be in the conference room to await the new Sheriff so he could address his employees and inform those who were to remain in the room and those whose services were no longer required to leave and turn in their ID badges, etc.

It was my second time I had gone through this process, and when names were called out of top-ranked officers, deputies and department heads, I was shocked to watch what I called a political massacre of employees who obviously did not support this Sheriff politically. There was total silence in the room as I watched dumbfounded while friends who had families depending on this job were shaken and some in tears after being on the job for years. As best as I recalled, at least 10 to 15 were terminated that night.

Sheriff Stack then advised us that he was pleased to be our Sheriff and proceeded to introduce his new administrative staff. The Detective Bureau's new Chief of Detectives was an ex-NYPD officer named Robert Danner, Chief of Vice Squad remained as Lieutenant Cecil Stewart and Detective Lieutenant Norman Roehling, also a retired NYPD officer, was appointed head of the narcotics unit. The Sheriff introduced his Chief Deputy, Mr. Barney Lanahan (*deceased*) retired NYPD Commander. Once the introductions were made, everyone who remained in the room was sworn in by the new Sheriff.

We were fortunate in our squad to all remain on-board and were told to report to work the next day to meet our new boss Lieutenant Roehling at 9:00 a.m. We all left and amazed at what had just transpired. The vice squad and narcotics squad were not affected at all, thanks to our remaining out of politics during the election.

The next morning, I arrived at the office at 8:00 a.m. and met Sarge and the gang at the coffee shop next to the courthouse. The place was buzzing about what had transpired last night. Chuck made it clear to all of us that the new boss was a new face and part of the "New York Gang" as we called it.

Sarge said, "I want to make sure that we all keep a positive attitude with these changes. We had no idea about these new management positions, so let's see what the new lieutenant's game plan will be."

We all went to the office, where Betty greeted us. Lieutenant

Roehling was standing there waiting for all of us and said, "Why don't we all gather around in the middle of the room with your chairs and talk about these changes. First, let me assure you that nothing is going to change here. It will remain business as usual. Sergeant Stewart will remain in charge of you all and will keep me informed of what case we are working on. I will be the squad 'buffer' with the Chief of detectives, and he will respond to the Sheriff and Barny Lanahan.

"My policy is simple. Always be honest with me. Never lie to me about anything. If a problem has occurred, let's talk about it and get it resolved before it's escalated to the people upstairs. I will fight for you and have your back no matter what. Management has already been told what my work ethics are, and that we will not be micromanaged by anyone. I have been told that this is the best unit in this Sheriff's office and am proud to be appointed to it!"

Sarge introduced all of us to the lieutenant and said, "Welcome to the Mod Squad. We are pleased to have you as a boss, and I'm glad that somebody else will now take the heat and relieve me of some of the workload! One matter I have is that it has always been our position, since I and Joe Clarke started this unit, that we do not disclose our investigations to anyone outside this unit unless we feel and agree that management needs to be given a heads up when a major arrest is imminent. This way, we avoid possible leaks since it's necessary to do this to protect our undercover detectives and management from interfering with our jobs. Are you in agreement with us on this policy?"

"Sarge, you and the team have my total support on this, and this policy will continue to exist as long as I am in charge. Chief Danner was briefed on this by Lieutenant Stewart, and he fully concurred that the vice and narcotics units have to operate this way. So yes, we agree totally on this! Also, the Chief of detectives has discussed with the Sheriff the need for a new budget for this unit, since it was a low priority by the previous Sheriff. He will be going before the county commissioners to ask for an increase in investigative funds!"

"Thank you! That's what we wanted to hear. I promise that you will be busy because we are known to kick ass big time and have created a great reputation with prosecutors, judges, and police units throughout Broward County."

"Any questions from any of you, to me? Now is the time to ask, so don't be embarrassed. I have thick skin!" He laughed and waited for questions.

"Lieutenant, I'm Pete, AKA, Frenchy. As you have heard, we are a very tight group, and we work hard and play hard after work at times. Betty, our den mother, has a bar at her house that we use for R&R," everyone began laughing, but I continued, "and we would like, now that you're our new boss, to include you in our private club, that is if you drink? It's our way of blowing off steam after a case."

"Thanks, Frenchy. I have never met a cop who didn't have a watering hole, and I'm not going to break that tradition. "What we do and say together stays at Betty's place! And I'm honored to be asked to be in the club, so the answer is yes!"

"None of us here, I assure you, are ass kissers, but a family, and you are now part of this family as far as we are concerned."

"Well, I guess we are going to get along really well, and I like your boldness and bond as a unit! Sarge and I need to sit down to catch up from him as to what you have on your plate at this time! Are there any questions from the rest of you?"

"I have one. I'm Phil, also known as the 'Shadow'. We hear that Mr. Lanahan is initiating a NYPD policy that all detectives and deputies will have to carry a black book to record their activities when on the job and will have to produce it when challenged by supervisors or management. If it is not up to date than punitive actions will be taken. We have never done this, and personally, this is not doable for us because if attorneys ever got wind of this, they would have a field day with us in court to produce our books, and this would hurt us with ongoing cases. Is this true or just a rumor?"

"Glad you asked that. I won't lie to you and this stays among us! Yes, he is instituting the 'Barney Book' and did so in NYPD. Your concerns are valid, and I will discuss this with the Chief and go to bat for vice and narcotics to be exempt from this! I agree with your position on this and will go down fighting for this because I had to live with that in NYPD. It was a real pain in the ass, and it should only apply to uniform deputies and not the detective bureau. Great point! We will make this a priority!"

"Thank you! You just made our day on that matter. Sounds like you are like us. Ass kissing is not your style either!"

Laughing, the lieutenant responded, saying, "Never have and never will. Thank you all. Let's get to work!"

Within one week, the Barney Book issue was settled, and we became exempt from using it! We were still all issued one, but it stayed in the bottom drawers of our desks.

✦✦✦✦✦

The unit continued to make sensational cases, and hardly a week would go by without our making headlines in the newspaper of our narcotics arrests in Broward County. Lieutenant Roehling turned out to be a great boss and made sure that we had all the necessary assets to our disposal in order to do our job effectively.

One of the last big events in which I was involved before major changes occurred to my career was when we got news that there was going to be a second hippie festival occurring at the Hollywood Sport Atrium, located West of Pembroke Pines. This event, which was being advertised as the Second Woodstock Hippy Festival created a massive influx of Hippies from all over the U.S. and Canada.

To handle the coverage of this type of event, Sarge, Lieutenant Roehling and Lieutenant Stewart got together organized a meeting for us to come up with ideas on how to infiltrate the event grounds and covertly arrest drug dealers and users. Sarge suggested that our mod squad needed to blend in, and that we needed hippy vans to stay in the camping ground park so we could lure the dealers to our vans and do drug deals inside to be able to discretely arrest these assholes. The dilemma immediately came up that we did not have the financial resources to buy vans!

Sure enough, our wildly sadistic Lieutenant Cecil Stewart, with his crazy sense of humor, immediately said, "This is a problem, but I will get us three vans before the end of the day!" Our meeting ended, and we waited for Cecil to perform his magic!

"Sarge," I said, "what the hell is he up to?"

"God only knows. If anyone can get us the vans, it's him! Let's wait and see!"

Lieutenant Stewart came back two hours later wearing a devious look and smiling as he entered the squad area.

Lieutenant Roehling came out of his office with Sarge, smiling like the rest of us, and Phil said to me, "Frenchy, bet you ten bucks that he didn't get them."

"You're on! You got 20 because I'm doubling that bet. Might as well fork it over now if you want because this nut case always comes through!"

"You're on!" he said, shaking my hand.

Betty, who was standing next to us, leaned over to the Phantom and whispered softly, "Asshole! You just lost that bet!"

"Ok!" Cecil said, "listen up. I couldn't get two. The Phantom immediately looked at me and Betty wore a large smile as Cecil continued, "I got three brand new customized camping vans!" he announced laughing.

The Phantom said softly, "Son of a bitch."

As he gently breathed out those words, I reached out with my right hand, palms up and said softly, "Pay up now!" I laughed with Betty. Phil had already gotten the 20 out and handed it to me, shaking his head.

Cecil heard the commotion as he looked our way, smiling as he saw the hand-off and said, "Frenchy, I'll take half of that bet! Phil, you should know better to bet against the old man," he bellowed as everyone else in the room broke out into laughter, and Phil turned red with embarrassment.

Cecil than said, "Besides getting these brand-new babies, the dealership is getting two of them painted with full-blown psychedelic colors and Peace Signs, weed symbols and lettering 'Make Peace and Love!' We have them for the whole week! We got two weeks to prepare for this. We will have a prisoner holding area away from the festival grounds and BSO prisoner vans to transport the prisoners to the SO

Booking Desk. We will have deputies processing the prisoners and judges holding bond hearings after they are processed at the booking desk. The judges had agreed that due to the possible large number of prisoners, that this process would be lengthy and take at least three to four days for arraignment.

Lieutenant Roehling and Sarge had been making calls to the Fort Lauderdale Police Narcotics Unit and the Hollywood Narcotics Unit, and they were providing additional UC narcs to work with us. This news caused smiles on all of us, and we could feel the excitement to start right away. We all pitched to devise forms for the arrest, packages for evidence, cameras to photograph the defendant with the Arresting UC agent who made the buys, along with photos of drugs sold, etc. Within four days, we had everything ready. We discussed how we would walk the grounds for offers to buy dope, bring them to the vans, and once inside and the dope was produced, how we would immediately grab and muffle the suspect, subdue him or her to the floor of the van and slowly depart the area to the holding area so that we could turn the suspect over to uniformed deputies.

Three days before the start of the festival, a unit member (*name withheld*) had left the office to go meet with Hollywood Narcotics Unit members about the festival arrangements. We drove down US-1 from Fort Lauderdale. When we came to a traffic light south of Dania Boulevard, I observed a hippy-looking character driving in the right lane with Canadian tags. I rolled down the passenger window, and as the light turned red, we stopped side by side. Driving, I yelled at him in French and asked him where he was from. He responded, Montreal, and I told him to pull over at the Crystal Burger place on the right. He was smiling and immediately drove in as I did. I told my partner that this guy is coming to the festival and we are going to make a dope deal with him. "Just watch me," I said.

We pulled into the parking lot and parked next to this individual and began speaking in French to him, "*Ça va?*" I asked, extending my hand to shake his. *"Moi, je m'appelle Pierre."*

He responded in French, *"Ça va bien. Je m'appelle Gérard.* (PN)

"Pierre, do you speak English?"

"Yes, where are you from?"

"I'm from Montreal, originally from Valleyfield and Lachine! I live here now in Hollywood. This is my partner!"

"Hi! How you doing, man. Nice ride you got there! Are you here on vacation?"

"Yeah! Heading to my motel a couple blocks from here. I'm here for the festival in Hollywood. Should be a blast. Are you guys going there also?"

I responded, "Yeah, tomorrow. We're just meeting a couple of contacts in an hour to buy some stuff to make some money while we can. Should be a lot of people, time to cash in while we can!"

"I got you. That's why I'm down here. What have you guys got? I may be interested in doing business with you?"

I looked at my partner and smiled, saying to myself, *Oh Yeah! You took the bait, you asshole, and we are here to bust your ass! Let's play!*

"We only do White Snow from Columbia. How about you?"

"I got some acid hits, hash, and pills! All Oz packs for smoke-hits! A hundred a sheet, and pills, meth and barbs. A hundred a bag!" he announced while smiling the whole time.

"Man, that's cool," I commented. "How about we meet here in an hour? Can you handle five of each and how much?"

"Hits, normally $10 a piece. I can give you a deal for us Canadians!" he said, smiling. "For $5, and hash $150 per oz, and pills $50 per bag @ $2.50 per pill. Cash only, no trade!"

"Sounds good to us. See you in an hour right here, my man! *À bientôt!" yeah, really soon, asshole!* We shook hands and went on our way.

We left and headed south on US 1 while our Canadian friend fell behind us and pulled in a motel a block away from our meeting point in his black Charger.

"That asshole deserves to be taken down, for being stupid," I said.

"God Almighty! You called this one right! He'll pass out once we badge him!"

"Ok, let's make a pass back and see what motel room he's parked in front of?"

"Yep. I'll get the room number, and you call in the cavalry for some money to flash this guy."

"You read my mind, my man!"

I got on the phone and briefed Chuck telling him to bring $5K in $100 bills for the flash roll, and we can meet at the Dania Ice Cream Parlor on US 1. Sarge advised that they would be rolling in 15 minutes, and two of the guys would set up on this guy at the motel.

We met the cavalry at the ice cream parlor lot and briefed everyone that once the deal was made and goods in hand, the signal to take him down would be when I gave him a high five and went to the trunk of my car to get the money.

As planned, we pulled into the Royal Castle parking lot and waited for our friend! Just like clockwork, he arrived as planned and parked next to my car.

Sarge and Phil were inside the RC, sitting facing the window to the parking lot, munching on their order.

Gerard arrived right on time, and my partner and I exited our vehicle as did he.

I said, "*Bonjour, mon ami*! Are we ready to deal?" I smiled.

"Yes, no problem. All I need to see is that you have got some money to pay?"

"No problem. Show our friend some green!"

"Come over to the car, Gerard. It's right here!" Phil opened the passenger side door and reached into the glove compartment, where he pulled out a bank envelope with $5K of $100 bills.

Gerard verified the cash, placed it back in the glove compartment and locked it.

"Ok! I got your merchandise here in the trunk of my car. Come on and check it out!" he told us as he walked over to his car and opened the trunk. Gerard opened up a brown leather overnight bag, which contained several envelopes of exactly what we asked for.

"Man, looks like you know how to do business nice and quick, with no hassle! That's the way we like it. Now I need to verify it, and we have a deal!" I checked each item, and everything looked great.

"Ok, mon ami," I said. "we have a deal! Let's go to our cars, get your money, bring your bag, and we can meet later at the festival grounds tonight and party!" I raised my hand up to give him a high five, which he returned. My partner also high fived him as we walked to our cars.

Instantly out of nowhere, Sarge, Phil and the Calvary rushed up to us with guns drawn yelling, "**POLICE ON THE GROUND NOW!!**"

We immediately responded as well as Gerard, who said, "Aw, fuck!"

Once Gerard was handcuffed, he stood up, then we did. After we were on our feet, I said to him, "Sorry, pal, but we are also cops!" Gerard flushed and kept shaking his head, saying, *"Merde!"*

The defendant was taken to the BSO booking desk, and this case turned out to be one of the largest busts prior to the start of the Hippy Festival. Gerard refused to cooperate, so a search warrant was executed on his hotel room with additional drugs found in his suitcase.

———————— ++++++ ————————

With some cases such as this, everything goes smoothly and quickly with no problems. This is an exception to the normal cases that we work on. Because we never know what we will uncover from one day to the next, narcotics investigations are fascinating with never a dull moment.

———————— ++++++ ————————

When the festival opened, we situated ourselves at three different locations on the grounds and blended in and for three days, 24 hours a day, making numerous drug buys and arrests, totaling close to a hundred. There was so much drug activity that deals were being made every hour we were there.

All we had to do is dress like hippies and agree to buy drugs then bring them back to our vans. Once inside and see the drug, we'd immediately arrest them and use good old Duct tape across their mouths to keep them from screaming as we drove off the festival grounds to take them to the processing center.

After three days of work, we were exhausted, and everyone was given two days to recuperate from all the crazy activities. The team consisted of agents from BSO, Fort Lauderdale PD, and Hollywood PD.

Top Row Left to Right: Bobby "LNUK",
Harold Prior, Dennis Nichols, Larry "LNUK",
Art McCullum. Bottom Row Left to Right:
George De Carlo, Pierre "Pete" Charette,
Phil McCann, Gorman Brennan, Bob DiCarlo)

Because of the good prior planning, teamwork and great law enforcement cooperation, this was a new chapter in narcotics investigative work that became a model for future festivals such as this.

During this period at BSO, my career was slowly starting to change. I decided that I needed to enroll at the Broward Community College to pursue a degree in police science and technology. I used my military GI Bill benefits to pay for my night classes in which I enrolled.

In addition, I started dating a BSO Fingerprint ID employee, Chris Lawrence, whom I married after she was transferred as a Detective in the vice squad. Chris was a great investigator and worked undercover in vice and at times with our special squad. She made one of the biggest heroin cases for BSO and was highly respected by everyone in the department.

During this period, Lieutenant Roehling and Sarge asked me to meet with them in private. "Pete," said Roehling, "Sarge and I are nominating you for Officer of the Year for the Broward County law enforcement community. This is the highest award given to a police officer by the Coral Ridge Kiwanis Club of Fort Lauderdale. The award ceremony will be held on September 25." Once again, I was speechless and dumbfounded as to what I was hearing. The lieutenant continued, "Pete, I want to read to you this memo that we are submitting to our Chief of detectives Robert Danner:

Date: 21 July 1970
Memo to: Robert A. Danner, Chief of Detectives
From: Lt. Norman E. Roehling, Narcotics Unit
Subject: NOMINATION FOR OFFICER OF THE YEAR AWARD: PIERRE A CHARETTE

The Unanimous selection for the Officer of the Year award by the Narcotics Unit of the Selective Enforcement Squad is Detective Pierre A. Charette.

A. Background

1. Detective Charette sworn in as a Deputy Sheriff, September 1966, promoted to Detective September 1967.

B. Education

1. Detective Charette has completed all Police Courses at Broward Jr. College and is currently working on his Associate Degree in Police Science.

2. Graduated from the United States Department of Justice, Bureau of Narcotics and Dangerous Drugs School, August 1968.

3. Completed Vice Control Operation Class at Broward Junior College, December 1967.

4. Completed F.B.I. Finger Printing and Classification School, November 1968.

5. Attended Police Seminar on Scientific Evidence, Broward Jr. College, in May 1970.

6. Represented B.S.O. at a National Conference of District Attorneys in Chicago, Illinois, May 1970

7. Has given lectures on Dangerous Drugs on off duty time to various Municipal Police Departments.

C. Detective Charette has received recognition from his fellow police officers by receiving an award for Meritorious Acts in July 1970, by the Fraternal Order of Police, Lodge 32, for making the largest purchase of LSD in the history of Broward County, resulting in the arrest of (5) Defendants, some of whom were armed.

D. In the past year, Detective Charette has given freely of his time and effort to aid other police agencies in combatting drug abuse in Broward County. He has also been directly or indirectly involved in the arrest of 172 defendants in the past year, who were sellers of or in possession of illicit drugs or involved in other offenses.

E. When engaged in the act of making narcotics, Detective Charette, although covered from a distance by fellow officers, has put himself in personal jeopardy. Going unarmed into areas where confrontations could, and in some cases did occur, when he was recognized by narcotic sellers he had previously arrested.

F. He has given unceasingly of his time, in an effort to rehabilitate young drug addicts, who gave indications of wanting to be cured.

G. He has proven his faithfulness to duty by being on call 24 hours a day to aid other Municipal Police Agencies and has been called out in the early morning hours many times to help and assist them.

Summation:

In summation, the finest tribute that can be given a dedicated police officer, is the recognition and high esteem that he is held by his fellow officers. Detective Charette has received this recognition not only from his superiors and fellow Detectives, but from various Police Chiefs and men of the many Municipal Agencies within Broward County. His faithfulness to duty, his constant dedication to his work should now be recognized by all citizens of Broward County

Lt. Norman E. Roehling
Selective Enforcement

Credit: Copy of Original memo Labeled: Edward J. Stack, Sheriff Broward County P.O. Box 8069 Ft. Lauderdale, Florida 33310 Phone 525-4321 Dated 21 July 1970

"Pete, you deserve this and from the Sheriff on down, everyone concurs that you deserve this award. Congratulations! The competition is large and will be announced by the Kiwanis Club. We feel that you are deserving of this, and we will know soon!"

"I don't know what to say. I'm honored that you all feel that I am worthy of this, and I will continue to do what I do best, which is to put drug traffickers who are the scum of the earth and are spreading havoc on our community in jail."

"The Lieutenant and I will always have your back, and I know that there's no doubt you will beat the other nominees hands down for this well-deserved honor!"

"Thanks, Sarge. I owe this all to you for having had faith in me from the start!"

On August 24, 1970, the Sheriff put out a memo to all personnel that The Kiwanis Club of Fort Lauderdale has nominated Detective Pierre A. Charette to be the recipient of the Officer of the Year Award and Major Thomas E. Atkinson to be the runner-up. The date of the Eleventh Annual Dinner would be on September 25, 1970.

Needless to say, I was excited and honored and got one hell of a reception from our detective bureau and office team! Throughout the day, I received calls from all of my friends from various police agencies in the county and from BSO employees who came by to congratulate me.

I thanked everyone and went over to the vice squad, where I received a standing ovation from all my friends. Lieutenant Stewart came out of his office and walked over with an extended hand. He said, "Frenchy, I knew from the moment I told you on your first day on the job to arrest your lieutenant for me that I had picked the right man for the job! You never let me down, and you deserve this honor. You have made us proud, and I know that you will continue to do so. I know that this 'ride' is not over for you! Keep up the good work, my friend."

"I will and thank you and all you for this honor!" I was all teared up and have never forgotten this day. "You had faith in me, and I owe my career to you. I will always continue to make you proud!" I made sure to immediately call my parents to give them the good news. As predicted, Mom was in tears and Dad was all choked up.

On September 25, my wife Kristine, Dad, Mom, Father-in-Law and Mother-in-Law Jack and Ella Lawrence, were honored at the Kiwanis

Club Dinner with an attendance of numerous dignitaries and friends. I received telegrams from FDLE Nick Navarro, BNDD agents and police Chiefs from Broward County congratulating me on this award. I was overwhelmed and humbled to receive this award and never forgot that evening.

Officer of the Year Award with my wife
Christine at the Kiwanis Club Dinner

An amusing incident occurred while I was behind the speaker's podium that evening. During my speech, unbeknownst to me, a rat was hovering over my head on a wooden beam! Chris later advised me that had her mother seen this rat, she would have screamed at the top of her lungs, causing mass panic and possible evacuation of the dining room. Her mother had a deadly fear of rats. She discretely told her dad, who looked up slowly and told her not to draw people's attention to the rat, or Ella would die or go into full panic mode. Thank God, I never knew about it either!

About a week later, I was asked to report to the Sheriff's assistant, Mr. Barney Lanahan's office. His secretary told me to go in, and when I did, he said, "Peter, have a seat. We need to talk about your passing the Sergeant Exam when Michell was Sheriff. As you know, Peter, we are very proud of you and feel that you deserve to be promoted to detective Sergeant as a result of your fine work, but there is a small problem about this and the concern that you are not registered as a Republican!"

"Sir! I'm aware that I am not registered, and the reason is that I firmly believe that as long as I am an officer, I don't need to get involved in politics and will support whoever is the Sheriff loyally and not let politics interfere with my job!"

"Peter, I fully understand that, but managers need to show that there is a total commitment to this office. I hope you see where I'm going, and this would lock you in for your promotion!"

"I'll make it easy, Mr. Lanahan, for you. I withdraw my request to be considered, but thank you for the opportunity. I will remain loyal to this agency and to the Sheriff in power!"

"Peter, are you sure about this. I hate to see you miss out on this opportunity?"

"Thank you, I'm positive. Politics is not, in my view, that important for a promotion. Promotions should always be done on the merits of one's accomplishment and job performance. I have learned this from my distinguished professors in college and mentors on the job. No need to pursue this any further. Again, thank you and the Sheriff for considering me! Is there anything else you need from me?"

"No, Peter. I appreciate your honesty on this matter. Have a good day. I will advise the Sheriff that you have withdrawn your request!"

I left the office and went back to the office and briefed Lieutenant Roehling, Sarge and Captain Stewart on my encounter with this issue! Captain Stewart said, "Frenchy, you got a set of balls, to have stood up to them! You nailed it perfectly and did the right thing!"

"Pete! As your boss in this unit, you have my respect and support on your handling of this matter and if they approach me, I will back you 100%! Good job!"

"Frenchy, wow! That took balls like Cecil said and keep up the good work. I'm sure there's got to be some red faces right now. Just watch your back because politicians have a way of striking back and when they do, they shove it up your ass!"

"Thanks, guys! I have no regrets, and thanks for your support!"

28

Shield 328 Resignation

I knew after this meeting that they would be gunning for me and find a way to let me go since the Sheriffs can fire you 'without cause' at any time. I discussed this with my wife and friends and made a decision on December 1, 1970, to submit my resignation to be effective December 11, 1970. My reason for resignation was to go to college as a full-time student to pursue a police science degree.

I should note that this was a hard decision to make, fully knowing that I would miss being a narc, which I dearly loved. My goal and dream after working in this area of law enforcement was to someday become a federal narcotics agent and get assigned overseas to France where all the heroin was being produced by the Corsican mob and shipped to the U.S. mob for distribution on the streets.

I enjoyed being a full-time student and being one of the oldest ones in my night class. There was a benefit of having a law enforcement background. Some of my professors would ask me to give the classes on narcotics/vice/ uniform patrol/detective work since I had an expertise in those areas. I was told by doing this, I would receive an 'A' for the courses. That deal was a no brainer!

One day while attending class, I received a message that Police Chief John Ballantyne (*deceased*) of the Pembroke Pines Police Department wanted me to call him. The Chief was a retired NYPD officer who was a good friend and whom I had helped on numerous occasions. When I called the Chief, he requested me to come to his home because he wished to talk to me in person. I left class and drove to his home. John was about 5'10", burly built, a grey-haired Irish gentleman. He had a great personality, and I admired the man immensely.

Upon arrival at his home, he greeted me wearing a bathrobe and pajamas and, with a broad smile, said, "Frenchy, how the hell are you, son? Come on in. It's great seeing you. What's this I hear about you resigning from BSO! What the hell happened?"

"John, let me tell you what happened. I saw the writing on the wall after I turned down a promotion for political reasons!" After filling him in, he was appalled that this occurred. I told him that I was fine and glad to pursue my education on a full-time basis. He then told me that he recently found out that he had cancer that could not be cured and wanted my help.

"Frenchy, I found out recently that some of my officers may be involved in possible illegal activity, and I want you to come to work for me to verify if these allegations are true. You can name your hours so it doesn't interfere with your classes. I want this done before my time is up, and I am asking this as a friend!"

"John, you know I would do anything for you, and I am sorry that you are faced with something like this. I will accept without any hesitation. Give me a week to rearrange my courses and put me on the 4-12 shift as a patrolman. I will keep you posted and verify if this is occurring for you, my friend!"

"I knew I could count on you and would not want anyone else for this covert assignment. No one will know about this. I will simply tell the mayor that I have an open position, and you are the man I want. Right now, I got an officer running things, and I will advise him that you will report next week for the 4-12 shift. I will get your uniform ready for you and swear you in next week."

"Chief, I need total secrecy on this. It's between you and me and no one else. If the word was to leak out, my ass would be out to hang, and it could get dangerous and physical as you well know from your New York days?"

"For sure, no problem and thank you, my friend!"

The Chief and I enjoyed a drink together and I left feeling sad that my good friend was heartbroken over this. He did not deserve this. I drove home tearing up to see him suffer like this. I asked God to watch over him and to give me the strength to resolve the matter for him quickly and safely.

I reported for duty two weeks later in April of 1971 until September of the same year. The police department was located at the small Pembroke Pines City Hall adjacent to the Florida Turnpike and Pembroke Road. The police department was in one room with three Sergeants and six officers. The Chief welcomed me, and for the next 6 months, I worked the 4-12 shift, patrolling the city. During the six months of employment, I was able to gather information that some officers were accepting cash for traffic offenses and dismissing the citations. In addition, some officers were involved in turning their backs on violations involving the sale of alcohol to minors and receiving gratuity from local businesses.

Of the nine officers, only two voiced their concerns to me about various doings by officers in the department.

After a period of time, I decided to speak with one of these officers and take him into my confidence. I told him that I was conducting an internal investigation of the department and asked for his cooperation should I need help in case my cover was blown. He agreed and I further advised him that if I am ever called by any supervisor to meet away from the city, I would click my radio mike button twice for him to slowly head to the location and give it a five-minute delay.

The investigation came to an end when I received a radio call from the lieutenant who was off duty for me to meet him at the Hollywood Sport Atrium located west of the city on Hollywood Boulevard. Something did not sound right to me, so I clicked my mike button twice and headed for the meet.

Upon arrival, the parking lot was empty except for three cars parked together and five officers gathered together awaiting my arrival.

Exiting my car and approaching the off-duty officers, I was advised immediately by one who stated, "We hear that you are doing us in and that you're a plant, investigating us, you son of a bitch!"

"Ok! You're right!" I responded as I placed my hand on my weapon. "Everybody calm down. You don't want to make it worse. I've been requested by the Chief to investigate possible corruption in the department and it ends tonight. You all calm down and don't do anything that you will regret and go to jail for!"

Just then my back up pulled up, turned on his blue light, and pulled up next to me. Then he got out of his unit.

"Guys, the Chief has been called and is waiting at the station, and I have called the state attorney's office along with the mayor's office. They will be at the station." The look on their faces told me everything I suspected. They all looked at each other with flushed faces and said nothing. "Let's all go to the station now before things get out of hand. See you there!" As I turned around and got into my car, my back up followed me to the station.

Arriving at the station, the Chief was there with Maggi, a member of the city council.

"Frenchy, what happened?" he asked as the off-duty officers drove in. When they came in, he said to them, "You all please go into the council room now and wait for us. That's an order!"

They all responded solemnly, "Yes, Sir!"

The Chief said, "Maggi, let's go in my office with Pete, and I'll explain everything." After briefing her completely and discussing the findings with the state attorney, it was agreed that those involved would be given a choice to immediately resign and agree to sign an affidavit that they would never seek employment in law enforcement, or they would be brought before a grand jury on charges.

After a meeting was held with all seven officers, all agreed to the conditions and officially resigned.

Maggi stated, "Chief, you're on sick leave, and as we discussed, you're not able to come back, and now, with this situation, I need to get us a new Chief. And Pete, the Chief and I have talked and feel that we would like to offer you the Chief's job at this time. You are someone who we trust, and we would be honored to have!"

"Wow, I wasn't expecting anything like that!" I was at a loss for words. "I am honored, but Chief and Maggi, I feel that I'm too young to accept this position, and I need to get my degree as I planned, but I can give you the name of someone who could be a great choice for you.

That person is the BSO Chief of Detective Floyd Hall, who has high integrity and would be ideal for this city!"

"Pete, thank you, and the Chief and I will contact him in the morning and talk with him. I don't know how we can thank you enough for what you have done!"

"Maggi, you don't have to thank me. It's John who deserves the thanks! I'm proud to have helped and will always be there for you all!"

"Frenchy! You did what I asked you to do for this old man!" he said, laughing! "Now I can retire knowing that my department is clean! Thanks, my friend" We hugged, and I left feeling that John will sleep well now!

Floyd Hall became the new Chief Hall!

29

Unexpected Dream Comes True

After accomplishing my work at the Pembroke Pines Police Department, I continued my study for my degree on a full-time basis. I stayed in contact with my friend Gerard, who advised me that the Miami Bureau of Narcotics and Dangerous Drugs was now becoming very active with new agents and now had five enforcement groups, a new special agent in charge (SAIC) named Ben Thieson, AKA The Batman *(deceased)*, a deputy ASAIC, and two assistant special agents in charge (ASAIC).

Miller asked me for a favor for the new boss who needed temporary lodging until he purchased a home and asked if I could get him lodging at my father's motel on Hallandale Beach for three months. I told him to consider it done and to give me the date he wants to check in and my dad will fix him up.

Ben Thieson checked into my dad's place, and Miller asked me to come to the office to meet the Batman. A few weeks later, I went to the BNDD office to meet Miller and Mr. Thieson at a local watering hole near the office. I walked in the bar and spotted them sitting against the back wall of the bar at a table. Miller motioned me over and made the introduction, "Ben, this is Frenchy. He is crazy and a pain in the ass!" He laughed.

Frenchy, all I can say is you hang around with dangerous company with this crazy German! I have heard a lot about you from my people and also from your dad! I appreciate your help on getting me fixed up at the motel."

"My pleasure, Sir! I agree this guy is a pain, I've been making him famous once a month with cases, and then what does he do in return? He steals my best female informant from me and makes a large hashish case! I don't know why I do it, but I can't help myself. He's become one of my best friends along with the Mad Cuban Navarro!" I replied.

"That's what I hear. Try to keep him straight if you can!" he replied with a smile. "Let's drink while you tell me about how you got into doing this type of work!"

Our get together lasted till 9:00 p.m. when we all left and agreed to hook up for drinks again. The Batman was unique and was my kind of guy. He stood about 5'10", looked like an Italian mobster, with jet black hair, a deep raspy voice and a good build and could be a movie star! He spoke his mind and expected people to work and play hard after work. Gerard contacted me the next day and told me that The Batman enjoyed our get together and would enjoy getting together again. He said, "Batman usually is very distant from new people, but you made a hell of an impression on him. He told me that his close friend, Supervisor Pete Scrocca (*deceased*) AKA Pete, the Blond, had told him that you were one of the best narcs that he had worked with. I'm glad that you met him because now you have been accepted in our circle by the man who is a legend in this agency. Frenchy, I'll call you later. In the meantime, keep working on that damn degree!"

"Don't you worry. I will and thanks, my friend!"

⁺⁺◆◆◆◆⁺⁺

About a month later in December 1971, while in class, a message was delivered by phone to our professor that I needed to leave immediately and go to the BNDD office in Miami, that a Mr. Thieson needed you at his office as soon as possible. I left and immediately drove to the BNDD office arriving around 8:30 p.m.

Mr. Thieson's secretary was waiting at the reception desk and took me immediately to his office.

"Come on in, Frenchy. Sit down and keep quiet!"

"Get me headquarters on the phone! Frenchy, bear with me and I'll fill you in after I speak to this boss in DC!"

"Sir, he's on the phone!"

"Yeah, he's here with me now, and he will not accept anything except a grade 9! He has ten years as a cop and is fluent in French! You can run it to Administration. He will have his associate degree by the end of December in Police Science & Technology! That should satisfy the waiver of a B.S. degree. Call me back and let me know. This is the guy that you're looking for. My word is good, you know that. I'll be waiting!"

"Ok, Frenchy! Here's what's going on. We received a teletype today asking all regions to find a fluent French-speaking officer to go to France to work on the French Connection Organization. I called DC right away and told them not to look any further, that I had the man for the job. After talking to my staff and people, they all agreed you were the man for the job!"

"Sir! DC on the line!"

Dumfounded, and I'm sure with a look of disbelief, I could not believe that this was happening. I had dreams of becoming a BNDD agent someday, but not by this type of surprise. I felt like this was a dream, and my heart was beating fast, and yet I was saying to myself, "Please God, make this happen!"

"Bill, what's the word? Ok, sounds good. I'll get him in and start the process! You won't regret this one, trust me! Thanks! Later." Ben hung up and turned to me. "Frenchy," reaching out with a handshake, "Congratulations! You're being hired as a GS-9 Special Agent with us, son!" he beamed.

"You're joking, Ben! Aren't you? Come on, is this a joke?" I asked in astonishment.

"No, this is real. I'm proud to hire you, and I know you won't let me down. You're now part of a special group that, not too many enter into our circle!"

"Ben, I won't let you down and will work my ass off to make you all proud of me!"

"Just remember, your integrity is the most important part of this work, and you had three guys vouching for you on this: Miller, Navarro, and Scrocca! Of course, I also felt the same in the short time we knew each other," he said, reaching out and shaking my hand. "We need to end this tonight. Be here Monday morning to do the paperwork, and we will talk some more. One thing, mum's the word. Don't discuss any of this with anyone except Agent Miller, Navarro or Scrocca!"

"Yes, Sir!"

"Sir, only at work, to you when off work, it's Ben!"

"Ben! I fully understand. Have a great weekend. I'll see you Monday at 9:00 a.m." I couldn't contain my smiling. I left floating on cloud nine, still in shock. I hurried home and told Chris, who was also elated and shocked.

I called Miller, but before I could say anything, he said laughing, "I told you that someday you will be on this job!"

"I'm still in a daze. Thank you, my friend. I won't let you down!"

"I know. That's why I knew you were the one for this. Just maintain a low profile and Ben will clue you in about how to proceed on this! Just remember, some people will be upset as to your GS Status. Just shrug it off, and no need to explain anything! Mum's the word. See you Monday for coffee! Enjoy the weekend."

I next called Nick and thanked him, and the Mad Cuban said, "You deserve it! We groomed you for this, and that's what friends are for!"

I have never forgotten that day. I was anxious to take the ride all the way to the top of the criminal underworld ladder wherever the job took me!

I called my parents and broke the news to them. My dad was speechless, and I detected a slight choked up reaction. He and my mother were excited. And the first question my mother asked was, "Is this more dangerous than the Sheriff's department?"

"Mom, it's the same but on a bigger scale in the criminal underworld. I'll be working all over Europe. Don't worry, I will be safe. It's what I always wanted to be." Needless to say, I couldn't wait for Monday to come.

•◆◆◆◆•

On Monday morning, I met Gerard for coffee and discussed all of this. I was nervous and he also reminded me about keeping this under wraps. He brought me into Mr. Thieson's office.

"Well, Frenchy, how was your weekend?" he asked with a smile.

"I'm still in a daze, to be honest and anxious to start this new career."

"You will be fine, so let me explain what this involves. As you well know, heroin addiction is our number one problem in the United States. Most heroin, about 90%, is coming out of France. The Corsican mob controls all the production and exportation to the U.S. The Labs are mainly in the Marseille area, and the white heroin is shipped to the U.S. for the mob to distribute it throughout the country. President Nixon has ordered that BNDD needs to put all their resources into breaking up this French connection, and BNDD is making this its highest priority worldwide.

"We were tasked to send agents to France to work hand in hand with the French government to dismantle this organization. Our agents currently in France, are not fluent in French, so we need someone like you who speaks French fluently to be assigned in Paris and work with the French Narcotic Unit. They are not allowed to work undercover due to the Napoleon Code of Law, which forbids this. The statute is called Agent Provocateur. This is where you come in and work undercover with cases we develop with informants of ours and theirs. Any questions!"

"No, sounds pretty clear to me. I'm in, and hopefully, we will destroy these death merchants." I let out a nervous, quiet laugh.

"Now, we will process you through the system today and swear you in sometime in January. Then you will attend BNDD Agent School in DC on January 10. Agent Miller will take you downstairs, and an agent is waiting with the paperwork to process you ASAP! If he asks any question about your employment, just say they needed some fluent French speakers. No mention about France understood?"

"Yes, Sir!"

"Good, Miller, he is all yours. Stick with him today, got it?"

"You got it! Let's go, Frenchy!"

The agent and I had met on prior occasions and began, "What's up, Frenchman? Mr. Thieson asked me to process you. Welcome on board! Glad we got you with us. Let's get started. Sit down, and I will type your application. Just answer the questions, and I'll do the rest." Then he turned to Miller and said, "I got him and will call you when we are done in about two hours!"

"Ok! See you guys later. Go easy on him!" He turned laughing and exited the room.

"Ok, let's do this. I need your full name, date of birth, Social Security Number, etc. Now your grade level will be GS-5 Special Agent, Grade Series 1811 correct?"

"I hate to stop you, but Mr. Thieson advised me I was starting as a GS-9, not GS-5."

"I think he's wrong. All new guys start at GS-5!"

"You need to call him because that's what he told me!" I said, shrugging my shoulders with palms up.

"Ok! I'll call him!" he said as he dialed and told the secretary he needed to ask Mr. Thieson a quick question. "Mr. Thieson, I need to clarify an issue with Pete's grade entry. He said that you told him he was starting as a GS-9. I told him that was a mistake. All agents start as a GS-5!"

I could hear Mr. Thieson say to him, "Pete is right. Thanks for asking!"

"Yes, Sir!"

He hung up and said," You were right, man! They must want you bad!" he said, laughing.

⁺·⁺◆◆◆·⁺

The process took several hours, after which Miller and I went out to lunch at a Howard Johnson restaurant across the street from the office in downtown Miami on Biscayne Boulevard. Sitting there when we walked in was Pete Scrocca (*deceased*), Aka "Pete the Blond," the group supervisor. He smiled and said, "You don't have to say anything. The word is out, and you are now one of us!" He smiled and gave me a hug. "Pete, I know you spoke up for me to the Batman, and someday I'll repay the favor, my friend!"

"Bullshit, you deserve it, and we knew you were the guy for this job! Once you're there, give them hell, you lucky bastard! Paris of all fucking places, me I got New York when I came on," Pete the Blond said.

Miller responded, "You deserved New York, you crazy bastard. I had to work with this mad man! He's nuts! And dangerous!"

We all had lunch together and returned back to the office to finish the paperwork. I was advised to report for work on January 3, 1972, at 9:00 a.m. I left and pinched myself to make sure this was not a dream. *Thank you, GOD*!

On Monday, January 3, I arrived at the Miami office at 8:00 a.m. and was told to report to Mr. Thieson's office. His secretary greeted me and smiling she said, "The boss wants you to get with Ruthie May Jones (*deceased*), our administrative clerk who will get you started with other paperwork for your life insurance benefits and ID, weapon issuance, and all of that stuff. She will get your reservation for DC Agents School Hotel, airfare, and per diem advance for the next 12 weeks. So, come with me and meet Ruthie May!"

As we entered her office, this beautiful forty-something tall lady, light black skin, wearing glasses and a smile that melted you on the spot said, "Pierre, I knew from the first time I met you that someday you would be one of us and the good Lord answered my prayers!" she said as she gave me a big hug!

"Ruthie! I made it, and I am so happy that we will be working with you all!"

"You will do fine, and Ruthie May will make sure that you are well trained and taken care of! Now, see that empty desk by the window? Frenchy, this is your temporary desk. Then it's DC Agents School, and then you come back here to work in Group Three and report to the Group Supervisor (GS). You will meet him in a while. See this big BNDD Agent's Manual on your desk here? That's your bible, and you will spend the next three days reading it completely. You need to familiarize yourself with it, and if you have any questions, ask me!" said Ruthie.

"Yes, ma'am! I'm one to ask questions and not ashamed to say I don't understand, and I need to know."

"Frenchy, there's no shame in asking, and you have the right attitude. Some of these new guys act like they know it all, and I have seen these types fall flat on their asses sooner or later, if you know what I mean?"

"Yes, I do!"

"Ok! I'm doing your paperwork, and when I'm done, you can sign all these forms! Right now, sit and start learning the manual!"

I sat at my assigned desk. The BNDD Manual was at least 8 inches thick and about 350 pages long.

--------‹·♦♦♦♦·›--------

I had learned quickly by my mentors that the manual for some was looked upon as the gospel, and those who lived by it were what we called not real or "suck ass" agents. They only wanted to move up the management ladder and were unable to be real agents in the eyes of those of us, who had brass balls and didn't suck ass, but who kicked ass, made cases, worked undercover, and devoted 12-16 hours a day including weekends without complaining. We learned that the manual was a reference tool only and not the gospel. Having common sense and being street smart were always the best guides for being a good agent.

--------‹·♦♦♦♦·›--------

Lunchtime came around when my new group supervisor came in and said, "Frenchy, you're allowed to go to lunch. So, let's go!" As he reached out to shake my hand, he continued, "Good to see you. I got the word from Agent Miller and damn! We sure are glad that you're on board. Ben told me he was putting you in my group so you could train some of my new guys in undercover work and take them out to get their feet wet with making buys when you get back from agents' school!"

"You got me, and I will do whatever it takes to break them in! I'm anxious to start!"

"Good. Let's go! The gang is anxious to meet you. Some of them you already know, and they are anxious to see you. The word is out that the frog is on board!"

"Great!" He made me feel right at home and was one of the best GS's in the MFD (Miami Field Division). The group was made up of eight agents whose names are protected from disclosure. All of them were great agent friends. The only one that I can name was a great agent, Charles Mann, who was killed in a disastrous accident when the Miami office collapsed, and he was killed along with several other employees.

————— ✦✦✦✦✦ —————

The next nine days were the basic orientation of the operation and administrative functions and requirements for agents. There was a lot to learn prior to leaving for my agent school, and I was anxious to get it done and start working. January 10 came fast, and the next chapter of my ride was about to begin, one that would last 26 years and take me on an unbelievable adventure around the world!

30

BNDD Basic Agent Class 23

My travel to Washington, DC, was filled with nervousness about what to expect and determination to succeed and be sworn in as a special agent of the Bureau of Narcotics and Dangerous Drugs. Achieving this would be a monumental task requiring discipline, physical exertion, massive instructional training from BNDD's best diversified expert instructors in federal law enforcement.

I arrived at the Sonesta Hotel located on Thomas Circle, 14th Street NW. Upon checking in, I was given a room on the seventh floor, sharing a room with another classmate.

BNDD in 1972 did not have an academy at that time. The classroom was located in our small headquarters building at 14th Street and I St. NW. BNDD was made up of approximately 700 agents worldwide. Assigned to us were three guidance counselors named Frank Tummillo (*deceased*) from New York (a great agent who was killed working undercover in New York on October 12, 1972), Baby (PN) and Shorty (PN). Their role was to help us throughout the 12 weeks with any issues we may have had. The class Leads were the head instructors. This included a Chief of physical training, an assistant PT instructor, and a firearms instructor. Our class consisted of 48 agents from various locations of the U.S.

We all reported to class on Monday, January 10, at 8:00 a.m.

The dress code was coat and tie. After introductions were made, each one of us gave a short background résumé to the class. We quickly learned that one-third of our class was ex-law enforcement officers, one third were new students, and one third were from other federal law enforcement and intelligence agencies. I was the only one who had a narcotics undercover background. We were given a brief overview as to what to expect and that any misconduct on our part would result in termination from the agency. The class courses would be three days a week, which included firearms training. The physical training was two days a week and was one of the most rigid trainings in all of federal law enforcement agencies. In other words, it was treacherous and a test of our most strenuous exercises we could ever imagine!

This was confirmed while we were there by the visit of the U.S. Marine General Commander when he was invited to observe our PT program. After a grueling workout for him, he addressed us and said, "I just want to say to you all, what I witnessed today was remarkable, and our Marines have never been put through this type of physical exertion. I applaud you all for your unbelievable determination as agents of this agency!"

Our training was the best and hardest I had ever experienced in my lifetime. A few funny incidents did occur, which showed that we were the best and could work as a team together and stand up for each other. In this line of work, we needed to know who would step up, and have our backs in any situation, and who would be ones on whom we could not depend or snitch us out to make points for himself.

One incident that proved that we could back up what we say and how we stood up for one another occurred on one of our firearm days. One of our agent friends (*deceased*) had a rough night and came in for coffee before class and said, "Frenchy, I feel like hell! I'm hungover, and no way in hell can I go upstairs to shoot. My fucking head feels like it's going to explode. I went up and signed my name in the logbook and put an 85 for my score! I'm going down to the hot tub to sober up!"

"I got you covered, and if the range Chief asks about you, I'll tell him you had the runs, and you're in the bathroom, and I'll go get you. Make damn sure you have the same story if asked!"

"Got it, thanks Pal."

The range was above the gym and after we all went through our range training, the instructor asked," Anybody know where our missing agent is?"

"Yes, Sir. I do."

"Frenchy, where is he?"

"He had to leave and told me he had a severe case of the runs, and is in the bathroom downstairs, Sir! I'll go get him right now!"

"Please do!"

I ran down two flights of stairs and went into the hot tub room. There was my friend, head tilted, back sleeping with hot tub bubbling away!

"Wake up!" I yelled. "The Chief wants you upstairs now! Put on your stuff and come up quick. I'll tell him you were in the bathroom shitting your brains out!" I said, laughing.

"Be there in a couple minutes."

"Ok!" As I ran up the stairs and walked in the firearms room, I advised that he was on his way.

A couple of minutes went by, and everyone stood around with a wondering look like, "Oh Shit, this is not good." I looked around and looked at JB and winked with a smile on my face. He had one on his face also!

Eventually, our agent friend, who was an ex-federal agent, walked in and said, "Sir, sorry, but I have a bad case of diarrhea!"

You do, eh? Well, I see that you shot an 85, and for some reason, I can't recall seeing you here. So, unless you can duplicate an 85 again, we may have a problem if you get my drift?"

"Yes, Sir! I will! He stepped up to the lane that had been prepared as we all stood back and he yelled out, "Ready on the right. Ready on the left. Begin shooting!"

Without any hesitation, we all observed him shooting and when he finished, he reeled in his target and removed it, handing it to the Chief for scoring. We all waited as he scored his target. He looked over at me and smiled and the Chief said, "All I can say is your score is 85. Next time let me know that you are not feeling right, understood?"

"Yes, Sir."

"Class dismissed!"

We all left and went to our hotel and met in our bar room where we had set up our bar on top of a clothes dresser. Our little group was made up of about ten of us, mostly all ex-cops.

"Ok!" I said. "How in the hell did you pull that off. I can't shoot that good! You're unbelievable?"

"Simple. I compete in police shooting tournaments, and I'm an expert champion!" The whole room exploded, laughing and shaking their heads in disbelief!

As I mentioned above, some people in every class somehow show their true colors and try to suck up to management by snitching on fellow agents. We had one incident that was reported to me by one of our great counselors who will not be named.

A few friends and I were returning from supper one night, and as we walked in, I observed two counselors sitting in the lobby. One of them stood up and said, "Frenchy! I need to talk with you for a minute outside!"

"Sure, what's up?" I answered as we walked outside.

"Frenchy, you didn't get this from me, understood?" he said, smiling. "You guys have a snitch who's keeping watch on you and your friends and reporting back to the head of training. He's reporting time you guys come back from bar hopping and if anyone walks in a little tipsy. All I can tell you is to watch out for this guy!"

"Son of a bitch! I got you, I'll make sure the word gets around, and I owe you!"

"No, you don't owe me. You guys are great, and we watch out for one another in this agency! It's assholes like that you have to watch out for! You're spoken for already, my friend!' Have a great evening and be careful!"

"Got it! See you tomorrow!"

I went upstairs to meet the guys for a nightcap at the bar-room and told them about the snitch. One immediately said, "That son of a bitch! it's blanket party time!"

"No! If we did that, this asshole would report us, and we all would get kicked out!"

Our expert shooter said, "Guys! I got this. Let me handle this. By the end of the day tomorrow, he will know that he's been ID'ed as a snitch, trust me! Mum's the word."

• • ✦ ✦ ✦ ✦ • •

The next day, our friend was observed having coffee with the snitch at the hotel restaurant. We sat down at our group table and could tell that the snitch had a red face and kept nodding as our expert shooter was engaged in what looked like reading him the riot act.

Our friend came back to our table and told us all to turn around and give him a thumbs up and smile. All together we turned and looked at him, gave him a thumbs up and smiled then turned back around. The snitch never finished his breakfast and left. When we got to class, the snitch moved from his front-row seat to the back corner of the room. I learned later that he had told the head of training that the class had heard that he was reporting behavior information to management and that he could not continue doing so! Still, he remained an outcast for the duration of the school. As a good friend of mine always said, "No good deed goes unpunished."

Unfortunately, we lost two of our classmates during the 12 weeks of training, one due to a physical injury and another who requested to return to his previous intelligence agency. He had advised me that he could no longer keep quiet about his appointment to BNDD. He said, "Frenchy, I can't do this to you guys. We have become great friends." And with tears in his eyes, he said, "I'm a plant by the agency, and I am to report any corruption and such while I'm assigned to BNDD."

I looked at him in awe and said, "Holy shit! I can't believe that this is happening. Look, don't say anything. Go ahead and return to your agency! I'll make sure that I talk with someone about this in confidence so it can go up to the boss!"

I was made aware by one of our classmates that there had been moles planted in our class by a well-known intelligence agency, which led me to report this to one of my trusted instructors who reported this to management. Needless to say, this caused quite a stir in BNDD. In later years, this came out in a book called *The Strength of the Pack and The Strength of the Wolf,* which confirmed this to be true. This was always a sore point for all of us who knew who these individuals were. Some of these individuals became close friends of ours, and some were held at a distance because they could not be trusted. In my opinion, they were snitches against our agency and were not totally loyal to BNDD.

⋅⋅✦✦✦✦⋅⋅

On March 17, 1972, graduation day arrived! For BNDD Class 23, it was one of the greatest days of our career. The Director Jack Ingersoll did the official swear-in ceremony. The guest speaker was President Nixon's (later implicated in the Watergate scandal) presidential advisor John Dean who handed us our credentials.

All of us had already checked out and booked flights back to our home office that afternoon. I went to Reagan National Airport, where I declared that I was armed and produced my credentials and signed a Firearm Declaration form as required before catching my flight back to Miami. While standing in line, I observed ASAIC Dave Connelly from Miami waiting to board. We sat together during the flight. When we got to Miami, Dave asked if I had a ride home. I told him I was taking a cab, after which he told me that he would take me home.

"Don't bother taking a cab," he said. Take me home and take my car. I'll see you at the office on Monday. On Monday morning, I'll just get a ride from one of our agent friends who lives close by."

Needless to say, I couldn't wait for the weekend to end so I could go to work!

31

First Office Miami Field Division

I arrived at the office at 8:00 a.m. and parked Mr. Connelly's vehicle across the street from the office. As I got out of his Cadillac, two agents said, "Look at Frenchy! First day on the job and already driving the ASAIC's car to work!" They jabbed with thumbs up. I started laughing as we shook hands and they said, "Great to have you officially as a new agent, Frenchy!" Needless to say, I was beaming with pride all day. Everyone greeted me and congratulated me as one of them. I felt I had finally achieved one of the highest honors in law enforcement to be a federal agent!

My day was spent with my two mentors. They took me around various police departments in Miami to introduce me to the narcotics agents, most of who knew me from BSO. We then went to Broward County, and the first stop was at the BSO special squad, where the gang was waiting to congratulate me and ask me how it felt to be a Fed. They knew that I would never change and that I would remain one of the guys always and be there for them without hesitation. I missed my old team, and the feeling seemed genuinely mutual. My assignment in Miami lasted from January to August of 1972, Group Three.

RD Ben Thieson advised me that they wanted me to set up some narcotics buys while assigned to the group and have some of the agents who had never made a narcotic purchase in an undercover capacity make buys with some of my informants. I was also advised that Miami had been selected to form a new federal narcotics task force named The Office of Drug Abuse Law Enforcement (ODALE), and that our group would be in charge of this new task force.

Needless to say, when this news broke, there were some concerns by the BNDD agents that we would be competing against them on case making. Mr. Thieson had an all-hands meeting and briefed everyone that this task force was initiated by the White House and Mr. Miles Ambrose, former Customs Commissioner, would be its director. Mr. Thieson advised that the unit would be located one block away from the BNDD office and would be made up of Group Three. With this group would also be the customs agents, state and local police officers. All investigations would be to target street level/ mid-level organizations and major organizations would be BNDD's responsibility.

Within a month, the transition was accomplished since it was a high priority by the White House, and money was no object along with equipment and cars, etc. All the agents had brand-new cars assigned to them, which caused envy and jealousy between us and BNDD agents. It took a while for the dust to settle and, as far as we were concerned, it was still BNDD no matter what. After five months of work with my friends, who made buys in an undercover capacity for the first time, we made numerous cases on the ODALE Task Force, and the office was a success and worked very closely with state and local agencies in Florida.

In July of 1972, my G/S advised me that the Batman wanted me at his office immediately. Upon arriving, his secretary said, "Frenchy, he's waiting for you. Go on in!"

The Bat in his typical rough scowling voice said, "Close the door and sit down! Your G/S has been keeping me posted on the ODALE work, and you guys have done one hell of a job in getting this task force off the ground. I heard that you broke in some of our 'virgin' agents who started working undercover, and I want to thank you!"

"Just doing what we agreed to do, and it was funny to see their scared looks somewhat, but they did great just like they were supposed to. We had a few laughs along the way, which embarrassed a few, but all in good fun!"

"Yeah, he filled me in. Wish I had been there to bust a few chops!" he smiled.

"Ok! Here's a copy of the job vacancy announcement application that just came out for the position of special agent Paris, France. We already responded and submitted your application. Don't do anything or say anything about it. If asked, just say you were told to put in and nothing else!"

"Great! No problem. I just do as I am told by my boss!"

"Good! This will go fast, and you will have to go to DC for an Oral Board Interview next week. Just start making arrangements to prepare for your move. Any questions?"

"No, I'm ready, nervous and anxious, Ben! Thank you for all you have done up to now. I won't let you down!"

"Oh, by the way, your dad has really made my stay a great one while I was in temporary lodging! The whole time I was there, the bartender never allowed me to pay for anything. He just kept saying, 'Phil says your money is no good here!' Just thank him also for his help on those wise guys from New York, the Gambino boys. Great Intelligence info!"

"My dad?"

"Yeah! Your German buddy had him keep tabs of their phone calls while they were staying at his place! Great info!" he said, laughing.

"Holy shit. My dad never said anything to me about this. I'm going to bust his chops on this one," I said as I was shaking my head and laughing! "My old man, working for the feds! Only Miller could pull that one off!"

"Frenchy, I told you that he is a con and a damn good one at that!" We both laughed. I thanked Ben and left.

Immediately, I made a beeline for my friend's office. When I walked in, he looked up from his desk, laughing and said, "I don't like that look on your face. Whatever you're going to say, it's not true and they are lying!"

"You son of a bitch!" I said first seriously, then broke into a laugh.

"What? What?"

"My Dad is a snitch for you, that's what! How could you do this? Behind my back! It's not bad enough you steal my female informants from me, but now my dad?" I had a hard time holding back from laughing.

"I thought it was pretty cool, and so did he! He only asked me not to say anything to you or your mom! You know me. If someone asked me that, I'm always obliged to keep my promises to my friends' parents!"

"Tell you what. Let's go. I will buy you drinks at the Playboy Club, and we can forget all of this! Call your wife, and I'll call mine, and we will let them know we have a surveillance and won't be home till 4:00 a.m. And I'll tell Ben to meet us there, and he can buy the drinks!"

"Wait a minute, you said you were buying!"

"Yeah, but I just thought this could be expensive, and Ben owes me for making him look good on your dad's info."

"You're insane! You know that?"

"Yes, I do and damn proud of it! Let's go!" We left the office and met the Batman at the Bunny Club.

I eventually spoke with my dad but not in front of Mom! He had a good laugh and said, "Damn! Why wasn't I invited for drinks also!" To this day, I have always wondered why he and I never had a cross word for over 50 years of friendship! I went home and broke the news to my wife Chris that the interview for the France position finally arrived.

⋅ ⁺ ⁺ ✦ ✦ ✦ ⁺ ⋅

Two weeks after the vacancy announcement, I was told that I was scheduled to go to Washington, DC, to appear before the Oral Review Board on the Paris vacancy announcement.

I arrived at BNDD Headquarters at 14th and I St. NW at 9:00 a.m. and proceeded to the eighth floor where I was advised to wait outside the room with two other agents who were sitting until summoned. I greeted them, saying, "Hi, I'm Pierre Charette from the Miami Office!" then reached out to shake their hands.

The first agent who introduced himself was a well-built stocky agent, 5'11', 195 pounds with a New York accent, in his thirties. He reached out to shake my hand. "I'm from the New York office. How ya doing?"

"Great, thank you. Nervous to be here, that's for sure!"

The second agent who was also from the New York office, reached out and introduced himself as we shook hands. Glad to meet you! That's a real French name. *"Tu parles français?"*

"Oui! Je suis français canadien!"

"Man, you're fluent! How long have you been on board?"

"Got hired in January. Was a Narc with the Sheriff's department in Fort Lauderdale."

"What? Usually, guys can't apply for foreign assignment unless they got five years' experience with BNDD. They must want you bad! That's great. Good luck!"

"My RD told me to apply and see what happens! I do as I am told." I smiled.

I could tell by the look on their faces that they were bewildered that I got to apply. Their interview lasted about 45 minutes. I was sitting there with all kinds of thoughts going through my head, and my stomach was churning with fear. All of a sudden, the stocky agent came out and wished me good luck and before he left, he told me to go in.

I entered the conference room, which had a long table. Sitting around the table were the Deputy Director, Chief of Intelligence, Head of Personnel and Head of Foreign Operations.

The Deputy Director welcomed me before the board and briefed me on the purpose of the interview for the position in Paris. He asked me to give them a short version of my law enforcement background and experience as an undercover agent. Once I briefed the members of the board, he began the 'interrogation.'

"Pete, why did you apply for this position?"

"Sir, I was directed by my regional director to apply for this position since he felt that I was probably the most qualified person because I spoke French fluently and had extensive narcotics investigative experience. He advised me to apply and would support my request."

"Pete, do you feel you qualified for this type of assignment, and would you be willing to work undercover throughout Europe?"

"Yes, Sir. I feel that I could contribute to our efforts to help dismantle the French importation of heroin to the United States and work closely with the French police with no problem at all."

The other members who were very receptive to my application also asked me questions. The final person to question me was the Chief of Intelligence.

"Mr. Charette, you have been an agent with us for only seven months. Who do you think you are to apply for this job with only seven months on the job? Are you aware that the minimum requirement to apply is five years?"

"Sir, I was aware of this, but my director in Miami, Mr. Thieson, ordered me to apply because he felt that my fluent French background was an asset for BNDD since we did not have a fluent speaking agent assigned to the Paris office. I was honored when he ordered me to apply and did what my boss ordered me to do."

The Deputy immediately responded by saying, "Pete, could you please step outside while Mr. Tartaglino and the members and I have a private discussion on this matter!"

"Yes sir!" I left the room and waited outside and could hear him speaking in a loud tone about this abrasive attack on me.

After a couple of minutes, I was requested to go back in and take a seat.

"Pete," the Chief of intelligence Andy Tartaglino said, "sorry for that. You were put in an uncomfortable position, and we have something to say to you!"

"Mr. Charette, I apologize for addressing you in such a manner and tone. We fully understand that you were only following orders by Mr. Thieson!"

"I understand your reason and no apologies are needed, Sir! I have thick skin, and it takes a whole lot more for me to be intimidated, I assure you!" I smiled.

"Thank you, Pete! I can tell by your response that we have hired a good agent. Thank you for coming and have a safe trip back!"

"Thank you all." As I got up to leave, the deputy asked me to wait outside for a moment.

He stepped out and shook my hand and said, "You did a great job and proud to have met you. You will be hearing from us in a few days. Have a safe trip home!"

Thank you, sir! You can depend on me anytime. I'm honored to part of BNDD!"

I left feeling great and headed for the airport, where I called Mr. Thieson and briefed him on the flare-up about which he laughed.

"Got it, boss! See you tomorrow!"

••••••••

I returned back to work the next day and briefed my GS, who was pleased that it went well and confirmed The Batman's assessment laughing.

Within a week, the HQS Teletype came out announcing that I had been selected for the position in France. I had 30 days before reporting to work in Paris. Needless to say, we all celebrated after work for my achieving another goal on my wild ride.

I called my wife to give her the news and told her to start preparing to go to France, that I had been selected. She was extremely pleased and submitted her notice to resign from the Sheriff's department.

32

August 31, 1972
Transfer to Paris, France

Augustﻬ 31, 1972, is a day that I will always remember in my amazing one-hell-of-a-ride career. My wife and I left the United States for our new assignment in Paris. This journey started off with a bang for having created my first international incident when we flew to London, England. As we left Miami, I made sure that I had checked my firearm– a Walter PPKS 380 weapon– in with the airlines. In those days when agents traveled, they were permitted to carry their weapons concealed on their body with no problem. We also traveled with a diplomatic passport, which allowed us to pass through foreign customs without any challenge.

We arrived at London's Heathrow Airport, checked in our hotel and stayed overnight without issues. The next day we went to the Heathrow Airport to check-in and went to the security line marked "Declaration Point" because I was armed. This was one big error! The moment I advised British Customs that I was carrying a concealed weapon with a diplomatic passport, all hell broke loose. The customs agent immediately hit an alarm button, and suddenly, we were surrounded by police and customs agents, then immediately taken to a detention room where I was frisked, and my weapon was seized.

I immediately produced my diplomatic passport and BNDD

credentials, advising them of my status and work assignment by the U.S. government. The panic in their faces looked as if I was there to kill the Queen! They immediately advised me that they would call the U.S. ambassador's office to verify my status. After an hour of detention, the customs director of the airport advised me that I was cleared, and he would escort us to the plane. The Captain of the plane agreed to place my weapon in the pilot cabin's secured safe. I was told that someone failed to get permission for me to enter the country with a weapon and never to do this without proper prior authorization through the British Diplomatic Section. I apologized for this error and thankfully left on good terms with them. *What a way to start my European Assignment!*

••••••

Upon arrival at Orly Airport outside of Paris, I was greeted by Special Agent Jim Collier, who smiled and welcomed us to Paris and said, laughing, "Pete! All I can say is before even getting here, you were off to start your job with a bang! The bosses Paul Knight (*deceased*) and Nick Panella (*deceased*) can't wait to meet you and discuss your incident in London. I got your gun, so let's get your luggage and go to the office. They are expecting you!"

"Shit, Jim! No one told me anything about clearance with the Brits. They just told me to bring my gun with me. I guess I'm either going to get an ass chewing or do a turnaround back to the States," I said, shaking my head.

"I think you are lucky that our boss Nick Panella told the guys that he knew you and that he and you had met in Montreal when you went there to visit family as a narcotics detective in Florida! He told us that you were a straight-up guy and went out drinking at the RCMP mess with the narcotics guys and got greased pretty well that night!" he said, smiling.

"God, I never forgot that night. Nick is a great guy, and he told me then that he hoped that someday BNDD would hire me! What a small world! Can't wait to see him."

"He told me to bring you to his office first before you two go in and see Knight.

Upon arriving, we came in through the back side of a two-story building. The building looked like a normal Parisian apartment building located at 51 bis Rue La Boétie, with no sign of being an embassy building. Upon entering, we were on the first floor with an open round hall. A U.S. Marine guard was sitting at a desk screening people coming into the building. We were waved through and went to the second floor, which was where BNDD, FBI, Customs and Secret Service had their offices.

We walked off the elevator and entered a coded door on the right. Immediately we were greeted by three secretaries. They led my wife for coffee while Jim and I walked into Nick's office across from Mr. Knight's office.

"Well, if it isn't the famous Pierre Charette or should I say ex-agent Pierre Charette! Sit down. Jim close the door. Ok! Be prepared to get drilled by Paul in a few minutes about the James Bond act in London!" he said then laughed hardily. He wants details on who told you to bring a piece here, and the ambassador wants an answer on this! Paul is a bit strange, but glad you're here, so relax. You're not in trouble, and I have spoken up for you since the beginning when The Batman approached you on this! Paul, DC and I spoke about you, and I told them that we had met in Montreal several years ago when I was in charge in Canada. I immediately told them that you are the one that we would want here and that your French was fluent as can be, and that I needed you here to solidify our relationship with the French Narcotics Unit and build up our liaison with them."

"I don't know how to thank you, Nick. I will do my best to meet your expectations and hope I can repay you someday!"

"Don't worry! Just buy me drinks once in a while!.."

"I will, but I don't know if I can repeat our last drinking episode with The Mounties. It took me a few days to sober up!" We all laughed!

"You will do fine, and welcome to France, mon ami!" he said, shaking my hand and getting up to lead me into Mr. Knight's office.

"Paul, this is Pierre Charette, the famous gun smuggler!" he said humorously.

"Pleasure to finally meet you!" With a stern look at me, he shook my hand and motioned me to sit down. Then he continued. "Let's hear your side of the story about this. Start by telling me who in BNDD told you to bring a gun with you? I want a name if you recall. Understand?"

"Well, Mr. Knight, pleased to meet you Sir! I'm sorry about causing such an incident and never thought that I was doing anything wrong since I was told by someone during this fast hiring process. I met so many people since January 1st, both in Miami, DC, along with all sorts of administrative personnel, that this was unbelievable for me to process since things were moving so fast! Mr. Knight, to be honest, I can't for the life of me recall who it was that told me to bring my gun. I am willing to accept whatever disciplinary action you need to do in this matter because I don't recall and will not name someone unless I am sure it was them with all due respect, Sir."

Paul Knight, BNDD European Regional Director and Nick Panella
Deputy Regional Director
(Photos were taken by me and are my property)

I waited for his answer, watching him look at Nick, not breaking a smile, then he paused for a minute. Finally, he looked at me and said, "Mr. Charette, this incident was unfortunate, but I'm pleased that your answer was what I was hoping you would say. Someone failed to write up this policy. Foreign agents need to make proper arrangements prior to reporting, and this will change today, I assure you, and pleased to have you on our team. *Bienvenue à Paris et bon séjour ici*. Welcome to Paris and enjoy your stay!" he said, smiling and shaking my hand.

"Thank you, sir! I won't let you down!" I walked out with Nick, and we went to Nick's office and talked.

"Pete, you didn't give up anyone, and Paul knows that. All I can say is that The Batman, Miller, Scrocca, and Navarro all said that you were a standup guy, and I totally feel the same. We are going to have fun and kick ass with all of us here, that's for sure."

Nick took me to the back office and introduced me to the greatest bunch of agents in this office. Each office had two agents per office. They were Jim Collier and Vern Stephen. Later, three more agents were assigned, two from New York and one ex-classmate from agent school who was a classmate of mine while there, and two intelligence analysts.

He then took me back up front and introduced me to ASAIC's office. He was a tall Italian looking man, in his forties who weighed approximately 195 pounds and who, prior to being an agent, was a casino croupier while going to college. He was well known to be a poker player on Friday nights with embassy staff members and usually cleaned them out every time.

I was also introduced to the two file room clerks, administrative officer and secretaries.

The Paris Office was the European Regional Office for BNDD. Mr. Knight was in charge of the Marseille, Brussels, Frankfurt and Munich, Rome, Milan, London, Madrid, Barcelona, and Vienna offices.

I was also taken by Nick to our U.S. counterparts on our floor, which was the U.S. secret service agents. Next to their office was the U.S. customs office who had three agents. Our relationship was excellent with them. Two FBI attachés were also located on our floor. I was then taken to the French Central Narcotics Office, which was a block away from ours. The office was covert and had a large door that closed after you entered, a French Gendarme greeted you and cleared you to go to the office located on the second and third floors. We went directly to the third floor and entered the director's office, where Nick introduced me to Mr. François Le Mouel, the new BCN head. Mr. Le Mouel (*deceased*) was a tall slim man approximately 5'11", partially bald with grey hair, glasses and a great smile, who proved to be extremely friendly.

I had the honor and pleasure to work in Paris with M. Le Mouel. He was imprisoned by the Germans in WWII when he was a tank officer and was facing death when the Americans liberated Paris and saved him from certain death. He was a great friend of mine and of the BNDD office agents. After he retired, he was hit by a truck while walking in his hometown and killed.

Mr. Le Mouel said in French, "Hello. You have to be Mr. Charette, whom we have heard so much about from Nick and Mr. Knight. Welcome to France, and I hope we will be working closely with you."

"Honor to meet you, sir! I have heard a lot about you and your office and anxious to work with you, sir!" I said as we shook hands.

"I can tell by your fluent French that you are a true Canadian!" He said, smiling. "Don't worry, it won't take you long to pick up our French accent, Mr. Charette."

"Please, call me Pierre!"

"Very good, Pierre. Please sit down. As you know, we are glad to have you here. We are prohibited by French law from doing undercover work, because of the Agent Provocateur Law. So, we are not restricted from authorizing you to work and assist us since you are an American agent, and you have full diplomatic privileges. Therefore, our relationship is extremely close and outstanding with your office. The only thing I ask is that you must advise me and my supervisors of any information received by your sources on the French traffickers, to be immediately shared with us, so we can surveil and monitor them with hopes to arrest them. Pierre, our goal and your agency's goal is to finally break the back of the so-called French Connection, which is mostly made up of French Corsican mobsters in France."

"I fully understand, and I am prepared to go to work with your office. Let's hope that we all can achieve this goal together!"

"I have no doubt that we will work well, and if Nick will allow me, I would like to introduce you to my team."

"Mr. Le Mouel, Pierre is at your service, and I will go back to the office to let him meet them all, thank you! Pierre, see you back at the office."

Mr. Le Mouel stepped out of the office with me and walked into the office of his assistant Commissaire Bernard Gravet and said, "Bernard, meet Mr. Charette, the new agent we have heard so much about!"

Pierre Charette, pleased to finally meet you," he stated in broken English. "Welcome to France, my friend." He wore a big smile. Bernard was a slim short well-dressed person, about 5'9", 165 pounds and appeared very energetic.

"We are pleased to have you here, and we will work well together, I assure you!"

"Thank you, and I am anxious to start work. I have heard so many good things about all of you!"

Le Mouel then introduced me to Deputy Lucien Amie Blanc, who was approximately 35 years of age, 5'10', with black hair, had a Corsican accent and was from the South of France. He was very active and also fair and dedicated to his agents, but not as open as Mr. Le Mouel with people, slightly cautious with all people he met and worked with.

"Thank you, Boss. I will take Pierre downstairs and introduce him to his new colleagues who are anxious to meet him!"

"Mr. Charette, you are in good hands, and we will be seeing each other soon. My door is always open for you, no appointments necessary at all."

"Thank you, Mr. Le Mouel, my pleasure. See you soon!"

"Ok, Pierre, let's meet our crazy gang," he said as we walked down the stairs to the second floor, which had two group offices, wooden plank floors, bare walls and two interview rooms.

We walked in the first office and the room was open, filled with desks, and had approximately six inspectors all dressed casually and varied from 22 to 50 years of age. As I walked in, Bernard said, "I want all of you to meet Mr. Charette, our new colleague! These are the group supervisors who you will be working very closely with!"

"Pleasure to meet you!" I said as we shook hands.

"The pleasure is ours, Mr. Charette. We have heard a lot about you from your colleagues, and we look forward to having a great relationship with you. Please call us by our first names, no more formalities!"

"Same with me. It's Pierre. Pleased to meet all of you!"

"I agree, Pierre. Our inspectors feel the same way."

All agents introduced themselves. One supervisor had a unique personality, to say the least. The best way I can describe him jokingly is to picture Inspector Clouseau in the movie *The Pink Panther*. He was 5'8" with a small frame and weighed about 155 pounds. He sported a mustache and was very hyper. He walked like a small Charlie Chaplin and had a fun personality. He was the nicest man I have had the honor and pleasure to work with.

After spending a few hours with them, I returned back to the office and settled in my group office in the back room. Nick had me review case files from the file room in order to get a clear picture of what we were facing at the current time with French heroin being imported into the U.S.

———————— ⋅✦✦✦✦⋅ ————————

The history of the French Connection basically was uncovered as early as 1937 when a French laboratory for heroin production was discovered in Marseilles, France, being run by a Corsican gang leader named Paul Carbone (*deceased*). Eventually, this network of mobsters sending heroin to the United States became known as The French Connection.

Marseille, being a major port in the western Mediterranean, made it easy for shipments of opium/ morphine base to be shipped and processed in the outskirts of Marseille into the highest quality of heroin ever manufactured.

The chemist who was famous for this quality of production was Joseph Cesari (*deceased*), who produced the heroin that was eventually seized on the shrimp fishing vessel *Caprice des Temps* on February 29, 1972. The seizure in the Port of Marseille by French customs, French narcotics agents and BNDD agents was the largest seizure of heroin made at that time, which was 415 kilograms of white heroin destined for the port of Miami.

When the arrest took place, Cesari jumped into the water and swam across the port, where he was observed by a couple as he was starting to drown. The man jumped in to rescue him while the lady called a Gendarme across the road for help. The police arrested him, and he was incarcerated at the police station where later the next morning, a guard found that he had hanged himself in his cell in the middle of the night. The BNDD agent on this case was country Attaché (name withheld for security purposes), Agent Al Habib (*deceased*) and one other agent.

Also, in the same month in February of 1972, the agent in charge of the Brussels, Belgium office, Jimmy Guy (*deceased*), posed undercover as an Army Sergeant assigned to shape headquarters in Belgium, was paid $96,000 to smuggle 264 pounds of heroin to the United States or the U.S. mob in New York. (*Note: I filled in for Jimmy in his position a year later and transported the heroin to New York with the Belgium police for trial in the Southern Districts of New York against five individuals. The heroin had a street value of 50 million dollars.*)

DEA statistics disclosed that drug arrests in France skyrocketed from 57 in 1970 to 3,016 in 1972. Because of cases developed and with documented intelligence, there was positive proof that through our joint combined efforts of drug enforcement agencies from various countries, the French Connection could be best disabled by the combined efforts of multiple countries such as the U.S., Canada, France and our other European counterparts. They worked together to achieve the success of bringing down the French Connection, which was finally realized in the seventies and eighties.

At this point, I need to recognize one individual who played a major part in BNDD to bring down the French Connection Organization when he was assigned to the Marseille Office. Agent Robert J. De Fauw is a great friend and legend in our organization!

* * * * * * *

Before I continue with my story, I contacted Bob (De Fauw) and asked him for some information about his work in Marseille and whether he could write in his own words what he encountered when he was the SAIC of Marseille from 1965-1968.

Bob thanked me for doing what I was doing with this book and agreed to write about his knowledge and participation during this infamous era that helped to dismantle the French Connection. I am dedicating a chapter of my book to Bob and copying his own words for his historical contribution, which will be in the next chapter! He furnished a signed permission document authorization letter to publish his story in my book along with personal photographs of his and permitted me to make any needed changes.

33

NDD SAIC Robert J. DeFauw
Marseille, France

B ob DeFauw's background is remarkable and due to his distinguishing service, he is highly regarded by all of us who served and worked with this man. Bob grew up in Michigan and graduated from Golden Gate University, San Francisco. He received a B.A. Degree in Administration of Justice (Cum Laude) in 1953. From 1953-1955, he was on active military duty with the United States Marine Corp. In 1955 Bob joined the Detroit Police Department.

In 1961 he was hired by the U.S. Treasury Department, Federal Bureau of Narcotics, Detroit District Office. From 1962-1965 Bob was reassigned to the Chicago District Office. He was chosen by the commissioner to be transferred to Marseille, France, to replace the agent in charge, who had to relocate back to the U.S. for medical care of his infant son.

From 1965-1968 Bob was the special agent in charge of the Marseille District Office and reported to the District Supervisor in Rome, Italy. Bob was responsible as a one-man office for southern France from Lyon south; in Italy from Milan north; in Switzerland, Spain, Portugal, Morocco, and Algeria. The Rome headquarters had jurisdictional responsibility for Europe, the Middle East and Africa.

Other district offices were located in Ankara, and Istanbul, Turkey;

Beirut, Lebanon; and Paris, France. All offices were one-man offices with the exception of Rome. This period encompassed the height of the infamous French Connection organization. As a result, an additional agent was assigned to the Marseille Office in 1967. The office worked with the French Police Judiciare Narcotics Unit in Marseille, which had seven officers and one supervisor who was a communist, an anti-American commissaire. Bob advised me that after a short period of time, two of the seven officers were deemed to be trustworthy and motivated to conduct investigations. Most of the cases made at that time, were results of exploiting raw intelligence furnished by the opium and morphine base country agents in Turkey and Lebanon. Overt and covert investigations were conducted within the framework of the French Code of Law that led to the penetration and neutralization of numerous high-level, opium, morphine base and heroin producing trafficking organizations that formed the famous French Connection in France.

Bob supplied me with this written knowledge of what the Federal Bureau of Investigation's role was when he was hired by them in 1961:

Federal Bureau of Narcotics (FBN)

The Federal Bureau of Narcotics' interest in deploying agents in foreign operations pre-dates the involvement of the U.S.A. in World War II. Under the leadership of Commissioner Harry J. Anslinger (*deceased*), FBN Agents were trained and excelled in their ability to pose covertly as members of the underworld, to penetrate narcotic organizations and purchase drugs directly as members of the underworld, and to penetrate narcotic organizations and purchase drugs directly from members of Narcotic Trafficking Organizations. As a result, the FBN enjoyed the reputation of having the highest criminal conviction rate (98%) compared to the rest of the federal, state, and local law enforcement agencies.

The value of undercover work was recognized prior to the Second World War when the Office of Strategic Services (OSS-predecessor to what is now known as the Central Intelligence Agency, the CIA). Chief William Donovan (*deceased*), asked Anslinger to provide seasoned FBN agents to help train and organize its agents to work undercover to avoid being identified by hostile security forces in an effort to carry out their intelligence-gathering missions.

FBN's foreign operations were formalized in 1951 when Agent Charlie Siragusa (*deceased*) under Anslinger's direction opened an office in Rome, Italy. At that time, the FBN consisted of about 200+ agents. As a result, overseas staffing was limited to less than twelve narcotics agents at any given time. In the 1960s, the Center for Addiction Statistics in Atlanta reported there were over 60,000 hardcore registered heroin addicts in the United States, and the number was climbing. Investigations revealed that most of the heroin was being clandestinely manufactured in Marseille and smuggled to this country by organized cartels of Corsican and Italian extraction.

An FBN agent's first priority overseas was focused on opium production and gathering intelligence about its origin from the poppy plant (papaver somniferum) to its final illicit conversion to heroin. In the late 1950s and early 1960s, Turkey and Lebanon stood out as the principal growth countries followed by Pakistan, Afghanistan, Iraq and Iran in later years. Through agreements with host countries, offices were established in state department facilities with one federal agent in each office. Offices were initially located in Ankara and Istanbul, Turkey; Beirut, Lebanon; and Paris and Marseille, France. Headquarters were located in Rome, Italy, staffed by three agents, a district supervisor, an enforcement assistant and a narcotic agent.

The primary mission of a narcotics agent was to work with and train assigned host country law enforcement counterparts to target and immobilize criminal elements engaged in the production, manufacture and distribution of narcotics from the place of origin in the poppy fields as opium, to the final destination in the form of heroin. Heroin was the choice for addicts in the United States.

Operations had to be conducted within the framework of each host country's rule of law. In some countries, the host country's laws created an impediment that an agent had to overcome. In this instance, it was

The Agent Provocateur Law in France, which created the impediments. It prevented a U.S. narcotics agent from using a flash roll, a normal tactic in the United States, during undercover negotiations to entice a trafficker to sell the agent narcotics. The threat of compromise and corruption among host country agencies was a constant problem and threat. In some instances, corruption was fostered by patronage and benign neglect by corrupt supervision or created as a result of the ravages of war, low pay and, /or an individual's ability to accept a representative of the United States as a viable counterpart.

When Narcotics Agent De Fauw reported for duty in Marseille, President and General Charles De Gaulle (*deceased*) had a standing order forbidding one to wear a U.S. Military uniform in France. The Commissaire of the seven Police Judiciare Narcotics Units in Marseille was a professed communist and advocate of Mao's teachings. On numerous occasions, he expressed his disdain for Americans and openly referred to Narcotics Agent De Fauw in fits of anger as a spy. Fortunately for Agent De Fauw, the commissaire of Narcotics reported to a Commissaire Divisionaire, who appreciated and supported Agent De Fauw's presence, contributions in investigative procedures and accomplishments. Based on the above, agents often withheld the sharing of vital intelligence with their indigenous counterparts to as close to the time of delivery as possible in order to avoid compromise and ensure success.

In 1968-1970, Bob was promoted to Deputy Regional Director, Foreign Operation, Region 17 Paris. During this period, FBN was renamed by congressional reorganization to be known as the Bureau of Narcotics and Dangerous Drugs (BNDD). The first order by the new Administrator was to move the Rome Headquarters to Paris. Narcotics agents were now referred to as special agents. District headquarters were now referred to as regional headquarters. With the reorganization, the budget was increased, which allowed for the gradual addition of personnel and offices. Those differences were recognized in the period of 1972-1978.

Bob organized the First International Narcotics Conference between France, Spain, Italy, Canada and the United States. This international attendance by foreign high government officials and police representatives was designed to establish the need for sharing intelligence relative to international narcotics traffickers and, in effect, targeting those who were mainly aligned with and formed The French Connection. The election of a new pro-American, French President Georges Pompidou, replaced Charles de Gaulle and assisted greatly in overhauling and assigning pro-American supervision and police officers to the BCN (Bureau Central de Narcotiques in Paris and the narcotics group in Marseille.

Mr. LE Mouel

Bob was responsible through his effort with others from BNDD and State Department, to encourage the Turkish government and pharmaceutical companies to place precedence in increasing the harvesting of poppy straw in the production of analgesics, antihistamines and cough syrup, thus making it, from an economic viewpoint, a less painstaking effort to achieve a more viable product than the exhausting practice of incising every single poppy pod to obtain the resin that transforms to opium.

Someone who also was a great contributor in the above efforts was Special Agent and former Regional Director of Paris, Jack Cusack (*deceased*). Mr. Cusack oversaw the monitoring of the poppy straw project in Turkey, and I personally attended a U.N. Drug Conference in Geneva, Switzerland, with the U.S. ambassador to the U.N. in 1976. After retirement, Mr. Cusack became a contracted narcotics advisor for the Bahamian government when I was ASAIC of the Caribbean offices for the Miami Field Office for DEA. Mr. Cusack was highly respected within our organization and a great friend.

Bob also worked with and encouraged companies that produced acetic anhydride, ammonia and lime–the precursor chemicals required in the transformation process of opium to morphine base to heroin–to report large, out of the ordinary orders to a list of authorities provided by BNDD.

Bob's cases were highly significant in Marseille in the effort to disrupt the French Connection. Three of the cases are notable. The cases were culminated by the Marseille office as a result of intelligence developed and the excellent teamwork provided by the eight FBN agents to District 17 from 1964 to 1967, namely Nick Panella (*deceased*), Ankara; Dick Salmi (*deceased*), Istanbul; Art Doll (*deceased*), Beirut; (*name withheld*), Paris; Mike Picini (*deceased*), District Supervisor; Hank Manfredi (*deceased*), Enforcement Assistant; S/A Joe Dino (*deceased*), Headquarters, Rome; and S/A Bob De Fauw, Marseille. All of these individuals were the ones who began the original history of the investigation of the French heroin connection that lasted for approximately 26 years. Bob supplied me with the three most significant cases that he worked on, which uncovered a massive international heroin operation in southern France, organized by members of the French Corsican Mob, later named the French Connection.

Narcotics Agent De Fauw and French Narcotics
Officer Claude Chaminadas

CASE: Morphine base Seizure:
(September 22, 1966) Seizure of 750 kilograms of morphine base, St. Julienne en Geneva's, French/ Swiss border.

Bob advised that he was contacted by Special Agent Dick Salmi from Istanbul, Turkey, who had intelligence information on three trans-international routier trucks (TIR) suspected in smuggling opium and morphine base from Turkey to France. Agent Salmi provided the tag numbers of the trucks. Agent De Fauw contacted Interpol and placed Locate/Report/Release alerts (LRR) along the European frontier. Three months passed. S/A De Fauw received notification from Interpol that a truck with one of the tag numbers carrying watermelons had crossed the border in Trieste, Italy. The driver reported his destination as Geneva, Switzerland. De Fauw said he notified the Swiss authorities and requested notification when it arrived at the Swiss/ French border.

Three days later, he was notified that the truck arrived at the Swiss

/French border town of St. Julienne en Genevois. De Fauw said he notified French Narcotics officers Claude Chaminadas (*deceased*) and Antoine Barbazza (*deceased*), trusted inspectors, and requested they contact French customs to hold the truck at the border until they arrived in the morning. De Fauw and the French inspectors drove all night to this border crossing. Upon arrival, the driver was detained. A secondary search was made of the truck, and the entire cargo of watermelon was unloaded. A thorough search of the truck was conducted, including the fuel tanks, but to no avail. The driver's papers were in order, but he appeared extremely nervous and evasive while being interviewed. It was agreed that with no evidence, the truck and the driver would be released the following morning.

Prior to reloading the truck the next morning, S/A De Fauw was walking around the truck when an elderly French Custom Inspector asked S/A De Fauw to assist him by holding a rope to measure the outside length of the cargo box. After recording the measurement, they then measured the inside. It was determined that the inside was approximately 1½ meters (4 ft 11" inches) shorter. At this point, metal panels were removed, and a trap was uncovered revealing a cache of (30) sealed ten-gallon metal containers marked 'shell oil'. Each container was opened, searched, and found to contain numerous, multi-kilogram bags of morphine base, representing approximately 750 kilograms.

An attempt was made to make a controlled delivery, but this was not possible since someone had called in to the newspaper disclosing that this was the largest seizure of drugs ever made in Europe at that time.

S/A Salmi developed information from his source that the driver corroborated that he was to check in at a hotel and would have been instructed to go to a location to offload his watermelons and the narcotics to another truck. He then would travel to the French/ Belgium border in the vicinity of Lille, France, with his truck, which would be reloaded with guns. The trap would be sealed, and the remaining space would be loaded with masonry bricks. Upon his return to Turkey, he was to take the truck to a construction site, and the guns, unbeknownst to the driver, would be delivered to the Kurds occupying the Syria/ Turkish border.

This case caused FBN to expand its scope of intelligence gathering from narcotic smuggling to include gun running, weapon merchant activity, and terrorist groups. The value of the seizure was estimated at that time at 600,000 Francs. At our current value in Euro, this would be a $6,845,197.01 @ 0.8763 per dollar.

Precursor chemicals were necessary in the clandestine manufacturing process of converting opium to heroin. Knowledgeable chemists under normal laboratory conditions could convert ten kilograms of opium to one kilogram of morphine base to one kilogram of heroin. The heroin averaged 98% in purity and was the drug of choice among addicts in the United States. To minimize detection in the smuggling process, clandestine laboratory operators preferred receiving shipments of morphine base to opium. Opium and morphine base from Turkey and Lebanon were normally smuggled overland or by sea to the Marseille area.

The *Iskenderun, Akdeniz*, and the *Karadeniz* were the most prominent suspect ships of Turkish origin used by trafficking organizations to smuggle narcotics contraband to the Port of Marseille.

CASE: Turkish ship KARADENIZ
February 15, 1967, 200 kilograms of morphine base seizure

Narcotics agents Nick Panella and Dick Salmi in Turkey furnished narcotics agent Robert De Fauw in Marseille with intelligence that the Karadeniz was scheduled to arrive in Marseille, allegedly carrying opium and morphine base, sometime in February, after making several stops en route from other Mediterranean ports.

Through a French maritime authority publication, Agent De Fauw monitored and documented the *Karadeniz's* progress and anticipated arrival. A determination was made that under normal weather conditions, the ship would arrive at the Port of Marseille sometimes during the afternoon of February 15, 1967. During the early morning of February 15, Agent De Fauw acquired the pier number where the ship would be docked and advised French Narcotics Judicial Police Officer Antoine Barbazza of the impending shipment. Barbazza notified and mobilized the remaining members of the six-man French narcotics unit.

Barbazza acquired a surveillance truck and parked the truck in a remote area, offering an unobstructed view of the pier. Barbazza, De Fauw and narcotics agent Anthony Morelli, who was on temporary assignment to Marseille, were manned with enough provision to sustain a two-day surveillance. Other French narcotics units set up covering ingress and egress to and from the pier. The ship docked and began unloading at 4:40 that afternoon and continued throughout the night. At around 2:30 a.m., thieves attempted to break into the surveillance truck, rocking it back and forth to no avail. But before leaving, they siphoned gas from the tank. The other units were alerted to the activity and were instructed to remain silent and undetected.

The unloading process appeared normal until about 6:30 a.m. From the surveillance truck, three men were observed carrying white canvas bags from a small door situated aft and just above the waterline of the ship. They piled the bags on the pier. From the vantage point of the truck, about forty bags were counted. A black 403 Peugeot sedan arrived. The driver exited the vehicle, engaged in a conversation with two suspects, and the three of them began loading numerous bags into the trunk of the car. As the car drove off, the two suspects returned to the ship. The other police units were alerted. The Peugeot was stopped about a kilometer from the pier. The vehicle was searched. Morphine base was contained in the bags that had been placed in the trunk. The narcotic was seized along with the car, and the driver was arrested.

Based on the above, the ship was impounded and detail searched. Two hundred kilograms of morphine base and opium were seized, and 23 seamen were arrested, including the driver of the Peugeot. Later the same day, the brother of the driver of the Peugeot was arrested. Both men were identified as known major opium and morphine base suppliers to clandestine laboratory operators in the Marseille area. Of the 23 seamen arrested, five of them, along with the two brothers, were convicted. The case represented at that time, and probably to this date, the largest narcotics seizure ever recorded from a Turkish ship in the Port of Marseille.

DEA SA Anthony Morelli, French Police Officer Antoine Barbazza,
DEA ASAC Robert De Fauw

CASE: George Louis Calmet *(deceased)*
Clandestine Heroin Laboratory, 1988 Marseille, France

In 1962, the Federal Bureau of Narcotics, headquartered in Rome, in an effort to curtail the clandestine manufacture of heroin, solicited the cooperation of chemical companies in Europe to report any suspicious orders of acetic anhydride to a specific list of indigenous narcotic enforcement agencies. Acetic anhydride is the principal precursor chemical used to convert morphine base to heroin. The request was reiterated, and the list was updated accordingly every year by BNDD.

————————•♦♦♦♦•————————

In early 1988, French Customs Marseille was alerted to an order placed for a 55-gallon drum of acetic anhydride to be delivered to an address in Les Beaumettes, France, a suburb of Marseille. French Customs alerted the special agent assigned to the Marseille District Office, who, in turn, alerted their Police Judiciare counterparts. A cooperative investigation was instituted. The delivery truck was followed to an upper-class villa. Investigation of the utilities indicated a large consumption of electricity, gas and water. Neighbors close to the villa reported at times breathing strong acetic odors and observing lights burning day and night. Surveillance revealed unusual foot traffic in and out of the villa during early morning hours, with the same individual going from and entering the villa daily. The combined information was reported to the Judge of Instruction. The judge directed a search of the villa.

The search revealed an active clandestine heroin laboratory resulting in the arrest of and the convictions of three laboratory operators and the seizure of hundreds of gallons of the following precursor chemicals: 13 glass biberons each containing two kilograms of morphine base in the first stage of conversion, ten five-liters bidons of acetone, 75 sacks, each containing approximately five kilograms of morphine base, gas masks, water pumps and other laboratory paraphernalia. Two drying bins contained a total of approximately ten kilograms of heroin (later determined to be 98% purity). The laboratory was determined to have the capability of producing 25 kilograms of heroin a week. It was the second laboratory seized since the Joseph Cesari lab was seized by the Police Judiciare and FBN Agent Al Garofalo, circa 1963.

Bob De Fauw said, "I would do it all over again" if he was ever asked. He paved the way for future agents to work in France but left Marseille in 1968 when he was promoted by BNDD to be Deputy Regional Director of Foreign Region 17 in Paris. He was transferred in 1970 by BNDD to be the Deputy Regional Director in Seattle and Washington until1971.

From 1971 to 1975, he was special agent in charge of San Francisco. From 1975 to 1978, he was the Deputy Regional Director of Paris Region 17 Europe, Near East, Middle East and Africa, where he supervised 38 countries and 35 cities with subordinate offices. From 1978 to 1981, he was promoted to Regional Director, Region 16 Bangkok, Thailand overseeing the Orient and Southeast Asian region. From 1981 to 1988. He was promoted as DEA Regional Director of Detroit Regional Office and retired in 1988. Bob was the NFL Drug Program Agent from 1988 to August of 2009. He also worked as an investigator for the Wayne County Prosecutor's Office and retired in 2009.

Robert De Fauw is one of DEA'S greatest pioneers. Those who worked with him from 1961 to 1978 also were pioneers who paved the way to the eventual destruction of the most famous international crime organization known as the French Connection. I am honored to call Bob my friend and be able to tell his story. Bob is what we were all about as narcotic agents during this era. Thank you, my friend. As we said, "We would do it all over again if given the opportunity! What a ride! The efforts of all the agents assigned to Europe, the Middle East, Asia, the Far East and Canada deserve the credit for having had an active part of bringing this historical crime organization to an end.

34

Time to Get My Feet Wet

After spending a week reviewing case files for eight hours a day at my desk, I finally felt that I was ready to start work. I went to Nick and told him that I was ready to get my feet wet.

Nick looked at me laughing, and said, "Are you for real? Ben Thieson told me that sitting around was not your strength! You had to be active, making and looking for cases. Pete, why don't you go tomorrow morning to the small café and sandwich bar to the right of the entrance of the CNO? The French narcs have their morning meet there at 8:00 a.m. I'll go with you. Jim, Dick and Vern will be there also. Good place to talk business. The owners are great friends."

"Great, I'm in, I don't believe in sitting in the office looking pretty and waiting for something to happen. It's not my style! You can't make cases by waiting for them to come to you. Between you and me, I saw a few agents like that and had no use for them. They sat around, trying to kiss ass with the bosses. That used to drive the Batman crazy!" I said, laughing.

"Pete, that's exactly my style also, and I always saw the Bat react the same way. That's why guys like us looked up to him, and the lazy ones resented being chastised by him if you weren't out on the street making cases. Keep your way of thinking like this, and you will do just what we hired you to do!"

"Thanks. I got to go to the embassy to see if they have any housing yet for us. I want to live on the economy, not in the damn government compound. I know that you and the guys all live there, but I want my wife to learn French and be on her own if I'm out of town."

"I know that the compound is full and that they have you in our building in a one-room apartment for the time being. It may take several months. Good luck! See you later and meet you at five p.m. at the Marine House upstairs for drinks."

"Sounds good to me!" I left and walked back to the back room to tell the guys I was heading out to check on housing.

I returned to the office, where the guys were ready to go up and have a few drinks while waiting for the crazy traffic to slow down. The marine barracks were above our office along with their bar and dance floor that was packed every Friday night with local girls lined up at times a half a block down Rue de La Boise. Girls were not allowed to have local male escorts. Great Rule! The marine Gunny (Gunnery Sergeant) was introduced to me, and he made it known that BNDD guys were the best friends of the Marines.

We left at 7:00 p.m. for the compound in Boulogne, near the famous Bois de Boulogne, a large wooded area and park on the western edge of Paris. My wife had supper ready, and we sat watching French television as I translated to her phrases she didn't understand. She was taking French classes to learn the language. She eventually became semi-fluent, and I was very proud of her.

＋＋＋＋＋＋＋

The next morning, Nick and the four of us rode together to work and went to have our café with our French counterparts. As we entered, the owner, a grey-haired, elderly tall man, wearing a white long-sleeve shirt, slacks, and smoking a nasty smelling Gauloise cigarette hanging from his lips, was sitting behind the cash register and said, "*Salut, les Américains! Comment allez-vous, les gars!*" How are you guys doing?

Nick said, "*Patron! Un nouveau! Pierre Charette.*"

I reached out as he extended his hand to shake and said, *"Enchanté, Patron!"* Pleased to meet you!

He said in French, "My God! Finally, we have not a Frenchman, but a real Canadian by the way he talks!" he laughed heartily as he patted me on the back.

We all laughed as one of the supervisors and his guys welcomed us for coffee.

Everybody had several laughs about my Canadian French, and I immediately realized that this was an asset to me. No one would suspect me of being an American with a broken French accent. I eventually adapted to refine my French to blend in with the Parisian accent and later the Mediterranean dialect. Eventually, no one would remark about my Canadian accent. I quickly adjusted to our morning rendezvous.

The one thing that I noticed was that some of the old clientele in the morning would habitually order a café Calva which was a demitasse (bold espresso) coffee cup with a shot of a white alcohol beverage. I asked my supervisor friend at his office later what this custom was. He laughed and informed me those who drink this Apple Cognac named Calvados are from the Normandy coast where it's made and very traditionally taken with coffee by workers in the morning before going to work. He said, "Pierre, it's a great Apple Cognac, but about 120 % alcohol. It packs a punch if you drink too many. Usually, it's a shot glass sipped with the coffee and swirled together and slowly swallowed to enjoy the aroma!"

The next day I walked in and said, *"Bonjour, Patron Un Espresso et Calva!"* There was a quick silence at the bar, and everyone watched as I was served. I took a sip of coffee with the shot of Calvados, slowly letting it slide down my throat as my sinus immediately cleared and I tasted this amazing apple cognac taste. I knew then that I was hooked, and for five years in France, I had my café Calva every morning! To this day, I have Calvados and enjoy it! My friends at the cafe bar nicknamed me Mr. Calva, and I was immediately accepted into this special circle.

Back at the office, Nick advised, "Pete, Le Mouel has a source he wants you and me to meet to work out details in order to introduce you to an opium trafficker who has five kilos of opium to sell."

"Sounds good. I'm ready to jump in, thanks!"

"Let me ask you, have you ever purchased opium"? He asked, laughing.

"Yeah! But only in gram quantity when I was in the Sheriff's department. I never forgot the smell, almost like shit with tar on it. I remember it was kind of sticky!" I couldn't help squinching my face and rubbing my right-hand fingers together.

"Yep! You know what you're talking about! When I was in Turkey, I saw and smelled a lot of it, and it's shit all right! These are in the shape of opium balls, about the size of a small bowling ball.

"Should be interesting! Anything else?"

"Get with the guys in the back and come up with a plan and location to do this so we can be ready to meet Mr. Le Mouel with our plan!"

"Nick, just one thing. I always had an agreement with my previous bosses when doing a UC deal!"

"What is it?"

"I'm wide open to any plan, but the final Ok is my call! If it doesn't sound right to me, I have the final say, no matter what, with your agreement. I learned that from Miller, Nick Navarro and Ben as a young narc. This came to light when the Frankie Tommilo (*deceased*) case in New York occurred. He was my counselor, along with two others.

"Pete, I totally agree and support you 100% on this. I feel the same way as you do!" He smiled.

"Thanks, Nick. I'll be in the back and get with the guys."

I spoke with the guys and asked for their input. They suggested the deal go ahead and have it go down on the Champs Élysées at the café sidewalk restaurant named Café George V near the Claridge Hotel. The location is great with large crowds of tourists and plenty of spots to set up surveillance in case the suspects try to rip me off in broad daylight.

We all agreed that the flash roll could be brought unannounced and taken away until I saw the dope. We briefed Nick of our plan to which he agreed.

Suspects delivered 5 kilograms of raw opium to me in 1973

CASE #- XA-73-0001
Case Agent Pierre Charette
5 Kilograms of Opium
UC Agent: Pete Charette
Surveillance Agents: James Collier, Vern Stephens, one other agent (name protected) and French CNO Inspectors

The next day we had a meeting with Mr. Le Mouel and his group, and our plan was accepted. I advised them that S/A Stephens would bring the flash roll $10K, and once shown, he would leave and go into the Claridge Hotel and be escorted out through the back entrance by CNO plain clothes inspectors where the money would be secured. Mr. Le Mouel advised that the informant would introduce me as a Canadian to the suspect, and after a brief conversation, he would leave to meet with Vern. Once the merchandise was brought to me for inspection, I would give the signal by removing my hat, and the arrest tram would move in with uniform French Police Gendarmes to arrest everyone. I was told that once the signal was given and the police moved in, I was to make my escape by fleeing the scene through the Claridge Hotel and leaving through the back entrance, then quickly departing the area to return to the CNO office.

Everyone departed to establish their surveillance position on the

Champs Élysées, and the informant and I sat down. He advised me he had told the supplier we had known each other in Montreal in a night club that I owned with my associates and we had done business together for the past three years. He also advised him that I was a serious buyer and was not to be duped or messed with. I then advised him that once the introduction was done, to let me do the talking, and I would tell him to go get Vern my associate, who at that time would come and show the money and leave right away.

The informant and I left the office and walked on foot to the Champs Élysées. Then we sat outside the café at a table for three. The informant placed a phone call to the supplier and told him to meet us at the George V café. He then told me that he would be here in 30 minutes. We both ordered a pitcher of red wine and enjoyed the scenery. I scanned my surroundings and was able to observe some of the team members at various location around me.

In approximately 35 minutes, a green Peugeot 4 sedan pulled up to the curb in front of the sidewalk, and the informant advised that this was him getting out of the front passenger's door. The driver then left the area.

The suspect, a dark skin Middle Eastern gentleman, 5'10", 190 pounds and wearing a greyish suit and overcoat, approached us and shook hands with the informant who then proceeded to introduce me to him and said, "Vadga, this is Pierre," as we shook hands.

The suspect sat down and ordered a glass of wine. In French, he said, "Pierre, my friend tells me that you are from Canada, and you are in the night club business. What part of Canada?"

"That's correct. I'm from Montreal, and I do have a partnership in a night club."

"I hear Montreal is a beautiful city. I would love to visit it someday! "Marcel (PN) tells me that you have done some business together, and that you are interested in my merchandise?"

"Yes, I am. I and my colleagues have a very well-established business. We are always looking for various products for Canada and New York, where we distribute our merchandise for buyers. I am prepared to buy the four shirts that you have. If the quality is good, then we can start to make monthly orders from your business. I guess Marcel told you that I get to the point fast. I don't like to play games." Turning to Marcel, I said, "Marcel, go to the hotel lobby, get Vern, and tell him to come and that everything is fine!" Marcel got up and left right away.

"Pierre, I see that you are quite direct and to the point. I am prepared to deliver what you are looking for as long as you can assure me you have your funds in order."

"I do as a matter of fact. Here's my right-hand man now." Vern, who was carrying an attaché case, sat down and set the case on his lap.

"Vern, this is Mr. Vadga. Show him what you have!"

Vern had already set the combination numbers and quickly partially opened the suitcase, turning it to Vadga, who observed stacks of $100 bills.

"My funds are in order, and now that you have seen that we are serious, it's your turn to show me the five shirts, and we will exchange packages here!" Vern closed the case, got up and left for the lobby of the hotel.

Vadga smiled and nodded in a manner of expressing pleasure to have seen that we were serious and cautious. He said, "Pierre, Marcel was right about you. You waste no time and are cautious, which I am also. I will call my associates to bring the merchandise, and you will be able to verify the quality of the shirts!" Vadga placed a call, and within five minutes, the green car arrived with three Middle Eastern males, stopping at the curb in front of the café. Vadga said, "Walk to the car with me and check out the shirts!"

The passenger got out of the car and opened the trunk as we approached and stood by. I observed five white plastic grocery bags in the trunk, with one that had a round, newspaper-covered ball partially opened, and I could see and get a strong sense of smell of raw opium from the ball. I reached up and removed my hat as I bent down under the trunk cover to get a closer look, which was the signal for the arrest team to move in.

I immediately heard French police car sirens with that familiar sound. I looked up and heard yells, "Police, Police! Hands up!" as they came running toward us. I looked at Vadga and said, "You set me up, you asshole," with a look to kill as I started running toward the hotel. The police kept yelling, *"Arrêtez!"* as I ran. I suddenly realized that I was being chased by a Gendarme through the large lobby of the hotel. Running out onto a backstreet, I ran to the right on a narrow sidewalk as fast as I could.

The Gendarme kept running after me yelling for me to stop and had a gun drawn. Luckily, he was middle-aged and was falling behind as I kept up my pace. I finally ran across the street and down two blocks where I could hear French police cars in the area, obviously looking for me. I immediately ducked into a small neighborhood café bar, sat down and ordered a Café Calva. For at least a good 30 minutes, sirens and police cars passed by, obviously still searching for the escaped Canadian.

After three cafés Calvas, I finally felt it was safe for me to leave, the sounds of blaring fading. I finally got back to the CNO office, and waiting for me was Mr. Knight, Nick, Mr. Le Mouel, the two supervisors and the guys. While all were wearing smiles and feeling relief, Mr. Le Mouel said, "Charette! Great job! We got them all and 5 kilograms of opium valued at $70,000. Thank you and your colleagues. Well done!"

"Thank you, Mr. Le Mouel. I have a question to ask, though. Why was I being chased by an armed, uniformed officer?"

"I'm so sorry about that. We did not tell the Gendarmes that you were working for us. We could not disclose your identity."

"I understand," I answered, "but maybe next time I can have a better escape plan. God forbid if he had shot me!"

I never mentioned that this Gendarme had actually fired one shot in the air. I did not want to create an incident with our French colleagues, but I wanted reassurance that we devise a better plan of escape in the future. The only person that I told was Nick, who agreed laughingly with me that we would not say anything to anyone about this. Nick and I had many laughs about this first time as an undercover agent in France!

35

Significant French Connection Cases Worked in France 1972 to1977

Being assigned to the Paris office from 1972 to 1975 was a challenging and exciting era of investigation. There are numerous cases that were worked by all of us, and during that time, we grew in size with additional manpower being assigned to Paris. We had new assignments with a great group supervisor Kevin Gallagher *(deceased)*who was transferred from the Marseille office, one new ASAIC (Named Protected) five new agents (three Names Protected) George Reucicard *(deceased)*,ex-customs agent, Walter Pardean *(deceased)*, ex-customs agent), one new ASAIC Vern, ex-custom agent who remained with BNDD approximately 60 days then returned to U.S. Customs Paris Office. As this office grew in size, so did the Marseille country office.

There were too many cases to talk about, but I have chosen some of the most significant ones that had major impact against the French criminal organization of the French Connection which led to the dismantling of this famous group of international heroin smugglers to the United States and Canada.

Case of Significant Impact 1: XA-72-0006
Case Agents: S/A Pierre Charette, James Collier,
other Agent's name protected
December 30, 1972- Seizure of 15 Kilograms of
Heroin, Paris, France
Value: $7.5 Million

In September of 1972, the French Central Narcotics Office started investigating the activities of a suspected heroin trafficker named Albert (PN) and his associates. Information developed through a confidential informant indicated that he was allegedly sending shipments of French heroin to Canada, destined for the United States to U.S. organized crime figures in New York. Through extensive coordination among the French Narcotics Office with BNDD and Canadian RCMP Investigators, and after months of investigations, undercover work, and surveillance in Paris, Mexico, Montreal, and Canada, this well-formed group was finally arrested on December 30, 1972, in Paris. Mr. Le Mouel informed Mr. Knight that he wanted our assistance with this investigation and requested that I, along with Collier and another agent, be allowed to work with his group until an arrest could be affected.

On November 28, 1972, we met with Mr. Le Mouel, who briefed us on their intensive investigation into the activities of two well-known suspected traffickers and their association with a Canadian organized crime figure named Frank Dasti (*deceased*) of Montreal. According to the CNO, between Nov. 25 and Nov. 27, 1972, the main head of this French organization had ten kilos of heroin delivered to Dasti in Montreal from Paris. That investigation had been ongoing for several months between the CNO and the RCMP. He noted that during the evening of Nov. 23, 1972, this target, Claude Dewachter, AKA Sling, was arrested in Paris on a robbery charge. During the robbery, he broke his left arm and had to be hospitalized.

On Nov. 26, he escaped from the hospital by jumping through a second-floor window, further injuring his arm and did not seek medical attention. Intelligence developed indicated that on Nov. 28, Sling was going to accompany one of his associates to Montreal for the purpose of receiving the money for this shipment of heroin. Since he was wanted, Sling was replaced on Nov. 28 by a John doe who was observed getting on an Air Canada plane with the partner to Montreal. Both returned on Nov. 29, and the CNO further intensified surveillance and investigations on this group.

On Dec. 29, Mr. Le Mouel asked if we could help in doing surveillance of Sling and his organization. We attended a briefing with our CNO colleagues and were given the latest locations that they frequented. Several meetings were observed between all of them, and a new figure was identified code name KiK who was followed to Cassis, France, a small seaport near Marseille. Surveillance was extremely hard to do since this seaport was no longer than a city block along the Mediterranean. The use of technical surveillance commonly referred by us as wiretapping provided outstanding results for all of us.

—————— ·⋆✦✦⋆· ——————

The French have fewer problems than we do in obtaining permission to wiretap a phone line. We have to be able to prove that all means of normal investigation have been exhausted before being granted the authority by our courts. This discourages investigators from having to do tons of paperwork and appear before a judge to lay out all the facts.

I can honestly say that our French colleagues with our assistance and undercover work were able at any time within 30 minutes to conduct technical surveillance on any suspects, phones, residences, offices, and hotel rooms anywhere in France with just one phone call. This, along with outstanding liaison and open sharing of information and daily physical contact with our counterparts, led to the destruction of The French Connection.

My only advice to DEA administrators, upper management, foreign DEA country attachés, and agents is that without close daily association and involvement with your host country counterparts, you will fail in getting honest cooperation. I have traveled to Europe and South America and spoken with foreign law enforcement agencies since my retirement and have been told that DEA, for the most part, has distanced itself from this form of relationship. Some have indicated that they are lucky if they see DEA once a month. I have spoken with some of our agents in overseas positions, and they have said that the only thing they do is exchange intelligence information and seldom go to their counterparts' offices. I was told personally, that they had heard from those who were working with us from the sixties to the eighties that we socialized every day and met them for coffee and after work for a drink, but that is not the standard anymore. I was saddened to hear that when asked how things were between them and DEA. The answer was jokingly, "What's DEA?"

As a manager, along with our agents, we, the 'old soldiers', insisted on daily liaison and work with counterparts. For having good solid liaison, we were on almost every news channel daily! Sometimes we needed to look at ourselves and ask, "What can we do to make things better and exciting!" Working overseas is not a paid vacation but requires agents to maintain contact with their counterparts in order to blend in and make them feel as if they are there, making an effort to work day-to-day with them.

* * * * * *

Kik was driving a metallic gold Porsche, with a license plate, which he had changed before making his trip to Aix-en-Provence, approximately 550 miles from Paris. Intelligence data revealed that payment was made for the purchase of 15 kilograms of heroin at that time. On Dec. 30, 1972, he was joined in Aix by The Tomato (PN), who was driving a dark blue Citroën sport Maserati that surveillance officers observed between 9:00 and 10:00 a.m. Kik was observed meeting with the same unidentified white male, whom he had met in Cassis on the 29th. The transfer of heroin was made at that time. Kik, who had been accompanied by his girlfriend, followed by the Citroën, departed Aix-en-Provence for Paris, followed by the CNO surveillance team at 10:30 a.m. and took the Paris AutoRoute.

Dark blue Citroen Maserati and gold Porsche

We were assigned to conduct vehicle surveillance to pick up the two vehicles as they passed through Péage de Fleury (toll station) at 3:45 p.m., approximately 30 miles from Paris. The team members consisted of BNDD Agent Jim Collier, one BNDD agent, five CNO inspectors and me. At 4:45 p.m., they were followed to 12 Rue Deodat Severac, the residence of The Sling. Kik parked directly in front of one of the CNO surveillance vehicles manned by CNO Officer and S/A Jim Collier.

The load vehicle driven by Kik remained parked across the street from the apartment. He exited his vehicle and immediately ran across the narrow street and entered the apartment. I was with a DST Agent, from the French Territorial Surveillance Bureau parked about 50 yards behind. Everyone remained at their positions and observed that around 2:00 a.m., all lights were off in the apartment, and once we felt comfortable that the occupants were asleep, my DST friend and I took a walk. We briefly walked around the block, passing by the Porsche. He took one look at the trunk's key lock as we continued walking around the block for a second pass.

He handed me his small leather bag, which contained various files. As we walked towards the car, he said in French in a soft whisper, "Pierre, give me the pointed file and stay watchful, mon ami!"

"Oui!" I gave the nod as we passed next to the supervisor's car.

The DST agent then alerted all units. "Pierre and our friend are good to go. Be alert on the apartment!"

"Here you go, mon ami. We have a go!"

We slowed down. My friend reached out with his left hand, held the pointed file out at a slight tilt, and quickly inserted it into the key slot of the trunk. The trunk opened up, and we both observed the travel sack inside. He retracted the file and quietly closed the trunk, never losing a step as we continued walking in a normal fashion! Mission accomplished!

We looked at each other, smiling and chuckled. I said, "That's worth at least four or five Calvas!"

He replied, "No, let's make it five apiece!"

We advised the supervisor by radio, "The gift is there; all is a go!"

"Bien! All units, we have confirmation!" We continued surveillance, and in the morning Kik came out from the apartment and waited on the sidewalk as The Tomato arrived in his car.

He parked and exited his vehicle looking around cautiously, and held a brief conversation with KiK as they walked to the rear trunk of the Porsche. Kik then retrieved a soft brown suitcase from the car, returned directly to the apartment building and entered by himself.

We all observed The Tomato get in his car, pull up alongside the Porsche and exit. Then he went to talk with Kik's girlfriend, who had gotten in the car. After a brief conversation, Tomasi left the area, followed by CNO surveillance units. He returned at 4:55 p.m. and parked in front of the apartment building from where Kik came out and had a brief conversation with him. Both left the area in their separate cars following each other while being followed by surveillance units.

Our team remained in a stationary surveillance position on the apartment building and was advised that technical surveillance reported that The Sling had a communication with his partner, advising him that "The 15 were there" to which his partner advised he would be there in 30 minutes. At approximately 6:15 p.m., he arrived in a yellow Austin Martin and immediately entered the apartment building.

At approximately 6:45, The Sling's girlfriend was arrested by CNO Deputy Director as she arrived and started to enter the apartment building. A radio message then came in from Supervisor Peru. "Pierre, you and Jim watch her while I advise everyone to prepare to move in."

"Ok, I'm going to ask if Sling is in the apartment!" I approached the girl and asked, "Micheline, is he in the apartment? tell me now!"

With a look of fear, she answered, "Oui, monsieur!"

"Good. Now give me your key to the apartment and hurry up. We need it now!"

She advised us that it was in her purse. I retrieved it quickly and gave the deputy director the key as a Gendarme took custody of her. All of this was done very quietly to ensure we didn't cause attention to our presence.

+ + + + + +

At approximately 7:00 p.m. CNO Officers, S/A Jim Collier and I entered the apartment and arrested The Sling and his partner. He was stunned as he stood there with his right hand in a homemade sling. Jim and I were asked to watch him in the living room while the search of the apartment was made.

One of our inspector friends came out of the kitchen and told us quietly on the side that the search so far was negative on the bag. He said, "Pierre, it's here, but that SOB hid it, and we need to find it!" Then he walked away.

"No problem, my friend. Give me a couple of minutes so I can have a 'moment' with our new friend." I looked at Jim and leaned down to Sling who was in pain from his escape fall and placed my hand on top of his shoulder as he grimaced in pain and said in French, "We will be here all night long, if that's what you want, until we find the suitcase. Do you want to tell us and help save time?"

"You are the Americans, aren't you? I wanted to come to you and should have done it, but I can't help. I think you know what would happen to me if I did! I'm sorry, monsieur."

"Ok! I understand!" I answered, smiling.

"Inspector, can you come here for a minute, please?"

"Oui, Pierre, what's up?"

"Jim and I need to talk for a minute in the kitchen. Can you watch him, oh, and he's in pain from his fall!"

Smiling, he said, *"Pas de Problème!"*

In the kitchen, Jim and I tried to get a good view of all possible places, where one would hide a satchel in a small French apartment.

After a few minutes, we came back to the living room and observed that Claude was in extreme pain, with sweat dripping from his forehead and he looked sickly white.

The Inspector was smiling and gave me a thumbs up from behind his back and said, "Pierre, Jim, I need to search the kitchen again. He's all yours!"

"Good. Let's hope we can find this bag soon!"

"Claude, how are you doing? You need anything?"

"No, thank you. I'm fine now!" he answered with a weak smile.

All of a sudden, a loud, "Yes! We found it" came from the kitchen area. The Deputy Director came over and said, "Our inspector was looking out the sliding kitchen window that overlooked the back yard and saw at the end of a clothesline the bag tied to the line." A test of one of the white 15-kilogram packages confirmed it was heroin. Mr. Le Mouel was notified and gave the order to the surveillance teams to arrest all suspects.

15 Kilogram Packages of Heroin in the bag tied to the clothesline

Surveillance CNO Officers located and arrested KiK and his girlfriend and The Tomato. During the morning of Dec. 31, Mr. Le

Mouel advised us that the four women had been released from custody, and no charges were brought against them.

Defendants Arrested – Alboreo, Tomassi, Marquette, DeWatcher

Our investigation continued in Southern France by the CNO and Marseille office, with additional suspects identified through technical surveillance in order to get to the principal source and location of the heroin lab. The heroin seized by us was destined to be transported to Montreal to the Frank Catroni organization. The follow-up investigation was done by the Montreal Country BNDD office and the RCMP Narcotics Unit in Montreal.

This was the first major case that I ever encountered in my career at that time. My determination prior to this assignment was that someday I wanted to work my way to the top of the heroin source of supply and make an impact on bringing down those who supplied heroin to the United States. Finally, with three of my colleagues, we made our first major case, and it felt great!

What an honor to have gained the confidence of the French Narcotics Bureau and to be able to work as part of their team for five years. They are the heroes of France, and I was honored to be part of this historical time with my DEA colleagues. This hell of a ride was continuing!

Commissaire Bernard Gravet - Mr. Francois
Le Mouel with heroin suitcase

BNDD Team/CNO Team

Working in the Paris Regional office involved various assignments throughout the Region. I was assigned on various deployments to

Amsterdam, Belgium, Germany, Italy and Southern France. Our day-to-day work in the office was to also handle numerous referrals from BNDD offices from the United States and parts of Europe on cases that had a connection to France by organized crime organizations, the Middle East and Far East offices of BNDD.

On the lighter side, Mr. Knight became concerned about our inability to meet our yearly firearm qualification and came up with a plan that surprised all of us. Paul came in on a Monday morning to the back office, carrying a medium-sized box, accompanied by Nick, who appeared to be holding back from bursting out laughing and Our ASAIC who was just smiling. He called a meeting of the troops and Paul said, "The reason I called this meeting is we are required to have firearm qualification every year, and we haven't been able to do this for obvious reasons. So, I decided that we would do our own qualifications here in the back office by having you all do target shooting practice with some pellet guns that I bought.

I looked at Nick, who was ready to burst out laughing along with the guys. Paul was dead serious about this. He opened up the box and pulled out two pellet guns along with a spinning metal bulls eye metal target on a metal stand.

"This is to start effective today, and I want you all to spend at least an hour practicing back here together. Nick will ensure that you do this, and we will report to headquarters that we met our requirements. Have fun!" Then he went back up front to his office.

Nick waited until he was out of sight and burst out laughing, saying, "Holy fuck. I think he has flipped out." We were almost all in tears from this. We always appreciated Paul's weird sense of humor.

I said, "Ok, Nick, we will start this most important requirement, Sir, and we will also make sure you get your turn as well." I said while we continued to laugh.

The layout of the three offices in the back was such that each one had two large glass windows that opened inward, overlooking a courtyard for our cars. We set up the target stand on a desk with a wall behind and started taking turns at shooting at the spinning target. As we took turns, it became really comical, and we were actually having fun, laughing at each other's skilled shooting capabilities. This came about one day when our Italian agent came into my office and was engaged in shooting practice when a pigeon flew past the open window. Suddenly and fluidly, he spun to his left and from the hip, shot the pigeon, which hurtled down until it impacted the top of one of our parked cars.

"Wow! Are you for real? Bet you can't do that again?"

"You're on Frenchy. Ten Francs?"

"You got it!" Dick waited, looking out the window until a pigeon approached the ledge of the window, and Dick popped him from the hip once again.

"You SOB! Here's 10 Francs!" This 'alternate' target practice attracted Jim and Vern, and before long, we began taking turns to duplicate this. Before we knew it, a dozen pigeon 'traffickers' had met their demise.

After that day, while at my desk, I would quickly reach for the pellet gun and pop pigeons on the fly. This continued for several weeks, and even Nick came to the back and would do some target shooting.

As the saying goes, "all good things must end." So too did our target practice one morning when Paul Knight paid us a visit in the back office with Nick, who once again was ready to burst out laughing!

"Guys, I got bad news. One of our French neighbors across the way in the apartment building has filed a complaint to the ambassador that his staff was assassinating French pigeons and requested that this horrible crime stop immediately!" he stated, laughing as he spoke. "If we continue, there will be some transfers back to the States. They are sending workers in the back to pick up all of our deceased traffickers, about 40 of them! Turn in your weapons to Nick. Have a great day!" he continued laughing as he left.

"Well, guys, it was fun, and I'll notify Washington that we all qualified as required!" Nick was almost in hysterics from laughing so hard. Needless to say, the word spread fast around the embassy families and French CNO, who all got great laughs.

Case of Significant Impact 2: Andre Condemine (deceased) et al. 60 kilograms heroin
Value $26 million, Case# XA-72-0004
(Mexican General Umberto Mirales- Cortes (deceased)
Case Agent: Nicola (PN)
BNDD Paris Team
November 28, 1972

This investigation started as the result of our outstanding relationship of doing liaison on a day-to-day basis with our French CNO partners in Paris and BNDD agent Nicola (PN) while at the French CNO in August of 1972. He was advised by one supervisor that intelligence on a major French heroin trafficker named Mario Denise Condemine AKA Andre Condemine (*deceased*) who was the subject of a Joint French/U.S. Narcotics investigation, was suspected of preparing a possible shipment of heroin to the U.S. The French CNO learned that two of Condomine's Lieutenants, Marcel Mouchigan (*deceased*) and Rashid Gharbi (*deceased*), had been observed in October in New York by BNDD agents and were suspected of receiving a heroin delivery from France, from Condemine.

Inspector advised him that, according to their information, the drug never made it to New York since it was seized in Rio de Janeiro. A seizure of 60 kilograms of heroin was seized from a cargo container on the *Le Mormac-Atair*, a ship on which numerous arrests were made. In October, the French CNO located Mouchigan and Gharbi's secret apartment in the 5th Arrondissement at 22, Rue de Pointoise, Paris. Inspector Sarda told Dick that a surveillance was now in effect on this location and requested his assistance with them. He advised all of us what was going on, and he was instructed to participate with the CNO.

He and the CNO team observed two new figures who met with Mouchigan and Gharbi were identified by the CNO. All four drove to a hotel near the Champs Élysées. A discreet check at the concierge desk disclosed that the suspects shared a large suite together with a Mexican identified by CNO. The two men also were in contact with another client who was lodging there identified as General Humberto Mirales-Cortes (*deceased*). General Mirales-Cortes was an Equestrian Olympian, who won a Bronze Medal in 1952 for Mexico. After his arrest in Paris for drug smuggling and awaiting trial, he was found dead in prison on December 7, 1972.

Mr. Le Mouel advised us that sources of information advised that a delivery of the heroin was going to occur soon. Surveillance was intensified on this hotel. They soon observed that Gharbi, Mouchigan, and one other suspect departed the hotel and followed them to Orly Airport, where they rented a Renault R-16 and followed them to Marseille, arriving in the middle of the night. Surveillance was joined by the Marseille Central Narcotics Agents at that point. The three suspects were observed meeting with a Mexican previously identified in Paris. He was observed carrying a suitcase which contained a large sum of money for the heroin, surrendering it to Mouchigan. All suspects remained under surveillance, but due to a major traffic jam, all four suspects were lost. The team alerted Mr. Le Mouel, and they immediately headed back to Paris.

The CNO team felt that the best option was to immediately place in Paris constant surveillance on the Mexican and General Mirales-Cortes. The two were observed leaving their hotel and went to the Champs Élysées to purchase four expensive suitcases and placed them in the trunk of the rented Renault. That night surveillance on Gharbi's residence observed the Mexican and Gharbi arriving and pulling up next to Mouchigan's vehicle, removing four suitcases from the Peugeot that had been purchased by the general. He then took them to his apartment. The Mexican returned to his hotel by taking a taxi. Surveillance was maintained all night, and on Saturday morning around 7:30 a.m. Mouchigan exited the apartment and opened the trunk of the Renault that he rented at Orly and started to remove five suitcases. The signal was given by Mr. Le Mouel to arrest everyone. The suitcases contained 60 kilograms of heroin in 120 sealed plastic packets, which were to be placed in the general's suitcases in Gharbi's apartment.

*Top left to right: PN The Hammer, S/A James Collier
Middle L/R Inspector George Barthe, Jean Marie Flori, Supv. Robert
Peru, Inspector Rene Baudin, last 2- Name Withheld
Bottom L/R S/A Pierre Charette & Name Withheld on last 2.*

CNO Inspectors arrested the Mexican and General Mirales-Cortes at their hotel, both in possession of airline tickets for that day, both for Mexico City, one via Amsterdam, and the other via London. A search of the Mexican revealed he was in possession of $17,000 in cash. Arrested later was Gharbi and his partne2r. The Marseille CNO Commissioner, Mr. Morin (*deceased*), and his team arrested four defendants in an apartment. Found in the apartment was one suitcase containing one machine gun, several guns, ammunition, 2,300 French ID Cards stolen from two Prefectures in Nantes and Montmorillon, France. The female who owned this apartment was charged with possession of stolen documents and unauthorized possession of weapons.

Case of Significant Impact 3 - CASE # XA-73-0012
VINKO (PN)
15 Kilograms of Morphine, Belgrade, Yugoslavia
Largest seizure of Morphine in a BLOC
COUNTRY
Value $4.5 Million
Case Agent Pierre Charette
UC Agent: Pierre Charette, Walter Pardaen
(deceased), BNDD AGENT (identity protected)
Surveillance Agents: James Collier, SAIC, Milan,
Italy; Vern Stephens

While working in my office on November 26, 1973, I was requested to meet with Mr. Knight in his office. Upon meeting him, I was introduced to a confidential source of his. Mr. Knight requested that I work with this individual who had a network of sources in France that had made numerous cases of theft for Commissaire Mathieu of the French Brigade of Paris. We agreed that this source could be utilized to set up a network of confidential informants in France, in order to gain useful intelligence as to the present trends in France, and at the same time, attempt to make cases for us.

Mr. Le Mouel was briefed by me about our plan and requested that verification be made with Commissaire Mathieu to ascertain his past assistance to his office. It was verified that the CI had made some of the largest stolen painting recoveries in Paris and was highly respected. The source advised me that he had already made contact with one of his past associates who had been offering to sell him multi-kilograms of Yugoslavian heroin. The CI advised that he had ordered 250-gram samples of heroin from this source at this time.

DRD Panella had disclosed to me that for the past year BNDD in Europe had been told that Yugoslavia was possibly trying to get involved in the making of illegal heroin, since they were legitimately producing opium for medical use and so far no indication of any such allegation ever proved that there was any criminal diversion ongoing at all. Nick advised me that this was a dead-end issue and doubted that this source could produce. I advised Nick that I had a gut feeling about this and for him to let me run with this, to which he replied, laughing, "Ok, Frenchy, you will see that I am right. Roll with it, but don't say I didn't warn you!"

I'm a firm believer that if one has a gut feeling in this game, then it is an obligation to pursue that instinct.

✦✦✦✦✦✦

The CI contacted me on November 23, and advised that he had made contact with the Bulgarian suspect named Vinko, who was a Bulgarian political prisoner for ten years prior to moving to France. While in prison, he made some contacts who are now in Skopia, Yugoslavia, and they are the ones who would furnish multi-kilograms of heroin to the CI. He advised me that Vinko's contacts would provide him with a 250-500-gram sample. Travel by Vinko would be within two weeks.

A meeting with Vinko and the CI occurred on December 5, 1973. Surveillance was conducted by CNO Supervisor, S/A Jim Collier and me at the Café de Roset, located at Place de Paris. The CI meet with Vinko, who was approximately 55 years of age, 5'10", 200 pounds with greyish hair. The CI was advised that Vinko was leaving Paris on December 8 or 9 for Skopia returning in about one week. I instructed the CI, in order to document that he did travel to Skopia, to tell Vinko that I wanted proof that he had gone there by sending a telegram to him from Skopia. I also told the CI to tell Vinko that My Canadian friend doesn't want a gram sample, which anyone can buy on the street, but a minimum of a 100-gram sample and nothing less. Vinko requested $600 to pay for his trip from us. I advised the CI that we would give him the money, and I would get my boss to approve it.

I approached Nick for the funds, but he looked at me questionably and said, laughing, "Are you fucking kidding me? This guy wants money to go home and will not come back, Pete! He's going to play you, and we won't see him again!"

"Nick, if I am wrong on this, I personally will pay out of my pocket the money back! Trust me, I know that he will deliver. It's my call. Please back me on this?"

"Ok! If he plays you for a fool, it's on you. And for God's sake, don't say anything to Paul about this until we see how it goes down!" he said, shaking his head.

"You got it. And if I'm right, you're buying the drinks at the Marine House and a night on the town with the guys. Deal or no deal!" I countered.

"You SOB, you're on!" We both laughed. "Get the paperwork request done and bring it down to Administration! Get the money to the CI. Now get the hell out of my sight!" he said jokingly.

I got the money, met the CI, and told him to tell Vinko that if he doesn't come back, I know where his wife and grandkids live, and I will make sure he will never see them again. Then I'm coming for him! The CI received a cablegram from Vinko, from Skopia. I insisted on this to properly document his travel. The cablegram stated, "Happy New Year-Good Health," which was the code set to mean "Everything is Ok–as planned."

On December 27, 1973, the CI contacted me and advised that Vinko had returned to Paris, with 150 grams of heroin and wanted to meet the CI to give him the heroin. The meeting was scheduled in an hour at the Café de St. Claude in Paris. I immediately tried to contact our CNO Inspectors, but all were off. My partner and I immediately went and surveilled the meeting. Vinko was observed ready to leave, but the CI remained seated at a table. Kevin and I entered as Vinko passed us on the way out. We remained at the counter ordering Café Calva and joined the CI at his table after 5 minutes.

The bar was busy with morning regulars who were enjoying their morning café Calvados along with myself! After ensuring that Vinko was gone, we sat down with the CI.

"Ok, the meeting went well, I assumed. Did he deliver our package?"

"Yes, he did, Pierre!" He reached inside his coat pocket and in front of all the people, handed me a rolled-up plastic baggie containing a greyish powdery substance which I immediately grabbed in order to avoid strange looks b,y the clientele. The CI was startled, and I said, whispering, "What the fuck are you doing? Don't ever do that in public!" I realized that he had never done any narcotics cases before. I quickly placed the package in my overcoat pocket, went to the restroom, locked the door and immediately pulled out an ampule test vial. As soon as I opened the package, I immediately smelled a strong odor of acidic anhydride. I tested the grayish powdery substance and got a positive purple result instantly, indicating a tentative positive for an Opiate. *Holy Shit! Now we have proof that Yugoslavians are getting started in the heroin market! Nick is going to shit himself!*

I walked out of the men's room, sat down and said, "We are in business! But it's not French heroin for sure, and I believe that they couldn't finish the process properly. It's strong morphine converted from raw opium!"

"You get hold of Vinko and tell him we want to meet him. Don't mention anything other than we are satisfied and getting it checked out and that we will be in contact, got it? Great job, and I will call you Monday. I will get you the $1300 for this sample to pay him."

We immediately went to the office. I called Nick at home and told him, "We need to meet you at the office right away and with Paul Knight also. Our CI just got delivery from Vinko and got 110 grams of smack from Yugoslavia! Nick, I tested it in the bathroom. The shit went positive immediately! We got the proof finally, Nick!"

"You're shitting me. This isn't a joke, is it?"

"Nick! It's fucking real, baby!" I began laughing with joy!

"Ok! I'll call Paul and get a hold of Le Mouel. See you at the office!"

"Were already here. See you soon!"

We were on cloud nine and ready to nail Their asses really good! All I can say is at that moment, I was on an adrenaline rush.

Nick and Paul arrived at the office, and Nick advised Mr. Le Mouel. We briefed both of them and produced the package. Nick immediately recognized the smell and appearance and said, "Paul, this is the real stuff, no doubt about it. Finally, we got the proof! Pete, you two did a great job!"

Nick added, "Guys, we need to get this stuff to DC lab right away. We will send it on the next TWA flight to Dulles. The last step must have failed to make it white. They probably couldn't get any animal black."

Now that we had the proof, plans had to be formulated and approved by the American Embassy in Belgrade, with the Embassy Narcotics Coordinator. The SAIC In Rome was requested to contact him and fully brief him on this matter. He requested that I contact him. He was briefed on this case and advised that he would pass this information on to the Chief of the Yugoslav Criminal Investigation Bureau director to see how the Yugoslav officials wanted to finalize this investigation.

⋅⋅✦✦✦✦✦⋅⋅

On December 29, 1974, the CI was instructed to meet with Vinko at the Tabac Bar at 100 Avenue D'Italie to advise him that the 110 grams of heroin was not heroin but morphine base. Surveillance assignments were made with the CNO supervisor and SA Vern Stephens, James Collier and me. Vinko was observed at 3:30 p.m. entering the Tabac Bar Café and met with our CI. Vinko told the CI that the 110-gram sample was given to him after telling them that the buyers wanted 50 kilograms of heroin. He advised that he stayed for seven days and waited while they hurriedly prepared the 110 grams for him, and it was possible that they had failed.

The CI informed Vinko that his friends still wanted to do business if they could sell them morphine base. Vinko advised that this would be no problem since they have been selling morphine base to their German buyers in Munich. He told the CI that this was no problem whatsoever, and they could immediately supply 100-150 kilograms immediately. He advised he would depart immediately for Skopia around January 3 or 4, 1974, to ensure they could get it ready and bring back a 10-gram sample. The CI advised Vinko to meet at 5:00 p.m. to meet with the buyers. Vinko then advised that the price per kilogram was 25,000 Deutsche Marks ($8900 per kilo), and heroin was 30,000 DM ($10,700). As a show of faith, DRD Panella agreed that he was to give Vinko $1000 for the 110 grams received. I advised the CI to inform him that he was to send cablegrams of his travels to and from Yugoslavia and Germany, as previously discussed. He was also instructed to remind him about his family if he fails.

So, he departed Paris on January 5, by train for Yugoslavia. On January 11, the CI received a postcard from Munich, stating he was getting his Visa to enter Yugoslavia. On the evening of the 11th, The CI received a cablegram from Vinko from Skopia, once again a coded message "Everything Ok! -as planned." He returned to Paris on January 21, and made contact with the CI saying he had the sample and was advised to meet on the 22nd at the Café Le Saint Claude in Paris at 2:00 p.m. S/A Collier, S/A Stephens, CNO Supervisor, and I observed Vinko meeting the CI at 2:00 p.m. He then left the bar at 3:15 p.m. with the CI and entered the metro station but due to massive traffic at that hour, the subjects were lost. The CI contacted me, and we met him at his residence, where he produced a 10-gram sample of morphine base to me, which tested positive for an opiate. The evidence was turned over and sent to our Washington lab for analysis and tested positive for 86% morphine base. (The test of the morphine by BNDD/French lab tested at 88% purity for morphine base.)

Vinko told the CI he wished to meet the buyers on January 23, in Paris at the Café Le Saint Claude, on the Left Bank in Paris, to discuss the plans for a delivery of 100 kilograms of morphine in Belgrade. I supplied this information to the SAIC in Rome, who set a date for January 30, in Belgrade. French CNO inspectors and one supervisor conducted the surveillance with BNDD Agent Vern Stephens and BNDD report officer.

Choosing Agent Walter Pardaen *(deceased)* to worked undercover with me came about as a result of a major agency reorganization by BNDD in getting approval to increase its manpower resources worldwide. This involved U.S. Customs. Rumors had been circulating that U.S. Customs Agents who wished to laterally transfer to BNDD could do so, and some would also be appointed by Customs to take management positions inside our agency. While I was working with the French CNO on a case, I learned that one of the investigators in the Paris Customs Office had been discretely working behind our backs on the same case and had asked the CNO not to tell us. U.S. Customs was not allowed to independently work a narcotics investigation without coordinating their case with BNDD, who had sole authority on federal narcotics investigations.

Needless to say, I confronted this customs inspector who was in the office of the supervisor. I took him aside and asked, "What are you doing working a case behind our backs? Do you realize that you could compromise my UC role on this case? I suggest you leave now and go back to your office." This inspector left, and I immediately went back to our office and met with Nick. He wasn't too happy, and he met with his SAIC George Cochran (*deceased*), who was a great friend of all of us. Along with one of his agents, Bill Rudman (*deceased*), within minutes, told Nick that this agent was no longer involved with this, and that his informant would be turned over to the French CNO immediately.

Within a few weeks, while the group was having a few cocktails at the Embassy Bar after work, Nick walked in from picking up an Alert Teletype from BNDD, Washington. He said, "You guys aren't going to believe this! let's get the hell out of here and meet Paul and me at the office right away!" Then he immediately left. We all looked at each other and I said, "What in the hell is going on? That is a rolled-up teletype, and it's big!" We finished our drinks quickly because it was not polite to leave a half-full glass, especially if you are a true BNDD Agent!

When we returned, we all gathered in Paul's office and Nick began, "This teletype is about new changes in BNDD and the reassignments of several hundred customs agents to BNDD worldwide effective immediately. I'll read off the names of those who are now assigned to this regional office!" We all looked at each other. The agents from Customs were Walter J. Pardaen, George Reucicard (*deceased*) and one other who was appointed to be an ASAC, replacing our ASAIC who was being transferred to the U.S. When Nick read that name laughing, he said, "Pete, it's your friend who you had it out with a few weeks ago, and he will be your new boss for you guys!" Nick continued, "Guys, Paul and I are just as surprised as you are, and it's out of our hands. We are going to work amicably with our new guys, understood? The positive side is that Pardaen and Reucicard both speak decent French, and we have always had fun with them. They will report to work on Monday. Have a good weekend. Oh, Pete, I need to speak to you in my office!"

"Ok, I know what you're going to say, so let me say it! You have my word that what happened the other week with this guy will not affect me, and I will respect him and work with him in a professional manner!"

"That's what I wanted to hear, so let's give the guy a chance. That's all I ask. If he holds a grudge with you, then we deal with it quickly, understood? And bring it to my attention immediately!"

"Ok, you got it! Want to join us at the Marine Bar upstairs in five? We all need to have a few drinks after this news," I said, laughing.

"Be up in 10 minutes. Got to chat with Paul!"

Needless to say, it was a long weekend!

On Monday, our Customs friends reported to work, and Wally set himself up in my office where there was an empty desk and said, "Pete, I asked to transfer over because I always wanted to be with you guys, and now I can truly say I'm a narc!"

"Wally, we're going to have fun. Here we work as a team with no backstabbing! If you have a problem with any of us, we are old school, and we immediately get it out front and resolve it quickly without having bosses get involved. I know that you have heard that the old-timers either settled their disputes in the office or took it out back, and once settled quickly, the winner would buy the drinks for the team and move on!"

"That's what I have heard, and I fully agree with that, Monsieur Pierre."

About an hour later, the secretary called me on the office intercom and advised me the new ASAIC wished to see me in his office. I walked back up front where Nick was standing in front of his door as I walked by and whispered, "Be cool. Let him talk!"

I entered the ASAIC's office. He was sitting back in his leather chair, smiling and said, "Shut the door, Mr. Charette, and have a seat. Well, what do you think about the new changes? I am sure you were as surprised as I was! I'm sure."

"I think it's great, and I looked forward to working for you and working with Walt and George also. Welcome to the team, boss!"

"Thanks! Appreciate that, and I want you to know that I haven't forgotten our conversation we had at the French CNO either and how you felt about me!"

"Sir, with all due respect, you seem to have an issue with what I said! I think that we need to move on. Do you need me for anything else? I have an appointment at the embassy."

"No, that's all for now!" I left and Nick said to go to the embassy and have lunch.

After a few weeks, our New ASAIC asked to go back to his old position with U.S. Customs. It's amazing how things have a way of working out!

Walt was perfect to work with me in a UC capacity as my brother, and I briefed him on what the case was about and where we were at this point. I asked him if he would work with me in an undercover role posing as my brother from Canada. Our undercover names would be Pierre and André Brissette. I said, "Walt, you're perfect for this role. You look like a mobster, and your demeanor is perfect. What I intend to do is to have you travel with me to Belgrade, and we meet these people and have you come back for the final delivery, removing myself from being there so I can keep my cover going."

"Sounds great, Pierre! Let's do it and get the merchandise delivered."

On the 23rd, Walt and I met with Vinko and the informant at the Café de Saint Claude, and seeing that it was crowded, I suggested we go to a quieter place. So, we went to the Glacier de France on Avenue D'Italie. A lengthy discussion ensued with Vinko, who then apologized for the morphine samples stating that after being advised that the sample was not heroin, was told by his associates in Skopia that they did a rush job trying to convert the morphine to heroin, but the final step was not achieved. So, they sent the morphine instead. Vinko assured us that his associates could furnish 50 kilograms of morphine base at a minimum price of 25,000DM per kilogram (approximately $8,900 per kilo).

I replied, "Something is not right with your price. Heroin can be obtained for $8900. Are you sure you didn't confuse the price because a morphine base can be purchased for 3,500DM maximum in the Munich area? I know because I have purchased it before there!"

"Pierre, I understand your argument. They told me that since there is a loss of approximately 200 to 900 milligrams during the morphine base conversion to heroin, there should not be that great of a reduction in price."

"Well, what are they selling a KG of Heroin for?"

Vinko answered, "30,000DM ($10,700). I assure you that 50 KG of heroin within a week, and he personally would bring a kilogram at the hotel to show the proof it was available."

"Ok! We are prepared to purchase 50 kilograms as long as it is high-grade for 30,000DM! When can you leave?"

"I can leave at the end of January, and I would like to ask you if it would be possible for you to help me pay for my trip to Yugoslavia?"

"That's not a problem since you did keep your word and brought back samples that we requested both times! I'll have 3,000FF for you ($600). What day do you want to meet at the St. Claude Café!"

"The 24th of January, and I'll leave that night for Munich to get my Visa."

"I have made contact with my Banker in Montreal, who is preparing for the funds to be transferred to a bank in Frankfurt, Germany, to pick up the DM funds."

"I'll send telegrams as I travel in Germany and arrive in Skopia. I'll be staying at the Tourist Hotel in Skopia if you need me!"

"Great! Once we get word and arrive in Belgrade, we will be staying at the Yugoslavia Hotel."

As a result of this meeting, arrangements began for the meeting in Belgrade. I conferred with Mr. Hill and advised him of our plans to meet tentatively with Vinko once he returned from Skopia. The embassy Liaison pointed out to the SAIC and also to me that this was a risky situation, which he strongly warned me to reconsider doing this UC operation. He further stated that should the local police, who were not advised of this, accidentally made an arrest, I and S/A Pardean would also be arrested, and the possibility would exist that the director may deny any knowledge of this. This would result in a major international incident.

I advised him that we were well aware of these possibilities, and that we were willing to take the risk and committed to proving that Yugoslavian criminals were now engaged in becoming another source of heroin supplied to the U.S. market. There was no way that we were going to back out of this case.

Vinko returned to Paris on March 9 and advised our source that the suppliers were ready to deliver 15-20 kilograms of morphine base, but only on the conditions that we take delivery in Skopia. Our source advised Vinko that we had returned to Montreal, and he would speak with us on this proposal.

I contacted The embassy liaison Chief in Belgrade and briefed him of the above. He advised that he meet with the director and see how they wish for us to proceed. I informed him of two possibilities: First, to have the UC agents go to Skopia and accept one kilogram of morphine as proof that they have the morphine and arrest them and get them to confess as to the location of the lab and suppliers by whatever investigative means they use. And second, see if they would finance this venture to identify all parties involved from the villagers in the poppy field to the location of the conversion labs, etc.

On March 11, the embassy liaison Chief advised that the director and his senior inspector were coming to an Interpol Conference on March 13 and wished to meet with S/A Pardean and me to finalize the UC plan. This was agreed to, and on the evening of March 13, we met in Paris with the director and his senior inspector of the Yugoslav Narcotics Bureau. Both were briefed about the two options. The director advised that the second option was preferred by his government since it would lead to the arrest of and immobilization of the whole group. He further explained that Kavadarci is a small village in the opium-growing area of Macedonia and would be extremely difficult in surveilling suspects.

He also suggested that it would be better for us to insist that we needed to see the 15-20 kilograms of morphine first before any money was shown or vice versa. We agreed that this was our way of handling these negotiations as a matter of safety and precaution, where we control the situation and not let them dictate to us how it would transpire. This way we protect ourselves from any hostage situation and theft of funds. The director expressed his government's sincere appreciation to collaborate with them on this extremely troubling enterprise. It was obvious that the Yugoslavians were very committed to prevent any future attempts by anyone in their country, and they would not tolerate anyone attempting to become an active participant in international narcotics trafficking. He emphasized that we could be assured that we will have their full cooperation at any time needed when it comes to these types of investigations.

I briefed Nick and Paul on the above, and they totally agreed with the plan to take down these people. Nick agreed that Walter should go there for the final delivery and to remove myself out of the delivery and arrest in order to keep my cover.

On January 31, 1974, the source contacted me that Vinko wanted us to meet him in Belgrade in order to make final arrangements for the delivery.

36

Undercover in Belgrade, Yugoslavia

T hings were starting to move in the right direction for this case. On January 31, 1974, Vinko called our source in Paris and advised him to notify me that we needed to come to Belgrade to finalize negotiations for the shipment of the morphine base. Nick gave us the green light to travel to Belgrade, and the Rome SAIC was notified and made all arrangements with the director and the embassy, advising them that we would be arriving on February 1. S/A Pardean and I flew to Frankfurt, Germany. Once at the airport, we were met by the SAIC, who handed me an attaché case containing 70,000 DM ($80,000). We were escorted to our plane via private access, bypassing security with SAIC and BKA State Police Narcotics Investigators.

Upon arrival at the Belgrade Airport, I noticed that the security forces were all over the airport complex, walking around with machine guns and were very alert of their surroundings. Meeting us and escorting us out through the diplomatic exit, the embassy liaison and Rome SAIC, immediately drove us to the Yugoslavian Minister of Justice building in a sedan with all windows tainted black. Once there, we were immediately taken to the director's office and met with him and his Chief of Narcotics. Greetings were extended, and he communicated with Walter and me in French since he did not speak English. He advised that Vinko had been under 24-hour surveillance since his arrival in Yugoslavia, and that he was in Skopia at this time. He was not observed meeting with anyone so far.

We were advised that he had obtained an undercover hotel room at the Metropole Hotel for two nights and rooms at the Yugoslavia Hotel for the following week. We advised him that we would be contacted by our source once he arrived at the Slavia Hotel. We were advised that under no circumstances were we to leave our hotel other than to step out for fresh air, and it would be preferable to remain discreetly at our hotel. We agreed and left to check in and await contact from Vinko.

Once checked in the hotel, we found the rooms to be quite small despite it being a five-star hotel at that time. It had a restaurant, a small bar, and nice lobby. Joe advised Walt and me that we needed to meet at the bar for a drink as he winked at me! The attaché case with a combination lock was turned over to the embassy to be placed in the embassy's safe. Only the SAIC, Wally, and I had the combination to it!

I then proceeded to Walter's room, which was a few doors away to get him. I knocked and he let me in. He said he'd be ready in a minute, and we did not speak any further. We went downstairs to meet Joe, ordered our drinks and sat away from the bar at a small round bar table. We all reached separately under the tabletop and felt for any metal box in case our table was bugged. Everything was good, and we toasted each other and hoped for success.

"Ok, Guys, here's the scoop!" the SAIC said softly as we leaned forward and kept smiling. Your rooms for sure are bugged, and we are being monitored and surveilled for sure by cameras.

"Pete, you are not new at this, so you know what I'm talking about."

"Wally, welcome to our world! Play the part just like we agreed on and be aware of your surroundings. Don't go out alone without us being together and no calls except to each other, short and brief to meet in the lobby!"

"Wally and I discussed this, and he fully understands. Trust me, he knows and fits right in," I asserted as we toasted each other!

"Oh! On a lighter note, the bar has a one-month supply of various hard liquor! So, as we all know, we have to play the part of hard ass! Canadian business types! So, let's at least stay sober! Joe added.

"We won't let you down, I promise, Monsieur." Raising my glass, I toasted, "*Deux fois le même à tous!*" (Two times the same for all!)

"Ah, shit! Here we go," Wally said, laughing out loud.

While we sat there and ordered food, we observed several young ladies sitting together, looking at us, and raising their glasses. We knew that these fine ladies of the night were trying to get an invitation and were part of the normal set up! Unfortunately, we did not bite and continued talking about various non-business matters about Canada. It should be noted that we registered as Canadians under the name of Pierre André Brissette. The SAIC was a muscular man in his late thirties, Italian looking, with jet black hair, 210 pounds, and dressed in a black shirt open collar, black slacks, Italian black shoes, and a gold-linked bracelet on his right wrist. Looking at us, people would no doubt suspect that we were mob-related people.

After several hours of socializing, we all went outside in front of the hotel for a smoke. Yes, I was a smoker like most everyone, and two to three packs a day was average! As we exited the hotel, the weather outside was in the thirties, and street traffic was almost non-existent. We discussed our plan once more, and as we looked around, all three of us noticed a dark black sedan, lights off, motor off, and windows tinted, about half a block away. The vehicle was parked on the left side of the street. I said, "We got eyes on us on the left!"

"Yep, I saw the driver light up a cigarette. Idiot! Not cool."

We smoked a few more cigarettes, discussing our escape routes, if needed, and rendezvous points that the SAIC had already checked out and pointed out directions to take. He had also scoped out three fire doors, exits from our third floor. He suggested we all use the one to our left since it was away from the elevator if needed. When working undercover, It's ALWAYS important to check out an escape route in case a quick exit is needed to avoid an arrest or compromise one's UC role.

The Director contacted me and advised that Vinko had arrived in Belgrade on Saturday and checked in at the Slavia Hotel. Since his arrival, he had not contacted anyone according to their monitoring of his movements. This meant that they were monitoring all of his communications from his room and anyone coming to his room.

On Sunday, February 3, 1974, I received a message from our Paris source that Vinko had called him and wanted us at his hotel for 7:00 p.m. I contacted the Director and advised him of Vinko's request to meet, but he cut me off and said, "Pierre, I know we heard him calling Paris and telling your friend to have you and André meet with him at 7 p.m."

"Very good. I will leave here and SAIC will remain with the money. I will bring him to André's room and do a surprise flash of the money as planned. Please alert your people if anything goes wrong, and it's a setup. Then my code word will be '*Merde! Alors tu es fou?*' (Shit! Are you crazy?) and André and I will handle it from the room and give us time to flee toward the fire escape across the other side. Have a car ready to pick us up while you do what you have to like we discussed."

"Good, he is waiting for you in the bar of his hotel now! Good luck. Be careful! We have everything covered, trust me!"

"Thank you. I'm on my way!"

"Ok, Walt, you stay," as I pointed silently, lifting the pillow next to the lamp table and showed him a fully loaded toy!

He nodded as I said, "If I knock three times on the door, then there's a problem. Do not open the door. Remain totally quiet! I will tell Vinko that you were probably at the bar. Go to the bar with him and tell him that something is not right. Go back to your hotel and wait for my phone call. If I knock twice, it's cool. Open the door!"

"Got it, mon frère!"

The SAIC was two doors away, and if everything was good, I would call him and tell him that we would meet you at the bar, which meant, "Bring the bread now!" Once he came to the door, he was to knock one time, the door would be open by me and intros would be made, and the suitcase would be opened. The contents of the money would be shown to Vinko and counted. Once counted, he was to leave immediately and secure the money.

I took a cab to Vinko's hotel, went to the bar, and told Vinko after greetings to come with me to my hotel by taxi. We both left and made small talk about our trip and arrived at the hotel. We had a drink at the bar, and I advised him that we would meet my brother in a few minutes, once I made sure that we weren't being followed by anyone. With my back to the wall, I could see anyone entering the hotel lobby, and I checked the patrons at the bar who appeared normal. After five minutes, I told Vinko, "Let's go up and meet with André and talk in his room!"

"That's good, my friend. I'm glad you are cautious. This is my first time doing something like this. I have hardly slept, and my nerves are shot!" He laughed somewhat.

"Vinko, it gets easier once we have established trust with one another! The first time is always the worst!" I smiled and patted him on the shoulder.

Getting off the third floor out of the elevator, we took a left and stopped at André's door and knocked twice. André opened the door. We walked in and exchanged handshakes.

"Vinko, how are you, my friend?"

"Good, André. Glad to see you and ready to do business finally!"

"Great! Have a seat!" André, sat on the side of the bed by the lamp table and phone, keeping him nice and close to the pillow.

"Ok, Vinko, where are we on this? We are prepared to get this over and to prove to you that we are serious. There's something we need to show you. André, call Joe and tell him we will meet him at the bar."

André called Joe, and within two minutes, a knock at the door sounded. I opened up the door, and Joe stepped in with the attaché case. "Joe, This is Vinko, our friend. Handshakes were exchanged, and I said, "Joe has something to show you!"

"Vinko, here's 700,000 DM for the shipment! You can count it and tell your friends that you have personally seen the money!" Joe opened the case and Vinko was amazed and smiling. Once he had counted the money, Joe departed immediately.

"Pierre, I was not expecting to see the money, but I will contact my associates as soon as I leave and advise them that it's been verified!" he stated. "My associates will have the merchandise ready in two to four days, and they could only furnish morphine base, not heroin! They could not make the final conversion from base to heroin! They can furnish 20 kilograms of base on the first delivery!"

"What the hell are you talking about? Not ready, my ass. Do you realize the risk we took to get here with this money? Are these people messing with you and us?" He could tell by the tone of my voice that I was not pleased now with this delay.

"I want you to listen to me very carefully. You leave now! And you leave for Skopia today! You contact your associates and tell them that we will wait until Wednesday. If things aren't ready, then we have to return to Canada!"

Vinko left the hotel with the agreement to return on Monday, the 4th of February and meet with us prior to his departure for Skopia. André and I met him at his hotel, and he assured us that he would be meeting the source at 3:00 p.m. and would send a telegram prior to leaving Skopia for Belgrade.

The Director advised that Vinko placed a phone call after our meeting to his associates in Kavadarci, which is the center of the opium-growing area. Vinko was observed meeting an individual identified as the Yugoslavian State Opium Control Officer for this area upon his arrival. Both left in a BMW sedan owned by this individual. They rode around for 20 minutes, after which Vinko was dropped off at the train station where he purchased a ticket back to Belgrade. On February 6, Vinko arrived in Belgrade and immediately called me and advised that it would be one week before the merchandise was ready.

"You stay in Belgrade until it's ready to be delivered. We are returning back to Montreal and call our friend in Paris to let him know when it's time for us to come back to Belgrade. This time everything must be ready, Vinko. Do you understand? If we come and there's another delay, then be prepared to pay a heavy price which will involve you and your family, do you understand? I will not be coming back on the next trip, André my brother will be here with members of my family to handle the purchase and delivery! I have to be in New York to prepare our buyers once you deliver. Have a great week, my friend, and I know you will make it happen! Right?"

"Pierre, it will be delivered on time. Please trust me!"

"Ok! I'll take your word on this. No more delays! Safe stay!"

The Director advised me that they would be doing 24-hour surveillance both in Skopia and Belgrade and thanked us for helping them make this case happen. We left for Frankfurt to return the flash roll and returned back to Paris that night. He also remarked, "Pierre, please do me a favor and tell your brother André to stop looking for the bug in the room. It's driving our people crazy. Tell him it's the light bulb on the lamp table next to the bed!"

"I apologize. He is new to this undercover work, but I will put his mind at ease, my friend!"

When I told Wally, he was a bit red-faced and apologized. I told him it wasn't a problem but just a normal instinct. "Just remember this. You're in a bloc country, and everywhere you go, you're being monitored. Make sure that if at all possible, you make your meetings in a restaurant of your choice at the last minute. If they pick a hotel for you to stay at, you accept, but be assured that your room has already been selected, and it's bugged. This also applies in Europe. Also, on these operations, your phone is always being monitored."

"I'll remember that, Pete!"

"Wally, I learned this quickly myself when I was told that our phones in our offices away from the embassy were being monitored by the French SDEC (Equivalent to our CIA), and I used to mess with them every morning as I came to work in my office. I'd pick up the phone, get a dial tone and say 'Good morning, SDEC! Mr. Charette is at work. Have a nice day!' then hang up! I told Nick about my little morning greeting! He burst out laughing and told me not to tell Paul! He will go nuts.

"About a month later, while meeting with Mr. Le Mouel at his office, he asked me to close the door and said, 'Pierre, mon ami, I need a favor. Please stop messing with SDEC every morning on the phone. They asked for you to stop your daily hello to them. They are pissed off and asked me to speak with you so back off, please!'

I was laughing and told Mr. Le Mouel that I appreciated his great friendship and would cease immediately! I love to play jokes on people, but I will stop. Thank you for the heads up! We both laughed, then he said, 'Only you, Pierre, can pull this off! That's why we all admire you and consider you our friend. We trust you, and you keep nothing from us, which is why you have earned our total respect! Merci, mon ami!'

"I told him I was honored to be part of his team and I would never let him down.

"Wally, that was the greatest compliment I got from the CNO Chief, and they also have remarked to me that they are happy to have you on board! You keep your relationship with them open and, trust me, you will get cases referred to you to work on with them! Mr. Le Mouel and his handpicked team are the best we have had, and the proof is visible with all the cases that we have been making since 1972."

⋅⋅◆◆◆◆⋅⋅

A week passed before Vinko made contact with our source. He advised that 10 kilograms of morphine base were ready for delivery and for André to come to Belgrade. Arrangements were made for S/A Pardean to travel along with our Rome SAIC. Vinko and his associates made the delivery to S/A Pardean, who was able to leave to go get the money after which the director and his agents arrested five defendants along with Vinko. S/A Pardean was shown as escaping arrest and left the country immediately for Paris.

This was the largest seizure ever made in a bloc country, and Interpol was requested to arrest two Canadian brothers named Pierre and André Brissette immediately if located. The embassy liaison advised us that the first report in the paper indicated that the morphine might not be morphine and further analysis was being made. Finally, the government acknowledged that it was, in fact, morphine base manufactured in Macedonia illegally, and further arrests were anticipated.

The Director thanked us for this major investigation, which brought about an outstanding relationship between BNDD and the Yugoslavian Narcotics Bureau. Arrested on April 4, 1974, in Belgrade, making the delivery of morphine base, were Ilija Velkov, born in 1895; Georgi Mitrev, born in 1943; Nikola Liptov and Kiril Andonov, all from Kavadarci, Yugoslavia.

Nick Panella advised me that the Director of Interpol Mr. Jean Napote (*deceased*) wanted to speak with me about our knowledge, if any, about two Canadian brothers involved in a large smuggling case from Yugoslavia. Nick said, "Frenchy, meet with him and tell him that you have researched our intelligence database, and we have no mention of the Brissette Brothers. You and the whole team did a hell of a job on this case, and you stood your ground to make it happen!"

"Thanks, Nick! Everybody made it happen, and I will go over and be back in a couple of hours!" I left and drove over to Interpol in La Celle St. Cloud, outside of Paris.

Mr. Napote was the J. Edgar Hoover of the world and was a short, stocky Frenchman in his early sixties and extremely pompous! His secretary waved me to go in.

"Mr. Napote, *Comment allez-vous?*" We shook hands.

"Mr. Charette, Bonjour. In French, he said, "I hope you are doing well. Please sit down and let's talk. Nick told me that you would research this matter for me on these two Canadian brothers that are wanted by the Yugoslavian government."

"Thank you for asking. I'm doing well and keeping busy since my arrival back in France! I researched all of our databases in Europe and in the U.S. and have no record on these two persons. We will continue to inform all of our offices, and our agent in charge in Italy will immediately contact his counterpart in Belgrade to get details and descriptions of the two individuals."

"Thank you, Mr. Charette, I have a copy of the international warrants for you. Let me ask you a question on this matter! How should I respond to them as far as our attempts to locate them are concerned?" he asked, smiling and directly looking at me in a questioning manner.

"Mr. Napote, since you asked, if I was in your place, I would respond with a simple message saying, 'Unable to locate.' I'm sure that those names on this request would probably be most satisfied with that!" I answered, smiling at him.

"Bien, Mr. Charette. I appreciate your input, and I will send your recommendation, which seems like the right one, immediately. I won't take any more of your time. You have a good day and please stay safe!"

With a broad smile and while shaking my hand, he said softly, "Keep up the good work, Pierre!"

"Merci, Mr. Napote. Always a pleasure working with our Interpol service!"

••••••••

I returned to the office and briefed Nick and Mr. Knight. They both were pleased, and we all went back to work and celebrated afterwards at the Marine Bar upstairs with everyone! Nick made sure to tell everyone that the case agent always buys once he is successful! With everyone agreeing, it cost me a few bucks, but it was well worth it with such a great bunch of guys.

37

Compromised by French Inspector and by BNDD Agents in New York

Case of Significant Impact - XA-73-0002 Salvatore Lamanna
20 kilogram of heroin seizure Paris, France $10 million seizure. February 14, 1973 Case Agent: Pierre Charette, Assisted by BNDD Agents Jim Collier, Vern Stephens. (other names withheld for safety), Deputy Regional Director Paul Knight, Deputy Assistant RD Nick Panella,
ASAIC (name withheld), Surveillance Agents: Jim Collier, Vernon Stephens, French CNO Team.

The New Year started off with my being involved in one of the most significant cases of my career up to now in France. This international case involved three countries: France, Canada, and the United States. It resulted in the arrest of the biggest traffickers of heroin in France and New York with ties to suppliers, the Frank Catroni *(deceased)* Canadian criminal organization in Canada.

The day started off with our regular morning café Calva with our French inspector friends for an hour. Then we left and reported to the office, not knowing that I was about to make a ten Million-dollar seizure of heroin, destined for Canada and New York.

(If 20 kilograms of heroin successfully made it to the hands of the U.S. mob, the 20 kilograms of 98% pure heroin would cost approximately 500,000 Francs purchased from the Marseille lab. U.S. mobsters would sell a kilo in the U.S. at 200,000 Francs per kilo after having cut it with lactose, making 400 kilograms out of the original 20 kilograms.)

Sitting at my desk catching up on paperwork, Mr. Knight's secretary came into our office and said in her soft, beautiful voice in perfect French, "Pierre, there is a French person who wants to speak to someone who speaks French on line one."

"Oui, ma belle!" I smiled. "I'm on it, thanks!" I picked up and said in French, "Hello! How can I help you?"

"I need to meet with you as soon as possible, sir! I have information on a large shipment of drugs that will be coming to Paris in a few days. I can't talk anymore. When can you meet me today?"

"How about 12 noon in the 16th Arrondissement at the Café Bar, in front of the metro station Mirabeau and Avenue de Versailles?"

"Good!"

"I will come inside and will have a newspaper under my right arm. If it's under my left arm, it means that there is a problem, and I will leave. You stay put and call me at the office in one hour after I leave. I will be wearing a black overcoat, just be sitting at the bar. I will walk in and proceed to the back of the bar, turn around and walk back out and go right. I will stop next to a Volkswagen, grey in color with the passenger door open. Come out, just say 'Pierre.' Got it?"

"Yes, sir, see you then!" Then I hung up.

"My partner, who was given code name Hammer, was sitting at his desk. I said, "Hammer, the guy I just talked to on the phone sounded very nervous on the phone and said he had info on a load coming to Paris for the U.S. and Canada. Let's go see Nick and tell him we are meeting a possible source for a load."

I got up from my desk and we both went to Nick's office. As we walked in, Paul Knight was with him. Nick began, "What's up?"

"Nick, I just spoke with a French guy, who said he wanted to meet with me. He has information on a load coming to Paris in a few days, destined for Canada and New York! I'll take the Hammer and we'll meet him at noontime in the 16th at a bar near my place!"

"Mr. Charette," Paul spoke up, "sounds to me like a possible set up or a visual by him to see what we look like. I don't like the sound of this, so we will not make this meet! If he is serious, he will make contact again. Thank you! Nick and I need to talk!"

"Yes, Sir!" We returned to the back room!

"Pete, you and Kevin stick around, and I'll be with you in five!"

"Yes, Sir!" Needless to say, I was taken aback by Paul's abrasiveness and his 'spy' attitude, which always made it hard to read and understand his motives at times. Kevin and I both felt like he thought of us as being inexperienced in this line of work and not capable of handling a possible set up. I told Kevin that I knew when my instinct kicked in, that this was for real, and I would meet this guy! I would take the heat later. Obviously, this frog was pissed!

Nick arrived and shut the door to our office and said, "The look on your faces was worth a million! I thought that Paul was off on this and sometimes I can't read him!"

"Nick, I respect Paul, but he is way off on this. I have a hunch and feeling this is real, and we want to meet this guy, please! We can handle this. Let's go and feel this out! My plan is simple. I will walk in the bar, walk to the end, turn around and walk back out. He was told to come out. Once he turns right, to follow me.

"Hammer will have left the passenger's seat folded forward, and the Hammer will come out between the small alleys next to the bar, grab him by the back of his collar and shove him in the back seat. I will quickly turn around and jump in the driver's seat and he will push the seat back and jump in! I will take off and the Hammer will draw down on him. We will leave the area fast and go to the Bois de Boulogne to have a 'Come to Jesus' talk with this guy and let him know that it better be good, and he better have proof on this. If not, then we will drop him off in the Seine River to see if he can swim."

Nick seemed amused and simply said, "Sounds good to me! Leave through the back, and if Paul asks where you are, I'll tell him that you went to the embassy for lunch!"

"Thanks Nick! See you in a couple of hours!"

The Hammer and I drove to the meet location and parked two doors past the Mirabeau Café Bar in front of a small alley. As planned, we got out, and he positioned himself in the small alley passage next to the bar while I entered the establishment. Lunch hour in Paris is usually a two-hour ordeal, and the French take it seriously, enjoying a break from work and making this basically their main meal of the day.

As I walked to the café, I looked around for any signs of parked cars, with a driver possibly looking towards my location. All seemed safe. Entering the café and holding my newspaper under the right arm, I started looking around as if I were meeting someone and slowly did a visual scan of the patrons. Everything looked normal, except for one nervous person, a male, who immediately made eye contact with me. Bingo! I kept walking past the patrons sitting at the counter and turned around, walked out and made a right and returned to our car. Next, I opened the passenger door and pulled down the back of the front seat. I walked around the vehicle to the driver's side and stood by the driver's door, which I had opened. I looked in the café's direction and observed my nervous new friend, who started walking toward the car and said, "Pierre?" as he turned toward the car. The Hammer quickly came out of the shadow of the alley and grabbed our target by the back collar, shoving him in one push into the back seat.

I had immediately jumped into the driver's seat, started the car as the Hammer got in and closed the door, turning around with his weapon. As we sped off, I said in French, "I'm Pierre. Don't do anything to reach for a weapon or you're dead!"

"Pierre, I understand, and please don't do anything foolish, I want to help!"

"Good! We will be stopping shortly. I just need to make sure that no one is following us first!" We ended up at The Bois de Boulogne and parked by a beautiful lake.

"Ok, show me your carte d'identité so we can get information on you!" Once we verified his ID, I said, "Ok, my friend, speak to me about this load going to the U.S."

"In January, I was at a bar frequented by important figures that traffic in heroin going to Canada and the United States, specifically New York. While there, I was drinking and chatting with this guy called Paul (PN)who was telling me that he had been approached by a high-level French Connection trafficker named Salvator Lamanna, who was a fugitive from the U.S. who asked Paul to transport 20 kilograms of heroin from Marseille to New York via Montreal within two weeks. I told him that he was full of shit and he showed me an Air Canada ticket for Montreal for travel from Orly Airport to Montreal for February 16. He told me that he was getting $25K as the courier and that there would be more and that he could get me in to make money once he got back from this run. I don't have any more on this, but will keep you posted!"

"Why are you telling us this and what is your reason to call us?"

"Pierre, because of my association with these guys, I know that the French police will bust them, and my name may surface. Then they will grab me and put me in prison for 25 years for collaborating with his group on this matter. I have been arrested before, and no way in hell am I going back to the fucking Bastille prison again! I have heard that you Americans pay for information, and I only want a reward for the seizure."

"I can respect your request, and if we are successful, then I will put you in for a reward. You have my word!" We shook hands on it.

"Ok, I need for you to get me a telephone number from a street phone booth and for you to call us every day at noon to get an update. If anything comes up that's urgent, then call me at the office, ask for me and just say it's the Canadian calling! Here's 200 Francs for your expenses for now and take a metro or taxi. I don't want you to be seen with us!"

"Merci, Pierre! Au revoir! À Bientôt!" (Thanks, Pierre! Goodbye! See you soon!)

We left and returned to the office and met with Nick. When I told Nick the story and gave him Lamanna's name, he perked up with an excited voice and said, with a look of surprise and urgency, "Who did you say was behind this?"

"Salvatore Lamanna. Why, do you know this guy?"

"Holy Shit, Pete! This guy is a fugitive and a major figure in the French Connection organization!" He reached for the phone and dialed Mr. Knight's extension saying, "Paul, you need to come to my office right away. now!" Then turning to us, he added, "Come along with me, both of you!"

"Ok," Paul said as he walked in and looked at the two of us with his dry sense of humor. "This isn't good. I can tell."

"Paul, shut the door. Pete and Hammer, after your decision not to meet with the caller, talked me into approving them to go and check this guy out! I accept full responsibility, and thank god I did agree! Pete pleaded with me that he had a gut feeling that this could be good, and I believed him. The caller said he had information about someone who had been hired to transport 20 kilos of heroin for New York via Montreal, and the man behind this load is Salvatore Lamanna!"

"Whoa! That changes everything!" his demeanor changed, and he smiled. "Mr. Charette, I would say that whatever you do by your instinct, keep on doing it from now on! This is a stroke of luck. We need to get Mr. Le Mouel involved immediately."

BNDD had been looking for this guy since he escaped from Lewisburg Prison on April 26, 1972. He was arrested in October of 1967 with 6 kilos of heroin and was serving eight years.

The French learned on November 27, 1972, during the General Humberto Mariles/ Cortes (*deceased*) case of 60 kilograms of heroin seizure in Paris, that Lamanna was observed in that case and learned of his address at 341 rue Lecourbe in Paris. The French, through technical surveillance, learned that Lamanna was in the process of arranging a heroin shipment to the U.S.

"Nick, go over and brief Le Mouel with Pete and the Hammer. I'll get Le Mouel on the phone and tell him you're on your way."

Nick said, "Let's go. Things are finally popping around here, and we are kicking ass!"

Our meeting with Mr. Le Mouel and his staff lasted an hour or so, and everyone was pumped up on this one. Mr. Le Mouel advised us that their technical information indicated that Lamanna was receiving communications from New York from someone only identifying himself as Herbie. Mr. Le Mouel asked if we could ask our New York office if this name was familiar to them. Nick assured him we would get on this right away.

Mr. Le Mouel asked what we would like to do with this delivery to the courier. Nick replied, as agreed, that we would like for the shipment to be allowed to be delivered to New York. I would book myself on the plane to Montreal and coordinate with our Montreal office and the RCMP and New York offices to get the delivery done in New York and arrest all involved in one international arrest. Mr. Le Mouel agreed to this.

Surveillance teams were assigned on 24-hour surveillance on Lamanna and his associates. Nick asked me to immediately prepare a teletype request to New York's regional office international group to see if a Herbie was known by that office. Nick also placed a call to the regional director of the NYRO John Fallon (*deceased*), who advised that they would be the contact person for this. The next day, a teletype was received that no person by that first name or nickname was known by them. This was relayed to our French counterparts. Surveillance of Lamanna and his associates began immediately by the CNO and BNDD Paris agents.

The French CNO, through technical surveillance of Lamanna, learned that a well-known suspect of the French Connection organization mobster named Jacques Lacoste (*deceased*), 51 years of age, and a well-known mobster by the French police was going to be involved with the transport of heroin from France to the U.S. under the direction of a well-known Marseille French Connection mobster named Jerome Leca (*deceased*), in his fifties and residing at 11 Rue Lepic, Paris 18ième Arrondissment. This guy was well documented in our files in Paris. We had been trying to make a case on him for several years.

Surveillance of Leca and Lacoste on the 4th of January, 1973, by our team took us to the Gare de l'Est (east train station). They were observed going to a pay locker and removed two empty suitcases and left with the suitcases placing them in the trunk of Leca's car. My informant, who was in contact with Paul, learned that he was on standby to pick up a suitcase at the Gare de l'Est, which would contain the heroin and leave as scheduled to Montreal.

Both suspects were followed to Marseille by the team and were observed meeting with two Corsican French Connection mobsters, Joseph Boldrini (*deceased*), 64 years of age and Étienne Mateuci (*deceased*), 54 years of age. The two suitcases were given to them, and they departed the area. Leca and Lacoste returned to Paris, where surveillance was maintained on the suspects.

On February 12, 1973, our ASAIC and I went to meet Mr. Le Mouel at the French CNO to advise him that our source learned that the Canadian was to go to the train station and meet with Salvatore Lamanna and would get the suitcases loaded with 20 kilograms of heroin that afternoon. Mr. Le Mouel advised us that sources confirmed that the delivery was imminent, and everyone was on location. Wiretap information was overheard that one of Lamanna's men was being observed depositing a suitcase in a pay locker next to Lacoste's locker. The individual became very nervous as he observed a CNO supervisor watching him and was transmitted over the radio to all surveillance units.

At the same time, this message was received at Mr. Le Mouel's office where we were monitoring radio communications, Mr. Le Mouel received a call and was silent as he listened to the caller. I could see that he had a shocked looked on his face, and he said, "Merde" as he hung up then reached for his radio to give a quick order for all units to immediately arrest all suspects and seize the suitcase immediately! Mr. Le Mouel looked really disturbed, and my ASAIC asked me, "What's going on, Pierre?"

"Something is wrong! Hold on for a second!" I looked at Mr. Le Mouel, who said, "Mr. Charette, can I speak with you alone please and told my ASAIC to go back to his office. "I need to speak to Pierre alone. We need to talk now!"

"No problem. I'll go back to the office and brief Paul and Nick that something has happened, and we will wait for you! Mr. Le Mouel, I understand and will see you later! Merci."

"Pierre, please close the door! We have a problem, and I know you will respect my request! We intercepted a phone call coming from the downstairs' supervisor's office to Leca, telling him to 'Get out now, they are on to you!' and the caller hung up!"

I was, needless to say, shocked! Inspector Gravet walked in with a cassette recorder and put it on Mr. Le Mouel's desk.

"Pierre, listen to this!"

"As soon as I heard the voice, I recognized the caller immediately. I looked at both Mr. Le Mouel and Mr. Gravet and said, *"Merde, espèce de con!"* ("Shit, he's an asshole!")

(This inspector was the only one that I never liked from the first time I met him. His body language always made me feel that he resented us and was a phony every time he looked at us. I always had inside of me the suspicion that he could not be trusted and avoided close contact with him whenever he was around.)

"Mr. Le Mouel, Bernard, I am as shocked as you are and no need to apologize. I know that you will handle this SOB properly. You have my assurance that this person's name will not be disclosed and will not affect any of our trust and relationship whatsoever."

Mr. Le Mouel said, *"Merci, mon ami!* Pierre, Bernard advised me that Leca is on the run. We have Boldrini, Matteuci, Lacoste, Salvatore Lamanna, Antoine Lamanna, Charles Lucianni (*deceased*), André Kossayan (both from Marseille) and Gilles Lachere. All have been arrested and are in custody. In addition, we got the 20 kilos of heroin. At Lamanna's apartment, we seized five weapons along with false passports and identity cards.

The investigation based on evidence seized indicates that our joint investigation in November of 1972, of André Condemine and General Humberto Marilees Cortes in Paris, resulting in the seizure of 60 kilograms of heroin, were all connected to this organization.

Case Agent Pierre Charette with 20 kilos of heroin valued at $10 Million U.S.

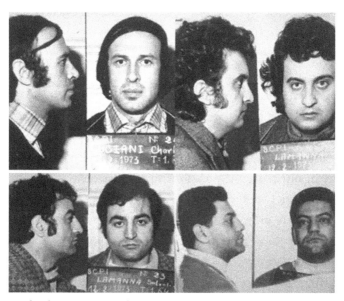

Charles Luciani, Salvatore Lamanna, Antoine Lamanna, Gilles Lachere, André Kossayan (Note: Arrest Photos taken by me at FRENCH CNO.)

"Mr. Charette, this is one of the most fantastic cases we have worked on. Thank you and your colleagues for helping us break this up!"

"Mr. Le Mouel, we are all a team. Thank you. I will go over and brief Mr. Knight, Nick and my ASAIC. Also, may I have your permission to take photos of all the defendants, please?"

Of course, you always have my permission on any case, Pierre!"

"Merci, Mr. Le Mouel!"

———— ·+ ◆◆◆·· ————

Once at the office, I briefed everyone, and Mr. Knight advised all of us that we were not to discuss this unfortunate breach by one of their own. Needless to say, the individual was immediately removed from the unit and dealt with in a timely manner.

Based on the review of Salvatore Lamanna's phone records and notes found, I learned that the denial by our New York office of no information on a Herbie was withheld to us by our own New York BNDD Office! We found out that this shipment was destined to be delivered to a famous U.S. mobster known to be "the biggest heroin trafficker in New York," identified as mobster Herbert Sperling.

I learned that New York BNDD was awaiting this shipment to be delivered, and we unknowingly foiled their attempts to make this seizure. Needless to say, Mr. Knight and Panella, our team and I, were furious to learn about this withholding of information. Mr. Knight let it be known to the New York director.

Mr. Knight had a meeting with Mr. Le Mouel and apologized to him. Mr. Le Mouel, being a great man unlike others we knew, let it be known that our relationship was solid, and this would remain in-house. What a great man! I think of him often and miss him dearly.

Failure to share and withhold investigative information is inexcusable, and agents who willingly withhold information from their own agents or departments should be suspended and relieved of duty pending charges against them. The actions by those responsible, whom out of professional courtesy I did not name, embarrassed us with our French colleagues who were furious to hear of this withholding of information. Thank goodness they were professionals and knew that we too were professionals, unlike those who embarrassed us and could have caused an irreparable rupture in our relationship. In my mind, those involved should have been fired or demoted for this. People who know me know that I have never held back from telling it like it is when an action needs to be taken. My advice is to never lie but to always tell the truth, otherwise, the price will be a heavy one to pay.

After this seizure by us in Paris, Sperling was indicted later. When the case went to trial, Mr. Le Mouel was asked to testify to show that the 20 kilograms of heroin seized by us and the French Police, was destined and purchased by Herbert Sperling for distribution in New York City. Sperling was one of the first drug traffickers to get a life sentence without the possibility of parole. He died in prison at the age of 79.

As a result of this famous case, I received my first letter of commendation from DEA Administrator John Bartels, Jr. I also received from the French police three letters of commendations as a result of this case. I was honored by these commendations, **but all of my colleagues in the Paris office deserved the credit as well!**

The work that our Paris Office did in 1972 was recognized by Richard Nixon, President of the United States, who wrote a letter of commendation to Mr. Knight and us.

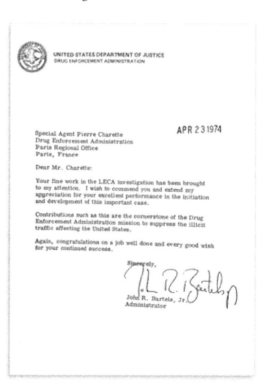

THE WHITE HOUSE

WASHINGTON

September 14, 1972

Dear Mr. Knight:

The Regional Office in France of the Bureau
of Narcotics and Dangerous Drugs has been
playing a central role in the global war
against heroin, and your leadership in this
effort has been outstanding. On behalf of
every American who is deeply concerned
about the menace of drug abuse, I welcome
this opportunity to express my appreciation
for all you and your colleagues are doing.

With my best wishes,

Sincerely,

Richard Nixon

Mr. Paul Knight
Regional Director
American Embassy
Paris, France

38

Saint Tropez, France
Train Station Undercover

Case XA-73-0006
Case Agent: S/A Pierre Charette

The Case # XA-72-0006 case previously described, led to the identity of several suspects that were involved with Sling in Paris. One person identified was a female friend of his named Claudine (PN)) and a male trafficker I'll call Plumber (PN). The French CNO had these two individuals on surveillance since that case. The CNO, through their source, picked up information from Claudine, who spoke with someone in Montreal that she was making arrangements with someone in France to have 30 kilograms delivered to her soon.

We had received information from our SAIC of the Marseille Office, Kevin Gallagher (*deceased*) that a Canadian Mounted Police Narcotics unit agent (name withheld) had contacted him and advised that one of his informants would be coming to Marseille to meet with the Joseph Boldrini (*deceased*) drug organization to arrange for a purchase of 30 kilograms of heroin. The CI would meet with Gallagher first. Mr. Le Mouel requested that the RCMP informant should come to Paris and meet with Mr. Le Mouel rather than ASAIC Gallagher.

On September 17, 1973, Mr. Le Mouel briefed my ASAIC and me

and told us that on September 14, Polombo had been lost by surveillance for a short period of time and later found in Paris, walking out of a store carrying two metallic suitcases. He met with Claudine and gave her the empty suitcases, which she took then left and was followed back to her apartment. That evening she called Canada and advised that "Things are going fine and ten contracts have arrived." Mr. Le Mouel deducted that 10 kilograms of heroin was in her possession. She further advised that the others would be ready soon. The Canadian told her to make sure the suitcases were metal ones, and he would let her know the exact flight schedule and date to send the suitcases.

Mr. Le Mouel advised that the plan will be for the heroin to be seized here in France and a portion sent in the suitcases to Montreal or the United States for delivery and arrest of the recipients. Mr. Le Mouel also advised that the informant had advised him that he has gone to Marseille on the 10th of September, and had met the Boldrini brothers, both who were in the hospital in Marseille. He was advised by them that they were financially in a bind and in dire need of money at this time. They needed to send a large shipment of heroin to the States and wanted to establish a trust with him. They agreed to use him for the intended shipment to the U.S. and advised that the heroin would be concealed in crates containing machine tools.

The Canadian source met with Mr. Le Mouel in Paris on September 14, 1973. Mr. Le Mouel briefed us and told us the source was meeting Claudine at the Grand Hotel in regard to final arrangements for the heroin. The source advised that he was instructed to travel to Marseille on the 15th to meet with Boldrini's spouse and get instructions from her on the delivery of the heroin. The source was scheduled to return to Montreal on the 17th. This information was passed on to SAIC Gallagher and the RCMP in Montreal.

French CNO Chief advised me that their source learned that Joe Polombo was going to Marseille on the 15th to pick up a key and instructions at a pre-rented apartment at an undisclosed location where the heroin would be picked up. Based on Polombo's previous prison incarceration, it was assumed that the location was outside Marseille since he was forbidden to go into Marseille as part of his condition of release from prison.

I learned quickly that cases such as this are seldom made instantly. This case involved an entire team effort on the part of the French CNO, RCMP, BNDD, and Marseille CNO and BNDD Paris Office team.

Mr. Le Mouel requested me to meet with him for our daily briefing on September 18. He advised me that Polombo had contacted a female named Madame AKA, Jossette (PN) who worked at the La Pompadour Bar, at 9 rue Mansard in the 9th District of Paris. The CNO Source advised that this woman is the one giving orders to Polombo and is in direct contact with the Marseille Connection. Once she was identified, surveillance was established on a 24-hour basis.

Mr. Le Mouel also advised me of the following, "Pierre, this woman received a call at the bar by a male who said, 'You and Joe should back out of the deal! Someone is talking! Sounds like someone may be on the take!' Since that call, Polombo has remained in his apartment not going out until later that night when he received a call from Claudine telling him to go to the Café de la Paix, where he will receive a call from the Canadian source."

"Mr. Le Mouel, I hope that we can identify who called quickly."

"Oh, yeah, I assure you, my friend!"

Polombo was followed to the café and received a call which once terminated, returned to his apartment and immediately called Claudine. He advised her that nothing was going to happen until Monday. He advised her that he was leaving for two to three days and would return to Paris on the 22nd. He informed her that the two suitcases had been purchased, and the heroin would be concealed in them this coming weekend.

On September 20, 1973, Mr. Le Mouel and I met, and he stated, "Polombo and an unidentified female left Paris for Belgium! Pierre, I got a phone call on the 19th from our RCMP inspector who told me I would be receiving a letter from their source, outlining the steps for the pickup of the 20 kilograms in southern France. They were as follows:

A. Polombo would go to St. Raphael on the coast of southern France. He was to pick up the heroin from a luggage locker at the St.

Raphael train station. He would have a key to the locker furnished to him by someone.

B. Polombo would retrieve the suitcase, which would be empty. He would then leave the area of St. Raphael by car and proceed to an unknown direction.

C. At this time, Polombo would drive around and ascertain if he was being followed. If stopped by the police, the suitcase would be empty. This was a security precaution fearing he was being watched by the police.

D. If everything was fine, Polombo was instructed to return and pick up the actual shipment. Polombo was then to take the suitcase to an unnamed airport in southern France and check in the suitcase to a flight departing from Paris on Air Canada to Montreal. He would board the plane and get off in Paris and allow the suitcase to go to Montreal, destroying any storage receipts, etc. Once the load arrived in Montreal, the RCMP would surveil the suitcase and have it delivered to recipients in Montreal and arrest effected at that point.

"Mr. Charette, we will not allow the total shipment to be flown to Canada only a partial portion!"

"Totally agree, Mr. Le Mouel. I will advise Nick and Mr. Knight."

On September 22, 1973, Mr. Le Mouel requested that Mr. Knight and I come over to his office for a meeting on this case. "Mr. Knight, Mr. Charette, thank you for getting here in such short notice, but we just learned that Polombo is going to be making his pickup at the St. Raphael train station. Mr. Knight, I would like your permission to have Mr. Charette be there to work undercover as a French baggage clerk at the train station with our close friend from the DST Département de la Surveillance du Territoire (Department of Territory Surveillance) with whom Mr. Charette has worked in the past. Mr. Knight agreed.

I had already packed my travel bag and told Nick about what the CNO wanted. He agreed to it. Mr. Knight, once I told him I was packed and ready to go, said, "Well, Mr. Charette, you are a step ahead of us, and your excellent liaison is working well!"

"Thank you, and I will make sure that it continues!"

On September 24, 1973, The CNO team supervisor and three inspectors and I arrived in St. Raphael and met with the CNO Marseille group, who had already obtained rooms on the second floor of the hotel directly across the street from the St. Raphael train station. Arrangements were made with the SNCF (Société National des Chemins de Fer) administrator to have the DST agent to work undercover with me, posing as baggage attendants at this train station. Information had indicated that Polombo would retrieve, first an empty suitcase from a coin locker, to test and see if he would be stopped by the police. This was a form of security check before picking up the suitcase in a locker that contained the heroin.

We met with the manager of the train station and were furnished with our blue smock uniforms with blue berets, work boots and credentials. At 10:00 p.m., the manager closed the station and advised us that coin locker #6 had expired its opening. We had him open the locker, which contained a new brown leather suitcase completely emptied. The suitcase was transferred to the baggage claim section. All suitcases were checked by us once a passenger brought a suitcase for temporary storage.

We were given a quick lesson on our job, which was to start at 5:00 a.m. on the 26th. We were to take charge of the baggage claim counter across from the coin lockers against the wall that faces the front of the train station. The station was old, made of large stone rocks as a foundation, with a half-moon driveway from the street and a small parking lot to the side. The baggage counter area had an open front with a counter where bags were put on the side for storage once the customer paid for storage up to 24 hours.

A numbered ticket was given to the customer, and my job was to collect the bag and give the receipt and place the payment in a cash register. The bag was then handed to my partner, who took it around the corner for storage. Once I gave him the ok that the passenger had exited the front door, the bag which he had placed flat on a table would be open by him. He was an expert locksmith! He would check the lock first by reaching in his small lock-picking bag and retrieving the proper pick. Then with one swift motion, he'd insert the tool in the lock, turn quickly, open the latch, lift the top up and do a quick feel of the top and bottom inside, lifting clothes to ensure that there were no kilos of heroin. He then closed and relocked the case; all of this done in less than a minute. The bag was then placed with other cleared bags.

Mr. Le Mouel communicated to all of us that one suspect, Daniel Marquet, previously arrested in our previous case (Listed as **Significant Case #1 –XA-72-0006**), who was released from French Prison on September 24, 1973, for lack of evidence, had placed a call to the Canadian source. He advised him that Marquet was awaiting the arrival of a baggage claim ticket at this time. This was suspected to be the ticket for baggage locker #6 found empty by us.

From the period of September 26 to October 2, 1973, no attempts were made to retrieve the suitcase. Mr. Le Mouel advised us that suspect Polombo remained at his residence throughout this period.

(While conferring among us, we began to suspect that Polombo may be leery of making a move based on the phone call he received from Madam Josse at her bar advising him that "Someone is talking." This leak could have been a major factor in placing this on hold.)

Suspect Marquet did receive a call from the Canadian who was inquiring as to when delivery could be anticipated. Marquet advised him that the suppliers had called him and requested that Polombo drive to southern France at an agreed location where the car would be taken to get the merchandise and return within 30 minutes with the merchandise. Marquet advised that he refused this plan and told the suppliers that he would only accept the delivery as originally planned in St. Raphael.

As a result of the intelligence information gained in this case, we suspected that the suppliers in Marseille might be part of the Migozzi organization because Madam Josse had been identified as the Mistress of Jean-Claude Migozzi (*deceased*), the subject, who was the supplier of 60 kilograms of heroin in Paris to Marcel Mouchigan. (See Significant Case #2 André Condomine (*deceased*) et al. XA-72-0004 also involved the arrest of nine defendants).

On October 2, 1973, we learned from the supplier, that the shipment could not be furnished for at least 2-3 weeks or longer. Based on this information, surveillance in St. Raphael was terminated at this location. On the third, Marquet made contact with the Canadian recipients, advising them that he was leaving Paris for Montreal on the fifth with forged documents. The Montreal office and RCMP were notified and took over the investigation, and surveillance was maintained in Paris by the French police.

This case was significant and tremendous intelligence was gained by the French CNO office and us. It finally showed that these cases made by us together finally disabled a major French Connection organization with the arrest of the highest members of the French Connection as a result of the great international relationship between the United States DEA/BNDD, RCMP, Canada, and the French Central Narcotics Bureau.

This bond goes to prove that through good relationships on a day-to day-basis among ourselves and with dedicated agents, and with the support from our managers without interference and micro management, cases are made. Moral and trust are impacted significantly, leading to major accomplishments like this.

Unfortunately, a lot of us who were on the battlefront during those years and since retired have seen a decrease in this type of cooperation. The mentality of "Don't rock the boat" seems to be the norm, and law enforcement needs to step back and reassess their operations in fields like ours. It appears that not all law enforcement is to blame. I blame those leaders who only have one objective in mind: to kiss ass and suck up to management in order to achieve upward mobility. Those are the ones who have caused a decrease in case making and destroyed the morale and camaraderie in our ranks.

Nick Panella told me something I will never forget. One day as we were alone in his office, he said, "Pete, I'm going to be straight with you. I've known you since 1970. Your FBN/BNDD friends spoke highly of you, and they were right! When your name came up for this, I immediately told Paul and HQs that you needed to be here. I assure you that you will have a great career, but you will never move all the way to the top of this agency because you're not an ass kisser. And neither am I.

"Guys like us are needed to make the heads of this agency look good! Don't change! Always remember, you started as a street agent! Treat others the same as you would want to be treated, and you will be respected by your peers and hated by those who are ass kissers who wouldn't know how to make a case if it stared them in the face!"

—————— ·✦✦✦✦·✦· ——————

Unfortunately, I was unable to stay on this case, because I was asked to go to the Brussels' office to cover for Country Attaché Jimmy Guy (*deceased*) for a couple of months while he returned to the U.S. for medical attention. Before leaving, he would show me the ropes.

I had met Jimmy on several occasions in Paris, and we hit it off from the start. Jimmy had made several famous heroin cases in Paris and Belgium. He was in his middle thirties, stout with a mustache, always smiling and cheerful. He had a weird sense of humor, and everyone loved Jimmy. You never knew when he was telling you the truth, or real facts, because, as Nick put it to me when he introduced Jimmy, "Pete, meet the famous Jimmy Guy, better known to us as Dr. Strangelove. He is the world's best bull shitter!" He laughed with Jimmy.

"Hi, Jim, a pleasure," I said as we shook. "Heard a lot about you."

"I'm sure you did. Don't believe a word of it. Nick is worse than me!"

The one thing I loved about him was that nothing ever phased him and if you told him that we couldn't do something as suggested, he would say "WOOF! No problem. We will worry about it after we do it!" and laugh. He meant every word of it. He was my kind of guy! No pun intended.

I went home, packed for a week and told my wife Chris that I would return on Fridays to Paris for the weekends. My wife surprised me, saying she was pregnant. This was a great moment! I told her it better be a girl! I didn't want boys because I had four brothers and always wanted a girl. I took a train to Brussels, which took about 1½ hours. I preferred this type of travel because riding the train in the morning and sitting in the dining car, having breakfast and café Calvas was the best. It was pleasant and relaxing.

39

Belgium

I checked in the hotel recommended by Jimmy, situated a few blocks away from the embassy and the palace. Jimmy was waiting at the train station with his close friends from the Belgium Police Judiciare, Inspector Frans Reiner (*deceased*), and his partner (name withheld). They were the narcotics inspectors for the PJ. Inspector Reiner was 5"10", 175 pounds, and had a big smile all the time. He did not speak English but spoke French and Flemish, his native tongue. On the other hand, his partner was tall, approximately 6'1", 225 pounds and very muscular. He could have been a great football player. He was a joker and extremely good at his work. Like Frans, he was Flemish and also spoke French.

We had lunch together at the famous Grand Place Square, where some of Brussels' finest restaurants were situated. Being briefed as to what was happening and cases being jointly worked, I realized that Brussels was also a well-known area for criminals from Germany, Denmark and France to meet and do business negotiations for heroin and morphine. This was also the place where the famous drug lord André Condomine AKA Mario Denise (*deceased*) used as his home base for his heroin organization.

Belgium was perfectly located between France and Amsterdam, between which a large percentage of drugs flowed. The Agent Provocateur

Law also applied in this country; therefore, the authorities depended on us to help them in a UC capacity. This resulted in Jimmy making one of the largest heroin cases, posing as a U.S. military staff Sergeant at Shape Headquarters. Jimmy was hired by French Connection drug lords to smuggle 220 pounds of heroin from an Army footlocker to New York.

After lunch, Jimmy and I went to the U.S. Embassy, where he introduced me to one of the most wonderful secretaries in BNDD, Dot (PN). I was also taken to meet the Deputy Ambassador and Ambassador John Eisenhower, son of President Dwight Eisenhower. I was welcomed and assured of their full support and assistance if needed while there.

Jimmy spent the rest of the day briefing me on cases and informants the rest of the day. He also advised me that the head of the Dutch Narcotics Bureau had been advised of my acting in his place and looked forward to meeting me with Jim tomorrow. Jim advised me that we were done for the day at 6:00 p.m. and that Dorothy, his lovely wife, was waiting for Pierre with joy! She was an outstanding cook whom we all loved.

We arrived at the house, and she welcomed me with a big smile and hug! The boys also greeted me along with their youngest daughter, who was five years of age and full of love. We all had a great supper, and as usual, Jim and I had coffee with Cognac. I was taken back to my hotel and Jim advised me he would pick me up to take me to Amsterdam at 9 a.m.

The next day, we drove to Amsterdam and met with the Chief superintendent of the Criminal Police Division. After receiving a briefing about the open drug policy in this country, I realized that Amsterdam was an open drug market for the people of Denmark and for the European population and a place where our military troops came for rest and recreation. The city was famous for its prostitution and sex clubs and where anything you wanted was available and lawful.

Our Belgium office was responsible for passing on intelligence information on organized crime figures from the United States, purchasing large shipments of a variety of illegal drugs, i.e., heroin, hashish, methamphetamine, LSD, and barbiturates for sale in the United

States. The U.S. Army CID from Germany with Jimmy Guy had an undercover criminal investigation agent (CID) making purchases of various drugs for intelligence in Amsterdam. This individual surrendered the drug to the Army CID Lab for analysis to ascertain its purity and toxicity in order to determine what area of Amsterdam needed to be off-limits to our troops.

I was introduced to this person, and he reported to me by phone and gave me weekly updates.

During my first week, one of Jimmy's confidential sources code name 'Crazy Dave' came to the office and advised us that he had met subjects at one of the strip clubs in Amsterdam, and after gaining their confidence after a few weeks, told him that they had received a large shipment of hashish, which they were willing to sell to his U.S. associates. He advised them he would speak with his boss in the States and give them an answer in a few days. They allegedly had 1200 kilograms to sell at $1500 per kilo. Dave was instructed to make contact with them and tell them that we would buy the load for $1200 per kilo and travel in a week to Amsterdam where he would have a truck in order to pick up the load, and that we would meet them at the Amsterdam shipyard revolving restaurant. If they asked why there, to say it was easier for us to have it put on a ship that was docked there now because we often use it for our merchandise to the States. Dave left and advised he would call us tomorrow. Jimmy and I discussed our plan and agreed that we needed S/A Hammer to be my partner from the U.S. and have Dave make introductions then remove himself from the negotiations so we could take over. Jimmy called Paris and briefed Nick Panella, who agreed on our plan. Hammer arrived the next day. Jimmy informed our Dutch police friends of this new operation. They agreed to our plan for a meeting and were advised that we would set it up for Friday.

We agreed to have the main suspect meet us around 1:00 p.m. at the Rotunda Bar & Restaurant on the ship docks of the Amsterdam port. Once we arrived, Dave was told that we would not meet the seller until we were assured that he was shown the load in their truck and verified that all was good and to call us at the restaurant payphone at 12:45 p.m. Once we got confirmation, he was to bring him to meet us.

Jimmy informed our police friends, who advised us that they would set up vehicle surveillance at each end of the street, and we advised them that once the truck arrived, one of us would stay with the money with a plainclothes officer in the bar to ensure no attempts were made by them to rob us. Once the truck parked along the sidewalk across from the restaurant and verification was made that the load was there, we would close the doors and give a thumbs up for the police to move in to arrest the suspects, and the informant would also be taken in custody. Jimmy would pick us up in his car, and we would leave the area immediately.

The Chief superintendent agreed to all of this and advised us of one thing we must understand. He said, "Jimmy, we need to have this all done before 4:00 p.m. Our agents can't work past that time, and if there is a delay, we will have to leave because we do not get paid after 4:00 p.m., understood?"

Jimmy said, "I understand, and we will insist on it with the suspect and give them an explanation that we have a deadline with our ship."

Hammer and I both looked at each other, not being used to having a deadline like this and simply smiled and agreed.

Everything was in place. We arrived at noon and took the elevator to the top floor and asked for a table for four facing the street below. We ordered a couple of beers, and Kevin had our money flash roll in a medium-size metal attaché case to show the seller that we had the money. Once shown, it would be taken to Jimmy, who would secure it. At approximately 12:40 p.m., I went out to the wall telephone and waited for the call.

Right on time, the phone rang, and Crazy Dave said, "Everything is there, no problem. Everything is clean! Me and my friend will be there in about an hour. We are a bit far, but we'll see you soon!"

"Good, cool on this end!"

I came back in, and we waited by ordering another round. As we looked out the half-moon glass window, we could see the surveillance trucks and cars in both directions. Time seemed to drag for quite a while until finally Dave and a middle-aged male with tan skin, wearing a leather jacket, and in his forties, possibly Middle Eastern, walked in smiling and was introduced by Dave.

"These are my associates from the States, Pete and Hammer, who I told you about!"

"Welcome to Amsterdam! Pleasure meeting you and hope you had a pleasant flight here?"

Hammer responded, "We did, and we are anxious to do business with you. We are on a tight schedule and hope that we can get down to business now. We have a delivery to be made by 4 p.m. to a vessel that leaves for the states at 5."

"Of course. Dave told me that you are quick with business deals and are on a tight schedule!"

My partner has something to show you. We have your funds, and I assure you it's all there!" Hammer placed the metal suitcase between him and the suspect and opened it to show him bundles of $100 bills. The suspect smiled and said, "Very good. I will go and get my people to bring your merchandise and return within the next hour!"

"Once you arrive, have your truck park across the street by the sidewalk, and we will come down and have you follow us to the docks to place the merchandise in our truck!"

"Great! I will see you soon!" The suspect left with Dave, and the money was given to Jimmy and secured. Jimmy communicated with the police and advised them it would be an hour, and everything was a go!

My partner and I returned upstairs to the restaurant and, while waiting, had two more beers. We kept looking for the truck to arrive, and time was getting close to 4 o'clock with no sign of our bad guys. I started to get nervous, and at 3:55, as we were looking out the window toward the surveillance vehicles near the entrance of the port complex, they started to leave. "Oh shit! The cops are leaving!"

Looking a block behind them, we observed a tractor-trailer slowly coming our way! We both ran down the stairs, and as we came out of the building, three cop cars had just passed! We both started waving our arms, hoping they would see us.

Thank God one officer looked in his rear-view mirror and signaled to the others to turn around. We pointed toward the truck which was still two blocks away and slowly walked away as the police sirens started blaring. The police stopped both the truck and the car, then arrested everyone and confiscated one of the largest seizures of hashish ever made in that country.

We were both laughing in disbelief that the cops were actually going off duty as they had said. The Dutch authorities were extremely pleased and thanked us for our assistance in this great bust.

Jimmy met us, then we left and celebrated. Crazy Dave was released from jail a few days later and let it be known that he had been deported out of Denmark to the U.S.

I returned back home to Paris for the weekend with Hammer. We both felt good for making such a great case with some stress. All I can say is that we were determined to make this case, and the question was often asked, when people heard this story, "What would you guys have done if the cops didn't see you waving at them?"

"Simple! We would have met them, checked that the merchandise was there, and we would have taken them down on the spot and waited for the cops to arrive!"

Going home for the weekend was great to get away from it all. We got together for supper and told war stories. All of us were great friends, along with the rest of the Paris team.

"We played hard and worked hard."

While acting in charge, I received a referral from our County Attaché in Karachi, Pakistan, on July 25, 1973, that there were five Dutch traffickers presently in Ghent and Knokke, Belgium, who were in the process of selling 81.5Kof hashish from Karachi valued at approximately $300,000.

The Investigation with the Dutch police on the 25th through the week of the 27th resulted in the seizure of the 81.5K of hashish valued at $300,000. These types of cases showed that our working relationship worldwide was extremely great in those days.

40

Set Up to Be Robbed and Killed

Luigi Jepparelli (*deceased*) AKA Gigi
Undercover Negotiations for 20 Kilograms of
Heroin CASE # XK-72-0001
Case Agent: Pierre Charette
BNDD Agents: SAIC Jim Guy, S/A Hammer, Jim
Collier, Vern Stephens, Montreal BNDD/Canadian
RCMP, Belgium Police /French Police

When I returned to Brussels, Jimmy advised me that an informant of his had been associating with several well-known Belgium underworld figures named Luigi Jepparelli and André Bigini AKA Dede. The CI advised that they were looking to sell 20 kilos of heroin, and he had told these two that he had a Canadian associate from Montreal who was looking to buy a shipment at this time. He had told them that his Canadian friend had called him to keep a watch for anyone looking to sell some. The CI told them that he would call his friend and have him fly in for a meet. Jimmy told the CI to arrange a meeting for December 7, 1972, for 9:30 p.m. at the Watney's Pub in the Hotel Brussels on Avenue Louise in Brussels. Surveillance was coordinated with Inspector Reiner.

Jepparelli entered the bar at 9:30 p.m. He was Italian looking, 48 years old with brown eyes, jet black hair, 175 pounds with a muscular build. I was introduced to him by the source, and he introduced himself as Gigi. Drinks were ordered, and a general conversation for about 20 minutes was held, discussing my travel experience and living in Montreal and now in Paris. I immediately told Gigi, "Look, let's get down to business, if you don't mind?"

"Fine, I don't know you, so I have to ensure that we can know who my associates and I do business with! The reason being is that there have been a lot of arrests made lately here and in France in our business, and delicate situations have arisen from those arrests, which cause us to be suspicious and careful!"

"I am also concerned and was in Paris when several persons were arrested with large amounts. I immediately left Paris for Switzerland in order to avoid any confrontations with the police since I knew a few that had been arrested, which my family in Canada did business with!"

"You made a smart move, my friend! I would have done the same. I like the way you think!" he said, smiling.

"I am working as an intermediate for my friend Dede, André Bigini, who was associated with Mario Denise, André Condomine, Lucien Sarti, now deceased ex-drug kingpin in France. He can make a delivery anytime once arrangements are made. We want to do this deal as quickly as possible without any difficulties!"

"I agree, the last such transaction in Paris with my friend here of 40 kg was done in two days and went very smoothly."

"Dede is prepared to meet with you right away to finalize this. He is currently in Marseille. I will call him since he is waiting for my call once we leave. I will obtain for you the price and quantity. The price has gone up since all the seizures and kilos are now 250,000 Francs ($5,000 U.S). For your information, if you wish to verify my capabilities, two weeks ago, I was, unfortunately, part of an article that alleged that I was involved with 102 persons arrested in Germany for drug trafficking and 12 major narcotic heads, had been pictured in the paper and my picture was one of those 12. I just wanted you to know that I am capable of delivering the goods!" I explained with a smile.

"I have no doubts that you can!"

"Just like I can, if crossed, I take care of the problem within 24 hours, my friend!"

"Just tell your friend Dede that if we can do this in a week, I need 48 hours' notice to withdraw the family funds from our Swiss Bank account!"

"It's a pleasure, Pierre. I will be in touch soon!"

"The pleasure is all mine, Gigi. À bientôt!"

Our meeting ended at midnight, and we waited another ten minutes before the CI and I departed the bar. As we headed towards the front door, I said, "No, come with me." We continued down the hallway to the rear exit and grabbed a cab to meet Jimmy and our friends at the park near the palace.

I briefed Jimmy and our Belgium colleagues, and they advised that Jepparelli was well known by them and identified seven of his associates. Some were well documented as being involved in heroin distribution in France and Germany.

On December 8, 1972, the CI contacted me and advised me that Jepparelli wished to meet with me at The Grand Place Square in Brussels at the Chaloupe d'Or restaurant at 10:00 a.m. SAIC Guy was notified, and arrangements were made for him to surveil the meeting with our Belgium colleagues and to photograph the meet.

Surveillance

Jepparelli arrived at 11:00 a.m. and apologized for being late. Once settled, he advised me that his Marseille friend Dede had the 20 kilos of heroin and wanted me to go to Marseille and meet him to discuss prices and arrangement for the delivery. I told him I would rather meet outside of Marseille, due to too much police activity there. He advised me that this was a done deal, and he would travel with me. Responding, I said, "Look, no disrespect to you, but if I go, I will go with one of my associates and have you and Dede meet us at a place of my choice on the first transaction. And that, my friend, is not negotiable!"

"I understand and will tell Dede."

"I'm returning to Paris and call Roger, Jepparelli's brother, and he will call me with the details for this meeting."

After briefing ASAIC Guy, it was agreed for me to head back to Paris and brief Nick of the status, obtain a tourist passport and arrange to introduce S/A Hammer as my partner.

The CI was called, and he advised me that Jepparelli was still awaiting a call from Dede and would call me on Saturday at 12 noon on the 10th. I also told the CI to tell him that I spoke with my Canadian partners and they were pleased and had read in the papers that "The weather in Paris and Marseille was hot and that we needed to meet in a cooler place in France." (This was a code word for too much police activity for our type of business.)The CI understood, and he did not hear from Jepparelli for two days.

I was advised by Nick, for Hammer and me to get tourist passports from the embassy, which we did. Nick instructed Hammer, Collier and me to go brief Mr. Le Mouel and his supervisor of this newly developed case. Mr. Le Mouel agreed that if a meeting occurred, they would cover all surveillance and intelligence communications from all suspects.

On December 12, I called the CI, and his spouse relayed a message from her husband that Jepparelli had informed him that the meeting would be most likely in Lille, France, within the next two days. On December 12, I was advised that Jepparelli would meet with us in Brussels at the Polynesian Lounge in the Brussels Hotel on December 15, which he canceled due to an unexpected meeting he had to attend.

He advised the CI that he would meet us on December 16, at the Chaloupe d'Or restaurant at 10:00 a.m.

Eventually, Jepparelli met with us as scheduled on the 16th when I introduced Hammer from New York to him. After a few general exchanges of reasons for the delays, he further explained, "Pierre, due to intense police actions in Paris and Marseille, there is just too much pressure by the French police and U.S. authorities and is causing significant losses of our merchandise. We are trying to deliver your merchandise by the 22nd, most likely and shipped from Spain or Italy rather than from Marseille. If it can be accomplished, then it would have to be after Christmas."

I responded, "Northern France will be acceptable for delivery. We will return to Paris and be there until the 22nd of December then leave for Canada."

Jeparelli then said, "My associate, a chemist named Paul, who had been arrested in Montreal and had escaped prison, is in Spain and will be part of the delivery." Turning to Hammer, he continued. "I have been good friends with Joseph Gallo (*deceased*) and Thomas Eboli (*deceased*), who were recent victims of a gangland execution in New York. Their loss is very unfortunate."

On December 21, the CI placed a call to Jepparelli in the presence of S/A's Hammer, Collier and Stephens and me. Jepparelli said that Bigini told him there was no problem with the delivery of the dressers (heroin) but was running into a problem of money to finance the 20 kilos. Bigini would call him back on the 22nd. The issue was reaching an agreement on the money, since the heroin was available. So, he asked the CI to call him on Saturday the 22nd. At this, point the CI advised him that Pierre wanted to speak to him now!

"Luigi, I will remain in Paris for the holidays if I have too, but this needs to happen, or we are pulling out!"

"I fully understand, and I will hear from Dede tomorrow morning and will call my brother Roger."

"Ok, we will be waiting. Ciao!" I answered and hung up.

On December 23, the CI called me and said he had met with Jepparelli, who talked with Bigini on the phone and said, "Pierre, Bigini wants to talk to you directly and asked that you call him at 2:00 p.m. today in Lens, France. The number is ------------. He said it was urgent that you call him since delivery will be made on the 30th!"

"Sounds good. I'll handle it and get back to you soon, thanks!"

At 2:25 p.m., a recorded call was made in the presence of Hammer and Collier to Bigini.

"Hello, Dede, this is Pierre! How are you, my friend?"

"Bonjour, Pierre! Doing well, everything is going well! The shirts (20 kilos) can be ready on the 30th or 31st. My tailor had to take measurements for the 20 shirts but, without money, it's important that we meet. His associates were in Paris, and I need an answer from you since they have others that want the merchandise."

"I understand. Let's meet here in Paris!"

"Pierre, the weather in Paris is cold, and it's much warmer in Lens, France!"

"That's fine! We will be there on the 24th! Around 1:00 p.m."

"Either call me at this number or drive to the Manhattan Bar on Rue Berthelot in Lens."

"That's fine. See you at the bar!"

"Good, see you then!" Dede hung up.

Nick was advised of this call and told me to immediately call and meet the CNO. I contacted them and briefed them, and they listened to the phone conversation. Mr. Le Mouel advised his deputy, and his team would be covering the area and set up prior to our arrival by train.

On December 24, 1972, Hammer and I took the train to Lens, arrived at 12:30 p.m. and exited the train station. We looked around then walked across the street to Chez Yolande, a bar and restaurant. I placed a call to Bigini at his Manhattan Bar and spoke with him, advising him we were at Chez Yolande. At 1:00 p.m., Bigini arrived, greeted us, and sat down at our table. He immediately advised us that the heroin was ready to be delivered, but the suppliers wanted $30,000 advance payment just to ensure we were serious since all the recent arrests and seizures had hurt their business financially. No money had been advanced on these arrests and the French police and U.S. agents arrested suppliers before any money was advanced.

He stated, "Let me take your friend, and I will show him that I have the merchandise, and once he confirms this, you can deliver the money, and he will be given the merchandise!"

I translated this to Hammer, who was then willing to go with him!

Suddenly as I looked out the window to the square, I saw a CNO inspector on the side of a building looking in our direction and making a hand gesture across his throat, which was a signal to cut it off. Something was wrong! I immediately said, "Look, Dede. I know what you're saying. We also experience that back home!" I translated this to Hammer. "Look, there is no way that we are going to advance any money. If you were in our place, would you advance money, not knowing who you were dealing with for the first time?"

"No, I would not do it!"

"Look, we are not fools! I'm sure that certain people in Europe are masters at robbing people. I always follow my instinct, and I don't feel comfortable with all these changes. So, we are sticking to our plan, which is, no money up front!"

"I agree and I will get the 20 kilos by the end of January! I will finance the load myself and will contact you in Canada when it's ready! I will let you see it first before money is exchanged. You have my word on this! After we do the first deal, then I can arrange to deliver to you 60-100 kilos. My brother has bought a new sailboat that can cross over to South America for delivery, and we can make arrangements to use it."

"Sounds good. When ready, send me a telegram stating 'The 20th anniversary of our brother will be on _____ (date). We are expecting your arrival on that date.'"

"Great. I must leave but will be in touch. Call me when you get to Paris and furnish me with details to send the telegram! Have a good trip, my friend!"

"Great! See you soon. Get things going!"

Hammer and I took the train back to Paris and briefed everyone. Mr. Knight agreed on the plan and told me to get the Montreal office to set up a room at the Queen Elizabeth Hotel in Montreal for receipt of the telegram.

Upon getting back to Paris, we went to meet with the surveillance team and inquired why the signal to cut things off was given. We both got a surprising answer. Our CNO surveillance team had arrived early to see what Bigini was doing prior to meeting us. He had met with three individuals on the road leading out of town toward Belgium and conversed with them before returning to his bar to await our arrival. While we were meeting with Bigini, these individuals went to the local cemetery and dug up two new graves and waited there. It became apparent that these graves were prepared for us and had been pre-planned ahead of time by them. We realized that when Bigini asked that Hammer go with him, they would have held him hostage in order to lure me into delivering the money and then would have most likely killed both of us.

This close call reminded us all how important surveillance is in order to spot danger and alert other team members of any impending dangers. It was also a reminder that in this job, the other guy has only one thing in mind, sell the product or steal the money!

We kept negotiations going, and Bigini was called and told to send the message to the Hotel Queen Elizabeth, Place Ville Marie, in Montreal, Quebec, Canada. He was also advised that our associates definitely would not advance any money until verification of the merchandise was made. Bigini replied that the package would be ready for the end of January.

(An Interpol record check was made on BIGINI, which revealed that he had an extensive record for robbery, carrying a concealed weapon, extortion, and narcotics trafficking. Information also indicated that he was implicated in the murder of a Belgian police officer in 1966 along with a well-known French Connection trafficker named Lucien Sarti.)

The Montreal Office was asked to brief the hotel reception desk and phone reception to show a Pierre Brisette was registered in a suite. This was immediately taken care of by the RCMP and country attaché.

On December 29, I received a call from SAIC Jim Guy that Jepparelli had been arrested by the Belgium Police Judiciare for an outstanding arrest warrant for counterfeiting. This did not interfere with our investigation. Bigini contacted our CI on January 31, and asked if I was still residing at the Sheraton Mount Royal! He asked the

CI if I was going to produce the money upon delivery and was assured this would happen.

Things were moving slowly until February 11, when our CI reported he had met with Bigini in Lens. Bigini told the CI that he had been to Marseille and met with his heroin source and gave him the 15 million old Francs for final pick up of the 20 kilograms. Bigini advised that he had concluded a deal in Paris, which helped finance our shipment. He asked the source if I had received his letter yet. The source advised him on it.

--------------------◆◆◆◆◆◆--------------------

(This deal and arrest were a joint BNDD and /French CNO. This investigation resulted in the seizure of 10 kilograms of heroin seized from Thomas Solarik (*deceased*), who was arrested with two others in Paris on Feb. 8, 1973. The CNO found a letter in possession of Solarik from Bigini, which requested to know if Solarik knew a Pierre Brisette (my undercover name) from Montreal and was advised not. Solarik is well documented by the RCMP to be associated with Joey Horvath (*deceased*), who is a member of the Frank Catroni mob in Montreal. Solarik is a Canadian.)

The Montreal office was contacted, and the SAIC had a letter that came to my hotel, written in French that stated he had been to Marseille and his brother's birthday would be soon.

On February 16, 1973, the source received a call from Bigini, advising that the delivery of the 20 kilos of heroin would take place on March 1, 1973, in Lens. On March 5, Bigini contacted the source in Paris who was with us, and Bigini advised him to call us at the Élysée Hotel at 11:00 a.m. on March 6.

Bigini called and advised he was in Brussels and needed to see the CI, because his associates in Marseille were not pleased about the Canadians' position on this matter. He told the CI to meet him in Brussels on March 7.

On March 8, Bigini met the CI at the Mayfair Hotel in Brussels, and a call was placed by Bigini to me in Paris.

"Hello, Dede, how are things moving? I'm going to leave tomorrow if we can't do this within the next 24 hours! To be very honest, I am beginning to think that you are fucking jerking my partner and me around, and I don't like it one bit! I am ready to find someone else who knows what the fuck he's doing. I hate to be blunt about this, but once I reach the end of my patience, then sparks will fly, and bodies will be buried! Do you understand me?"

"Pierre, I fully understand, and I am with Roger at the hotel now and have 15 kilograms here ready to be purchased if you are still willing to do business. I will show Roger the merchandise, and you and your associate can come to Brussels and accept delivery."

"I will speak with my associate and call back in 15 minutes."

Hammer and I conferred with Mr. Knight and the French police, and it was agreed to try and get Bigini to deliver in Paris or somewhere in France. "If he refuses, then agree to Brussels. Once our source sees that he is with the merchandise now, have SAIC Jimmy Guy and Belgium police arrest them both now," Paul ordered.

Bigini was in room 509 of the Mayfair Hotel in Brussels. All agencies were on standby, and a call was placed at 5:00 p.m. I spoke with Bigini and Roger. "Roger, is he willing to come to Paris, to finalize this deal here?"

"No, Pierre. He has had too many losses there and associates arrested in the past six months! He wants to do it here at this place, and I am here with the merchandise next to me!"

"Let me speak to him, Roger! My associate refuses to travel, and the deal has to be here in Paris or any location outside Paris selected by us!"

"Pierre, I have spent a lot of money on this deal, and I am very upset that you refuse to come here. You owe me money for all of my expenses, and I will come to Paris to collect what you owe me! Give me a place to meet, and I and my associates will travel to settle this account!" The alternative can be that you come to Lens at my house and give me the money, and you will get your package after I have the money!"

"No way! Are you fucking crazy making such a ridiculous proposal, Dede! I'm sorry, but this association is over, and I'm returning to

Canada. Don't expect to do any business with us ever! Just watch your back!"

Agent Hammer was given a thumbs up by me while he had DRD Nick Panella on the phone, signaling him to give a go for SAIC Jimmy Guy and the Belgium police to arrest Bigini as he left the hotel with the suitcase.

SAIC Jimmy Guy, called back an hour later and advised that Bigini was stopped after he exited the hotel with a suitcase and was asked what was in the suitcase. After opening the suitcase, found inside were clear sealed plastic kilogram bags of a white flowery substance suspected to be heroin. Upon closer examination, the contents turned out to be 15 kilograms of pure white flour!

Bigini was carrying false documents and a concealed weapon on his person. The Belgium police arrested him and the French Police CNO Director Mr. Le Mouel put a detainer against him, pending French charges against him for conspiracy and participation in the 10-kilogram heroin seizure in the Thomas Solarik et al. case.

This case was highly significant and highlighted that our recent cases all tied in with one another, further showing that our efforts were now being successful in dismantling top French Connection mobsters.

I am honored to have had the chance to work with the best BNDD team of agents in Europe and the finest foreign police agencies, who never gave up on this case and saved Hammer and me from being possibly killed.

I was deeply honored to have had the pleasure to work with SAIC Jimmy Guy, Nick Panella, Paul Knight, Francois Le Mouel, Bernard Gravet, and Frans Renier, who became lifelong friends and now are all resting in peace with God.

41

Referral Cases

Working in foreign offices worldwide, we responded to inquiries and leads given to us from our offices worldwide as part of our duties. I was involved in several major referrals that resulted in agents from some of our offices, both foreign and domestic, where agents came into our areas of responsibilities and worked undercover to receive shipments of drugs.

Left image: L/R S/A Pierre Charette, S/A John Landrum, Inspector Michel Humbert, RAIC Dennis Dale
Right image: L/ R S/A Vern Stephens, John Landrum, Inspector Michel Humbert,
RAIC Dennis Dale

One significant case we received came from Charlotte, North Carolina, from RAIC (resident agent in charge) Dennis Dale (*deceased*) and S/A John Landrum (*deceased*). S/A Landrum had a confidential source who made arrangements for Dennis and John to purchase 3 kilograms of heroin from French suppliers in Paris. We coordinated this case with Mr. Le Mouel, who assigned a supervisor and Inspector Michel Humbert (*deceased*), to work with our team consisting of S/A Vern Stephens and Jim Collier.

Posing as U.S. mobsters, Dennis and John met the suspects on the Champs Élysées, and the defendants delivered the three kilograms to them, and all were arrested successfully, including Dennis and John. This case was one that happened in less than 24 hours. Needless to say, the French CNO office was pleased with this swift action. Both Jon and Dennis played their part perfectly and were great friends of ours.

Another significant case that was short and sweet occurred when I was on call for the weekend and received a call from one of our agents in Bangkok, Thailand. The agent advised me that while at the Bangkok Airport awaiting to pick up a friend, he observed a known suspected courier of Asian heroin checking in for a flight to Orly Airport. He advised me that this guy, without a doubt, was most likely bringing heroin to France. He furnished me with a physical description and name. I immediately contacted Nick and briefed him and said that Hammer and I would hook up with French Customs at Orly to have this guy tossed! He agreed and for us to keep him posted.

We met with French Customs officials who were elated to meet us and had heard about our work with the French CNO. We briefed them, and the inspector in charge asked us how we wanted this handled. We advised him that it would be best to allow him to go to baggage and pick up his bag and watch for any eye contact by the suspect with any others in the baggage area. If eye contact was made, then allow those persons to also pick up their luggage and be tossed for a secondary inspection of their person and luggage.

We posted ourselves at the exit from the immigration counter and were given the nod that our suspect was clearing and was followed to the baggage area pick up point discretely. Once inside the baggage claim area room, we posted ourselves at different observation points of the carrousel from this flight. While observing his movement and awaiting the baggage, the suspect walked around, slowly eyeing several passengers, males and females of various ages from their thirties to sixties, who he slowly gave a nod to. The customs supervisor was in communication by radio and gave IDs of possible suspects to several inspectors for them not to allow any of these passengers to exit until the suspects had a secondary inspection.

Our suspect retrieved his suitcase and was immediately taken to an examining room where he displayed high anxiety. Upon opening his suitcase, the inspectors found a few articles of clothing and toiletry items, but also a large quantity of packages, dried Chinese noodles rolled up tightly. There was no false section on the top or bottom of the suitcase. He explained that he was bringing the noodles for a family from Bangkok. We radioed one of the inspectors to break in half one of the dried-up noodles that was approximately 6 inches in length. To our surprise, neatly concealed inside the dried noodles were ounce plastic baggies that contained a pink-colored floury powder, which was tested and proved to be Asian heroin!

We immediately asked the Chief inspector to hold all passengers for secondary inspection, as we suspected that this suspect had a 'mule group' on the plane. Orders were transmitted by radio to examine all passengers' suitcases and perform physical body searches on all of them. Needless to say, we observed some very nervous passengers, and after two hours of delay, nine passengers were arrested, all carrying dried noodle heroin packages. The French customs were blown away with joy about this large seizure, which was approximately nine kilograms of Asian heroin and a major breakup of international mules from Thailand. From that day on, we were permanent friends of our customs colleagues at this airport. We notified Nick of this seizure, and he was overjoyed.

One lesson learned was that we had forgotten to notify Mr. Le Mouel, who congratulated us and advised that in the future, "Please, notify us first, and we will work together with customs!" Needless to say, we communicated the information immediately to our Bangkok agent, who made this case of the seizure, and Nick passed the same on to DC headquarters and the name of the agent that deserved all the credit for this case.

On the following Monday, I received a call from Jimmy Guy that the confidential source, code-named Eric the Red, escaped near death in Amsterdam being pursued by gang members in Amsterdam, alleging he was an informant for the Americans. Once the word got out, they came to his apartment and barged in. When he saw them coming into his apartment building with guns drawn, he immediately crawled out through his kitchen window, ran across the roof, down the side fire escape and fled the area to Brussels.

Jimmy said, "Pete, I'm putting him on the train for Paris and he is going to lay low for a few months. We will be in touch with you!"

"Crazy Eric! Tell him to take a rest for a while. He's the best, and I will keep you posted!"

"Ok. It's because he was helping our CID friend making introductions for him at various sex clubs there. A club member started spreading rumors that he may be a snitch for the Americans and putting the heat on our CID friend! I may need your help to cool down this nightclub manager, and I'll get back to you on it!"

"Sounds good! I hear you, and I'll run it by Nick and Paul about having Eric's bosses from the States pay him a courtesy visit! Our 'godfather' Wally is perfect for his part. We can have fun doing this and setting the record straight!"

"I totally agree! Get back to me on this!"

"Roger that!"

⋅⋅✦✦✦✦⋅⋅

It wasn't a week, and Eric the Red called me the first week of January 7, 1974, and said, "I need to meet with you right away. I have a deal lined up with a Lebanese journalist who has six liters of hash oil to sell. I told him that I had buyers for this, and they want to meet ASAP!"

"Ok, meet me and Vern at the Claridge Hotel bar, in 30 minutes, and we will discuss it!"

I told Vern that we had to meet the CI, and we advised Nick! I told Nick that the Lebanese is in a hurry to do this so we can make this happen at our bar on the corner of Franklin Roosevelt, across from the Church. Nick agreed and advised he will tell Le Mouel to expect us in an hour.

Meeting Eric was a joy! He was always full of excitement and a fast talker who had to be told to shut up and let me talk! I began to laugh.

"I met these three guys near the Moulin Rouge at a bar last night. We talked about where we were from, and eventually, this guy, a journalist from Lebanon, asked me if I had ever used hashish oil. I told him I had in Amsterdam and had American friends who were in Brussels and have been buying some to sell in the U.S. He immediately told me that I was in luck because they had just arrived in town a couple of days ago with six liters of hash oil. I asked them how much per liter, and he said 10,000 Francs ($2500 U.S.). I told them I needed to see the shit in order to have them come here for tomorrow.

"The Lebanese journalist, the dumb shit, picked up his phone and told someone, 'Bring the car out front and make sure our bottles are in view,' and he hung up! 'Let's go outside for a few minutes.'

"Ok," I said, "let's go!"

"Then a car pulled up, and a Lebanese male got out and opened the trunk. That's when I saw some hot water rubber bottles in a bag that had hash oil partially oozing out of one bottle! I swiped with my finger, and when I smelled it, without a doubt, I knew it was the real stuff!"

"Ok, slow down. You will get with them and tell them you called us, and we are taking the train to Paris tonight and will meet them at the Café Bar on Avenue Franklin Roosevelt on the square across from La Madeleine Church at 2:00 p.m. tomorrow! You will be with us and make the introductions, and we will tell him that we need to see the stuff first and that you will be at our hotel with the money, which is right around the corner here. Once we verify, it's a go. Then Vern will get you and bring the funds. Tell them we want to do it quick and simple and they can be assured of a monthly order from us."

"Got it. I'll go and meet them at the bar on Pigalle and call you!"

Vern and I went and met with Paul Knight and Nick to relay the plan to them. Paul and Nick knowing that Eric was good for his word, agreed on the plan. Paul was enjoying the hell out of this and said, "Nick! This can be fun. I want in on this. Let's tell Le Mouel that you and I will be at the bar drinking as clients, and we can have the girls from the office there also with us enjoying drinks at the bar and at tables with some of the French cops!

Once Pete and Vern see the merchandise, we and the French take them down, and since the CNO office is only two buildings away from the bar, we will walk them over to their new home," he ended by smiling.

"Paul, you know what? This is the first time I have seen you laughing and enjoying being your sadistic self! I love it; we will include our admit staff also and let everybody get a good view of what this job is all about!"

"Thank you, Nick. Now let's go and see our friends and present our plan." We left feeling confident.

Mr. Le Mouel and his inspectors all listened to Paul present the plan. The more he elaborated, the more laughter occurred, and everyone loved it! Mr. Le Mouel, Nick, Vern and I went to the bar and spoke with the manager and his wife, who were friends of all of us. We told them that everything was safe, and we would fill up his bar with all of us! They were amused and excited to do this.

Paul held a meeting with the staff, who were all anxious to be part of this.

· ✦✦✦✦✦ ·

(Nowadays it would not be done this way because if we had to have permission to do this, we would be denied immediately by management. Luckily, we were creative and our motto in those days was, "What happens here stays here." Those were exciting and dangerous and funny days! Wish I could do it all over again. And if they happened to draw guns? There would be 12 guns pointing at them instantly! Our seating arrangement was to have Vern and I sit at the only four-seat table available in front of the large window facing the sidewalk and square.)

Eric called me and confirmed that everything was a go for tomorrow at 2 p.m. He was advised to be there for 1:00 p.m., and everyone was going to be in place inside the bar at 11:00 a.m. in order to occupy all tables and bar stools for the regular noonday, two-hour lunches that French clientele enjoy. Lunch was on Paul Knight!

As scheduled, everyone was in place the next day at the bar, and we had every table and bar stools taken. Everyone enjoyed their free lunch, and Vern and I and the CI sat at our table enjoying a slow four-course lunch with a nice bottle of Bordeaux, courtesy of Paul Knight.

On January 10, 1974, at exactly 2:00 p.m., Eric stood up and walking in was a Lebanese male, black mustache, black hair with sideburns, approximately 30 years of age, 190 pounds, wearing a winter fur-lined leather coat and turtleneck sweater. Eric introduced Pierre and Vernon to him. He sat down with us and said to call him Aouni.

"I understand that you speak English and French. Which would you rather that I continue in?" I began.

"English is good. How was your trip from Brussels?"

"We had a great train ride and will be going back by car tonight and then make arrangements to fly back to Montreal tomorrow! Eric informed us that he had verified that the shirts are ready for us to take and to show them to our clients in Canada and the United States?"

"Yes," he answered in a low soft voice, "and can do deliveries every month, like you asked!"

Vernon said, "Excellent! Since we all agree, Eric, go next door to our room and get the funds as agreed and be back in 15 minutes!" Eric left the bar. Now, as agreed, have your associates pull up, and we will look at the shirts and do the exchange so you can be on your way!"

"Agreed. I will call them, and I will wait for them and bring in the hand-carried suitcase for your verification. I will be outside. It should only be a few minutes!" The subject went outside, and Vern and I both gave a thumbs up at each other, signaling for everyone to be ready.

Vern and I both were wearing overcoats, and I had my Walther PPKS 380 in my right coat pocket, safety off, one in the chamber just in case, God forbid, anyone attempts to rob us. A car pulled up with two Middle Eastern looking individuals by the sidewalk. The trunk was unlocked and opened, and Aouni removed a brown leather traveling satchel bag and came in the bar placing the bag between himself and Vern.

"Vernon, you can verify the merchandise?"

Outside the bar I noticed, two CNO inspectors looking at the bar lunch menu with their backs directly facing the car!

"Ok, let's see what you have!" Vern said, unzipping it. "Ok, perfect!"

I gave a thumbs-up to Vern, and as we both started to pull out our guns, all hell broke loose within seconds. At least six to seven shouts occurred!

"Police, hands up now!" Anoui was immediately surrounded by CNO officers and BNDD agents. Outside, the driver and passenger were immediately surrounded at gunpoint and pulled out of the car and handcuffed. All three defendants were marched to the CNO office, and the drug bag was seized.

The owner of the bar, along with his waiters and wife, all started clapping their hands shouting, "*Bravo les Gars*" (Bravo, you guys!) I looked at Paul, and he was smiling from ear to ear. Walking over, I jokingly said, "Boss, pay the bill." We walked out with the French police, giving each other high fives.

Arrested were four defendants, one from Beirut and three Moroccans. This was the largest seizure made in France at this time. The six liters of hash oil was valued at $20,000 (60,000 Francs).

(The six liters of hash oil is made with 100 kilos of hashish which is used to make the hash oil.)

L/R: BNDD- S/A Vernon Stephen and S/A Pierre Charette
with four liters of hash oil in a brown bag.

Defendants: L/R: Aouni El-Deiri & Khalil
Haouchine, Bottom- Idriss Amadoun

Tragedy struck during one of my undercover investigations. A source wished to introduce me to someone in Hallandale, Florida, who was looking for a courier to transport heroin from France for him. Arrangements were made for me to fly in from France and meet this suspect, and the meet was to be surveilled by a Miami BNDD office group. I traveled to the office located on the corner of U.S.1 And Biscayne Boulevard in Miami.

I arrived in Miami on August 2,1974, and was met at the Miami Airport by my brother John, who was the Administrative Officer for the BNDD Office. We drove to the office and met and socialized with all of my old bosses and agents. While there, I met with the surveillance group and briefed them as to what my role would be and agreed to meet the suspect at a famous steak house at the Inter-coastal Waterway on Hallandale Beach Boulevard. The meeting occurred on August 3 at 6:00 p.m.

L/R: S/A Vernon Stephens and Inspector Bernard Gravet!
(retired as the Central Director of the French
National Police Judiciare of France)

After finishing the meet, I briefed the supervisor and advised him I would see the suspect on the morning of the fourth after having breakfast with my oldest brother Gilles Charette (*deceased*) at the Howard Johnson across the street from the office. My brother Gilles was being interviewed on the morning of the fifth for a position as an agent at 10:00 a.m.

On the morning of August 4, I received an urgent call from Nick, telling me to book a flight for this evening to come back since I was needed for a case ASAP! Abandoning this meeting, I booked a flight out that evening from Miami to Paris. My brother Gilles took me to the airport right away. I left at 8:00 p.m. on TWA Airline in which I flew first class for free since the President of TWA for Europe was my landlord. (Pays to have a good landlord). I arrived in Paris and picked up by Jim Collier and taken to the office.

Once at the office, people were acting kind of strange, and asking how I was doing. The mood was quiet, which was unusual. Finally, Nick called me to his office and asked me to shut the door! Our administration officer was already in the office and I asked, "What is going on? Why is everybody acting strange?"

"Pete, sit down!" Nick got up and came around his desk, sat on the edge of the desk and said, "Pete, there's been an accident in Miami. The building of our office has collapsed!"

I cried out, "NO! NO! This can't be. I just left there!"

"Pete, the building collapsed at 10:25 a.m. So far, seven people are reported dead. They are trying to confirm this as we speak. Most were secretaries working for your brother in the Administrative Office. We're trying to reach them. Washington said all lines are out.

"Nick! My brother Gill has a 10:00 a.m. appointment to be interviewed for an agent's position. Please let me call my dad at home!"

"Go ahead. Do it now!"

Shaking and holding my emotions, my dad answered, and I said, "DAD! Please tell me that they are all right!"

"Pete, I just hung up with them. They are Ok. Gill's appointment was canceled and rescheduled for 9:00 a.m. another day, thank God!"

Nick looked at me, and we all hugged in relief! "God works in mysterious ways. I could have been in that office that morning.

Later on, my brother reported that he heard the ceiling collapse. A car from the rooftop parking fell through, and he observed his secretary being hit by the car while she was sitting at her desk. He quickly ran through the office, where his other clerks suffered the same blows. As he got to the hallway, he saw the floor underneath the carpet was breaking apart. He ran to the far end of the building on a suspended carpet. One of the surveillance agents, Nicholas Fragos (*deceased*), was pinned under the rubble and passed away next to an agent who I later had assigned to my office in Colombia, S.C., in 1977. Those who lost their lives will always remain in our memories and in our prayers. God bless all of you.

42

The Three Musketeers
Foiled a Robbery

Our CNO inspectors had asked a favor from us to buy them some police equipment that they could not get in France. An order was made, and on a Friday afternoon, the embassy mailroom called and asked us to pick up a box for our office before closing time. The package was police equipment such as handcuffs, leather holsters for guns, and handcuffs, which was purchased by all of us agents. The package was picked up by two of our agents who both lived at the American Housing Compound near the Seine River. Our families were invited for supper at one of the agent's apartments. I went home and picked up my wife, and we all met for a great Irish stew supper. In the middle of the evening, while enjoying ourselves, we heard a frantic knock on the door by our compound security guard, who was yelling, "Open up. Quick! Come quick. Three guys are breaking into your car parked outside the fence!"

The three musketeers swung into action! "Guys, let's go! Our box is in the backseat!" As we ran down the stairs and out the gate, we observed three males running away to our right, one carrying the box. All three of us took off running after them.

I yelled, "The guy running toward the bank of the Seine; he's yours!" Pointing to the other agent, I yelled, Get that son of a bitch running up the hill by the bridge. I got this one running under the bridge!" While in pursuit of my target, I saw another colleague catch up to his guy and doing a flying tackle, grabbed him as they both rolled down the hill toward the Seine, disappearing from view.

Shortly after, I caught up to my guy who had dropped the box while running full speed; I wound up my right arm, fist clenched and thinking *nail that bastard,* I thrust a full blast in the back of his neck. As he screamed, the force caused him to fly forward and land face down onto the sidewalk. I stopped, and as he attempted to get up, I stood by him and went for a three-pointer field goal right into his left side rib cage. Bingo! One loud moan, and he remained down, moaning in pain! *Damn, that felt good!*

Our other agent yelled out, "I got mine. He's all bruised up from trying to get away!" I could hear loud police sirens coming our way, called by our security man.

"Are you all Ok?" I yelled out.

"Yeah! I'm down here, by the river. He resisted arrest and isn't moving!" he was laughing.

"Ok!"

The police van pulled up, and five uniformed French police officers ran to take the prisoners in charge. The one caught by the river was screaming in pain, yelling, "My arm! My arm!" His right arm dangled loosely. The police physically flung him into the back of the van. This one let out a scream and lay on the floor, handcuffed and moaning. The other two were handcuffed and loaded up.

I advised the officer in charge, what had transpired, and he requested that we come to his precinct in the morning before they got off duty to sign the report. He thanked us and said, "We all have heard about you narcotic agents through the grapevine and appreciate and salute you all for your service to our country!"

"Merci, mon Commandant!" I responded, shaking his hand. We all went back and called Nick to advise him of our liaison of the night. He exploded, laughing and hung up!

The next morning, we met at 7:00 a.m. at the police office. The gendarme at the door said Saluting, "*Bonjour, les Américains! Entrez!*"

Waiting for us was the Commandant and his crew who began to applaud, saying, "Bravo, you Americans!" as he was shaking all our hands.

"Mr. Charette, I just want to say you and your colleagues are to be congratulated for the apprehension of these defendants. For your information, one is undergoing surgery. His right shoulder was dislocated apparently from his fall down the bank! The others, one suffered fractured ribs and one had several bruises to his face, we assumed also caused by their falls!" He smiled.

"Could you please sign this report, and we will let you go back to work! We verified the contents of the box, but we need to keep it for evidence if that is acceptable to all of you?"

"Commandant, you and your five men did an excellent job, and my colleagues and I can order a new shipment for our narcotics friends. We would like to give them to you all as a gesture of our appreciation and friendship!"

All of his group all smiled and applauded and said in one loud voice, "Thank you, our friends!" and we all shook hands.

We left feeling good and went for our morning 8 a.m. coffee Calvas. Our French CNO group was there, and Mr. Le Mouel was also there to greet us. Nick was laughing and Mr. Le Mouel said, "Gentleman, I was contacted by our Precinct Commandant of Police of the Boulogne District who told me of the incident and praised you highly for capturing these thieves. He stated, and I quote, "I would hate to mess with these American agents!"

"I have three injured defendants who apparently, Mr. Le Mouel, encountered some bad falls!" the commandant reported.

"With that said, I wanted to toast you three for your service!" Le Mouel said, holding a glass of Calvados. "What a great bunch of brothers!"

Jimmy Collier had invited a great inspector friend to lunch at our restaurant downstairs in our building. We all had lunch with our friend. During the course of our meal, the inspector with a serious look, said to me, "Pierre Every time Mr. Knight sees me, he always greets me in

English saying, 'Jean Marie, how are you?' and shakes my hand. If he comes today here, tell me something in English to say in greeting him!"

"That's simple. Just say this to him." I pronounced it for him several times. He was so pleased to learn this greeting that the rest of the guys were forcing themselves to keep a straight face. A few minutes went by before Nick showed up and joined us.

While we were having our dessert, who walked in but Paul Knight, who came over and greeted with his usual phrase smiling, "Well, how are you?"

Standing up and smiling proudly, Jean Marie responded with a handshake saying, "Fuck you, boy!" so proudly.

All of a sudden, I thought that Nick, who had just put something in his mouth, was going to choke and was laughing so hard he almost fell to the floor. We were all laughing as well. The typical straight man that Paul was, simply turned to me with a quizzical expression as if to say, "What's so funny?"

Smiling, Paul said, "Well, I see Mr. Charette has been teaching our esteemed colleague English!"

"You just told Paul to go fuck himself!"

"Pierre! Oh my God!" He Laughed and quickly told Paul in French that he was so sorry and to forgive him! Still laughing, Paul told him that "Revenge is justified, and I support you on this." Everyone had a good laugh, and I knew that he would get even. When we returned back to the office, the staff had already heard about the joke and got a good laugh out of it.

43

Unexpected Promotion

After a great lunch and much laughter, Nick called me and said that he and Paul needed to speak to me right away and to come to Paul's office. *Oh shit, I'm in trouble*! I continued to wonder while I was on my way up front. *What did I do wrong*?

"Pete," Paul said, "Nick and I need to talk with you about something extremely important. I have spoken privately with all the agents and the process I used, was to ask the most senior agent down, with the exception of one who is not extending his three-year commitment and the four others who are new, about being assigned somewhere else other than Paris.

"All decided that they did not wish to be relocated and wished to remain here. You are the last, and we were told by headquarters that the administrator has ordered to have a new office opened in France, which will require someone who is well versed in the language and preferably fluent. With that said, the director gave me the authority to select someone from this office."

At this point, my stomach was beginning to churn, and I was wondering why I was the last one. *It must be a lousy assignment.*

"Pete, I want you to consider accepting to be the new county Attaché of the Nice, France office, which will be responsible for the area covering St. Tropez to a part of the Italian Riviera when needed.

You can discuss this with your wife and let me know by tomorrow. We both feel, Nick and I, that you're the man for this job and hope you will say yes."

"Pete," Nick said, "You have done more than we ever expected in your three years, and I fully endorse this 100%. I know you are ready for this, and you have accomplished what others couldn't by being on the job only three years!

"Agents in this agency have never been promoted to this type of position with only three years overseas. The main thing is that your job will be to open this new office, establish liaison on the French coast, and make cases whenever the opportunity arises. I know you won't let us down and will do a dynamite job for us!"

"I'm honored, and I know that my wife will totally agree to this. It's something I have already committed myself to achieving down the road, never thinking that it would happen so fast. I'm proud to give you my answer now! Yes!"

"Great! I'll call Washington and advise the director that you accepted. You can go home and break the good news to your wife, and we will get started on the paperwork. Our administrative Chief will work with you to get the administrative paperwork going for you." Nick was excited for Pete.

"Pete," Paul broke in, "there are changes coming about here also that are going to happen, and I request that you do not discuss this with others in this office! I will be retiring soon! Kevin Gallagher from Marseille will be a new ASAIC here in Paris. We will be getting another ASAIC. Lots of changes are coming up! Congratulations, Pete!" he and Nick shook my hand.

When I returned to the back room, Nick tagged along and told all the agents the news. My friends were overjoyed and totally supportive of this assignment. Not only did I get this good news, but my wife, who was expecting a child, had to have a Caesarian delivery on June 23! I left the office, and all the guys kept saying that it was going to be a baby boy! I bet them "$100 that it'll be a girl. Three colleagues told me they would take that bet!

On June 24, 1975, at the American Hospital of Paris, France, my wife gave birth to the most beautiful baby on Earth, Miss Marielle Louise Charette! When the nurse brought her in all bundled up, I cried my heart out. My dream to have a girl had come true. Also, she brought me luck. Three hundred dollars from bets were paid. Even as a baby, she had the honor to be held by Princess Grace Rainier at a garden reception in Nice, France. She still is, to this day, my beautiful baby! Love you, Mar!

Things were moving quickly after my daughter's birth. We received notice in the office that Mr. Knight was retiring on August 1, 1975. Needless to say, I was extremely busy preparing for my new assignment to Nice, France. My promotion and start as country attaché, was effective on September 10, 1975.

Our Going-Away Party. Left to Right: Mr. François Le Mouel, SAIC Pierre Charette, ASAIC Kevin Gallagher, Mrs. Christine Charette, RD Michael Puccini

The office arranged to have a going-away party for my wife and me, which was spectacular, to say the least. Attending this party was Paul Knight's replacement DRD Michael Puccini (*deceased*), new ASAIC

Kevin Gallagher, New Associate Deputy Director Robert DeFauw, Retired BNDD Director Jack Ingersol (*deceased*), French CNO Director Mr. François Le Mouel, CNO Deputy Assistant Director, Associate Director Bernard Gravet, supervisors and all inspectors, DST Agents, and all of the other agencies' staff from Secret Service, U.S. Customs, the FBI, all with whom we worked. Most importantly, all of our team members and our wives, along with our wonderful secretaries and administrative staff, were present. Unfortunately, Nick and Paul were out of town and were unable to attend.

My French Colleagues presented my wife and me a beautiful hand-painted picture, which proudly still hangs in our bedroom and is cherished by us every time we look at it, never forgetting my wonderful friends. Merci, mes amis!"

During this transition period, I received a call from the head of the Paris Embassy Visa Office. He advised me that he had just been named the new Counsel General for the American Consulate in Nice, France, and would like for my wife and me to have supper with his family on the coming weekend. I was elated to get this news. He was the best friend of everyone in our office in Paris. I accepted, and we had a great evening with his wonderful and beautiful wife. His boys were great kids. One of his sons, the eldest, became a famous chef in New York, well known for having his own cooking show on the Cooking Channel!

Peter and his wife have remained great friends. He was appointed as Ambassador of the Order of Malta to Monaco in June, 2007 and retired July 14, 2016.

44

September 10, 1975
DEA County Attaché, Nice, France

T he move to Nice, France, occurred on September 10, 1975. Living on the French Riviera was almost like living in one of the most beautiful places on Earth! The Consulate had found us a penthouse apartment overlooking the French Riviera beach, a quarter-mile from Nice. We lived on the fifth floor of a beautiful apartment complex, only accessible by an elevator that allowed people to go up to the fourth floor only! To access our floor, we had a key for the elevator, which allowed us to push five once the key was inserted. The elevator stopped and doors opened directly into our kitchen. At times, we felt like we were living in a dream world. Our penthouse had large glass sliding doors all the way around the apartment, which slid open to a marble-floored porch. The front porch looked out unto the Mediterranean, and the backside overlooked the French snowcapped Alps.

Once settled in after a week, I finally came to the Consulate, which was a half block from the sandy beach on the famous Promenade des Anglais with all its beautiful restaurants on its boardwalk, five minutes, from Vieux Nice (Old Town Nice). I was greeted by the receptionist, who called Michelle Missud (*deceased*), my secretary, and told her that I was in the lobby. Michelle had been the secretary for our Marseille office, and her husband Guy *(deceased),* who was a narcotics inspector and great friend of ours in Marseille, had been re-assigned to Nice. When the official announcement was made, Michel, who had been Kevin Gallagher's secretary, asked for him to assign her to Nice, to be with her husband. She was immediately re-assigned to the new office in Nice. Michel spoke fluent English and French and was the best in France!

"Pierre! It's about time you came to work! Come, the Counsel General is waiting for you upstairs." The Consulate was a white, two-story house style building with tall black iron security pointed metal fence. The consulate had 24-hour police protection outside at the front and side entrances.

Standing by his office door waiting, he smiled and gave me a French hug and said, "Great to have you here finally! Come on in and let's talk! First thing, this Saturday, you and Chris are coming to our house for supper and a few bottles of wine to kick off our arrival here and enjoy our stay in paradise! My wife can't wait to see Chris again. They hit it off really well! Your office is next to mine, and Michelle and my secretary have hit it off really well! I have set up appointments for you to meet your counterparts, and I'm having a welcoming cocktail party with the Nice and Monegasque police of Monaco at our place next weekend! I hope that's ok with you?"

"I'm speechless. Thank you, my friend. I'm sure that you and I will break the ice and form a great relationship with them. I want you to know that I will keep you apprised of all that is going on with our liaison matters. I will have a monthly summary report for you so you can let the ambassador know about our work efforts to formulate a working relationship with our French counterparts against the French Connection mob in the Med area.

"This will take a few months to develop solid contacts, and I assure you that I will ensure that we don't overstep our authority but maintain a close working relationship with everyone. I understand that Mr. Mourey (*deceased*), the Commissioner of Police, is anxious to meet with me, and I will ask him to assign Michelle's husband, as my counterpart in all matters of investigations. I hope that you will support me on this. I would trust him with my life without any hesitation."

"Absolutely, Pete. You and I will work out fine! If nothing else, let's look at your new office, which Michelle has made look fantastic."

We walked in and Michelle was beaming and said, "Mr. Charette! Welcome to your first assignment!" As we walked into my office, she had beautiful flowers sitting in a vase, on my credenza, next to my chair.

"Now, we have here a bottle of Champagne to celebrate your new position and promotion!" We all laughed as I popped the cork and made a toast to our new future!"

It took me a week to get organized and settle down comfortably in the office. I received a call from our administrative officer in Paris, who told me to go to the BMW dealership and pick up my new car. I couldn't believe it! Needless to say, Nick was jealous! It was a beautiful forest green classic SE. A great undercover car! I spent the next month with the inspector traveling around my area of responsibility as he introduced me to various police officials and airport gendarmes at the Nice airport.

The cocktail party was a hit, and the Director of the French Police Judiciare for Nice, Mr. Albert Maury (*deceased*), and the Monegasque Criminal Director for Monaco were present with their narcotics inspectors. I can't say enough about all of them who became both close and personal friends on and off the job during my two-year assignment.

One of my memorable moments working in this socialite environment was the fact that the Counsel General and his wife were always attending various functions and cocktail parties in Nice and Monaco. It so happened that we were there for the American Bicentennial, which became a major event on the Riviera with an entire week of events occurring. Guy and I attended appearances on behalf of the U.S. The mayor of Nice had a reception at his residence that week, and with our wives, we all went to this beautiful summer day function that was attended by some of the wealthiest people in the world.

As we arrived in the company of my inspector friend and Michelle, we were introduced to a lot of people. Present was the famous Actor David Niven (*deceased*), who resided in Saint-Jean-Cap-Ferrat. I had previously met Mr. Niven when I drove him to the American Club of the Riviera, where he was a guest speaker.

David had asked me to drive him there and asked me privately if I could help him get out of there after he spoke. He explained to me that if he gets surrounded by people who wish to meet him and have pictures taken, he starts to sweat, and if not taken away, he will pass out! "Pete, if you see me start to get nervous and start sweating, find an excuse to get me out of there, please!"

"David, no problem, my friend!"

After his speech, people gathered around for pictures and autographs, and after about five minutes, I noticed he was starting to sweat and looked very nervous but still smiling. I immediately worked my way next to him, apologized and said, "David! We have to go, or we will be late for your appointment at the palace! Folks, I'm sorry, but Mr. Niven has an appointment in Monaco, and we must go now!" I said as I escorted him out and left so I could drop him off at home.

"Pete, great timing. I thought I was going to drop," he commented with a smile. I will always remember him. He was such a gentleman, and may he rest in peace.

The mayor's party also included the Actor Dennis Hopper (*deceased*), who was famous for his acting role in the movie *Easy Rider*. While involved in a conversation with the Counsel General Peter Murphy's spouse, one of the Consulate staff members told Jackie that Dennis Hopper was in the far back of the property, speaking to two young ladies smoking pot and people were starting to feel uncomfortable about it. Jackie looked at me, and I said, "I'll handle it quickly!"

Inspector Guy Missud (*deceased*) and I slowly walked to the back corner of the property where we found him. Hopper was wearing a leather buckskin jacket with buckskin pants. His long hair was in a ponytail, and he wore yellowish sunglasses and leather cap. As we walked up, he was taking a hit off a marijuana cigarette. I put my right arm behind his neck and my left hand on top of his right shoulder! He said in a slurred voice, looking at me, "Hey, dude! What's happening, my man?" He took another hit on the joint and smiled.

"My man! You're what's happening, dude." With two fingers, I pinched his collar bone muscle tightly as he slowly started to stoop down because of the pain. "See this?" I held my credentials to his face.

"Listen very carefully. We are leaving quietly, no scene or you will go to jail in the French prison for five years, asshole. Are we clear, dude?"

It was amazing how quickly he sobered up and smiled with us as we left the party. Once outside, we informed him that he had two choices to make, after showing him my badge as I informed him of his choices! "First one, agree to go to the airport and take a direct flight back to the U.S. tonight! Second choice, simply refuse, be arrested and prosecuted for possession of marijuana. (We had observed him removing a joint from a leather pouch attached to his belt and when seized, it contained over an ounce of marijuana.) You'll serve anywhere between two to five years in prison.

There was no hesitation on his part. He agreed to get on a plane. After his luggage was retrieved from his hotel, he was taken by the police to the airport. He left on a night flight for the U.S., and we returned to the party smiling, matter taken care of!

The week ended with the counsel attending the bicentennial ball and parade in Monaco. My wife and I, with the assistant consul general, were the Honorary Guests of Honor along with the mayor of Nice for the parade and the American ball. We will always remember this 200-year celebration of our country's founding.

Prince Rainier (*deceased*) was extremely proud to recognize the United States Bicentennial at the Principality banquet, and I received a personal invitation to attend the ceremony in Monaco. After the event, Prince Rainier sent to the counsel and me two bicentennial stamps, which he removed from a sheet printed in honor of Princess Grace and our American Bicentennial for his museum stamp collection. I have this stamp in a secured place, deeply honored to have received this.

During my assignment, I was able to get the deputy director of the Monegasque police to attend our DEA International School in Washington, for which his highness was extremely pleased. As a result, he was later named head of the Monegasque police, retired and was appointed Director of Security for the casino of Monaco. We have remained friends for life.

Once I announced my departure, DRD Picini and ASAIC Gallagher discussed with me who might I suggest for my replacement as country attaché. I recommended S/A in Paris who was a classmate friend of mine and now in Paris. The consul general held a going away reception for my wife and me at his residence. All of my French police colleagues were there, and my replacement attended the reception.

L/R: Agent, Edward O'Brien; Inspectors Francois Melis, Guy Missud, CA/ Pierre Charette, Director of Monaco's police, Robert Cassoudesalle; U.S. Consul General, Peter Murphy; Commissaire of French Police Judiciare for Nice, Mr. Albert Mourey; Chief of Public Surety for Monaco, Albert Dorato
(This is my personal photo taken by my wife with my camera and with everyone's permission for me to use.)

45

First Major Case on the Riviera 435 Kilograms of Hashish

October 19, 1975 - Seizure of 435 Kilograms of Hashish
Cagnes-Sur-Mer, France
Value: $300,000
Case Agent: DEA Undercover Agent, S/A James Collier, Paris, France
Surveillance Agents: Country Attaché Pierre Charette, Nice; French CNO, Paris; Commissioner, Bernard Gravet; Supervisors, Paris CNO/Nice; Inspectors, Paris French CNO Nice; Inspector Divisionaire Noël Vouret; Inspector Guy Missud; Inspector François Melis

In May of 1975, while working at the office, Michelle received a call from the Paris regional office! "Pierre, Jim Collier is calling from Paris and wants to speak with you!"

"Hello, Jim, what's up, pal?"

"Pete, I need to talk with you. I've got a source who can introduce me to an English subject who has 435 kilograms of hashish to sell. This guy and two British sailors who are associates are bringing a shipment of hashish from Morocco to your area for sale to me. They have a boat registered in England in the name of Steadfast, flying a British flag. I'm going to meet the broker and will advise Mr. Le Mouel and his team, who will work with us to get this cargo delivered to me in your area."

"That's great, Jim! I will get my counterparts on standby. I'm sure Mr. Le Mouel will get in touch with Mr. Mourey (*deceased*). I'll give him a heads-up as soon as I hang up! Just let me know how your meet goes and just tell me what you need from us. You got me, pal! Be careful, and I will wait to hear from you! Thanks Jim!"

I called the Nice contacts and briefed them on what was going on. Mr. Le Mouel appreciated my heads up, and his team became excited over this first case with us. I made sure the Counsel was also told, and he was also excited at this news. For the next four months, Jimmy Collier negotiated with the broker, and it was agreed that payment would be cash on delivery. The boat was set to return from Morocco to somewhere in the area of Cagnes-sur-Mer on or about the first or fifteenth of October.

Word was received by S/A Collier that the merchandise had arrived and that he was to have ready 1,500,000.00 Francs ready for payment of the shipment ($300,000.00). Arrangements were made for S/A Collier to stay on the Promenade Des Anglais in Nice, and the money to be used as a flash roll was secured in a safe at the hotel.

⋅⋅◆◆◆◆⋅⋅

On October 19, S/A Collier met the broker and insisted on seeing the merchandise. S/A Collier was told to come to an apartment building in Cagnes-sur-Mer called The Grand Large and took S/A Collier to the basement of the apartment complex. There he opened a car garage, that contained the hashish. S/A Collier, being surveilled, gave the signal that the merchandise was there, and surveillance officers were given the signal by Commissioner Bernard Gravet to effect an arrest. The arrest was made of the broker who was armed. The French police also arrested his associates. *The Steadfast* was also seized.

S/A James Collier deserves all the credit for such a significant case for his hard work and devotion on making this happen. Our French colleagues also remained fully committed to ensure the safety of S/A Collier. Without everyone involved as one team, this could not have been possible.

My next two years involved several cases, with my French colleagues, and our relationship continued to be one that has lasted forever.

Seizure

46

End of My Foreign Tour of Duty
January 18, 1977

In 1976, my tour of duty was coming to an end, and the office was now operating fully on track. I decided after I conferred with ASAIC Kevin Gallagher and my spouse that we wanted to return back to the States and hopefully return again for another assignment five years prior to my retirement. Kevin fully understood and briefed RD Picini on this matter.

Kevin advised me that our new director was coming to Switzerland to speak before the United Nations and wanted me to go to Geneva to help with his visit. I traveled to Geneva ahead of his arrival to ensure all hotel accommodations were properly arranged and to await his arrival with his wife and his aide. I made sure everything was organized, and he kept in contact with me to ensure that he was cleared immediately through the Swiss Customs with which we enjoyed a great liaison. For four days, everything went as planned so that he and his spouse would have an enjoyable time visiting Geneva and Zurich, Switzerland.

On the morning of the last day, while the director spoke before the UN Assembly, his aide took me aside and said, "Pete, the boss wants to have 15 minutes of personal time with you outside in the UN Garden area."

"No problem! Looking forward to speaking with him. I'll wait here and when he comes out, I'll go with him, Bob!"

"Good!"

Before long, the boss came out and said, "Pete, let's take a walk and spend some time together!" he smiled and shook my hand then we walked out into the beautiful garden and sat on a bench.

"Hope you enjoyed your visit, and that it was productive, sir!"

"Yes, it was great, and thank you for everything you have done for us. Not only for this trip, but for the past five years. I can't tell you how much this agency has appreciated all that you have done in Europe and in the bloc countries. You have surpassed all expectations, and I personally wanted to thank you!"

"Sir, thank you. That means a lot to me!"

"Pete, I know you're ending your tour of duty after five years. I know that your family lives in Florida, so I made sure that you go back home and enjoy your family again and continue working as a special agent!" he said, smiling.

That news made me stiffen up. People who know me know that I always speak my mind on how I feel if something bothers me! I said, "Sir, thank you for thinking about me and my family, and if you would permit me to be frank with you, I would like to give you my honest opinion on that decision."

Looking at me a bit stunned, he said, "Pete, absolutely! I appreciate your willingness to be upfront because most people are hesitant to upset the boss." He laughed.

"I have 16 years of law enforcement experience, counting my MP time. I have always done my job to the best of my ability, never complaining and always giving 100% and some. I know that I am good at my special talent as an undercover agent and making cases worldwide. In reality, I hated Florida all my life. I'm the only one in my family that did not like it! I was raised in Canada as a youngster, and I love the change of seasons. So, with that said, I'd prefer a different place up north if possible."

"No problem, Peter! I appreciate your honesty!"

"One more thing. I know you're on a tight schedule, but if I may?"

"Absolutely!"

"As you know, the DEA policy for Grade 13 Country Attachés is that when returning back to the U.S., we have to revert back to being a street agent again! This policy needs to be reviewed because it is outdated. The reason I say that, and I am not speaking just for myself but for the rest of our foreign agents worldwide, it that our job requires us to meet with ambassadors, foreign ministers, royalty, heads of international police, work undercover, make cases and do liaison for the DEA to ensure that we get their help in preventing drugs from entering the States. We do more than most RAICs. We also run the administration of our offices and do everything that RAICs do back home and more." I paused then continued.

"Sir, something is wrong with that. We will return and give the DEA our best work without complaint. We will work our way back to being promoted to what we were in our foreign post. I'm pointing this out to see if you could have this corrected if possible. I hope I haven't stepped out of line. I just needed to make you aware of this problem because it affects the morale of those returning!"

"Pete, this is the first time I have heard about this, and your point is well taken. I will have this looked at immediately when I get back. Thank you, and I look forward to seeing you stateside! I need to leave, but it was great talking with you!" he said, smiling and shaking my hand.

I wished him a safe trip then returned to Nice. This director was one of the finest ones we had in this agency.

Within less than 24 hours, a call came in. Michelle said, "Pete! Washington is on the line. It's the DEA Comptroller, and he sounds upset?"

Picking up the receiver, I began, "Pete Charette, how can I help you, Sir?"

"I just want to know, who do you think you are telling the director that our transfer policy needs changing for agents returning to the States? I don't appreciate getting a call from the director and being told to find a RAIC office for you!"

"Sir, I don't appreciate being questioned about the director's directive to you or your abrasive tone! If you have a problem with his instructions, then address it with him, not me! Have a good day, Sir!" And I hung up on him!

After I hung up, I called Kevin Gallagher and gave him a heads up on what I just did. He laughed and said he would tell Picini to expect a call! He told me, "Pete, I got your back, and I would have done the same thing."

Approximately 25 minutes later, Kevin called and said to expect an apology call from the Comptroller! Then he laughed quite loudly into the phone.

Not long after, the phone rang, and Michel nodded for me to pick up. I said, "Pete Charette."

"Mr. Charette, this is the comptroller. I want to apologize for my outburst and just wanted you to know that a teletype is being prepared to be sent out DEA-wide that you have been selected as the new resident agent in charge of the DEA Colombia, South Carolina office. Sorry for the way I acted!"

"No apology needed, Sir. I can understand your concern and have a good day!"

All I can say is that the director watched out for his agents and was one of the best directors we had. I was able to thank him later, and the policy was subsequently changed for our country attachés.

————— ·•••••· —————

In briefing the replacement for his new assignment, I advised him that from the day I opened this office, I carried around a photo of Fugitive Jean Jehan *(deceased)* AKA, The French Connection. I advised him that the word in this area was that he was living somewhere in the Nice area. I furnished him with a photo of him and asked him as a favor to find him for me.

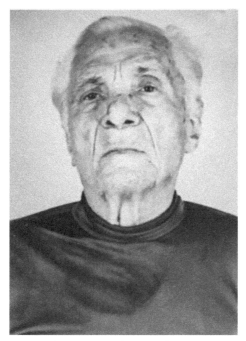

Jean Jehan AKA, The French Connection

He called me approximately a year later, telling me that while stopped at a traffic light, he observed him sitting at a café and followed him to an apartment in Nice. With the Nice police, they eventually followed him to a country castle on the Italian coast and arrested him after finding a heroin lab at this castle.

Jehan was in his nineties and died in a French prison.

· ◆ ◆ ◆ ◆ · ·

Leaving France was sad for us, since everyone treated us with respect and love, something we have never forgotten. These five years were some of the greatest experiences in my career. I never thought that I would get an opportunity to work on some of the most famous cases of the French Connection.

All information written by me along with photographs, copies of documents in the books, are from my own personal notes, photographs and records kept throughout my career. I traveled to France for some of my documentation and conferred with numerous colleagues named in this book.

One Hell of a Ride continues with my next book *One Hell of a Ride II.* Stay tuned for its release date.

ONE HELL OF A RIDE ENDS AND THE NEXT ONE BEGINS!

Arriving back to the United States felt wonderful for us to see family. The second part of the Ride would turn out to be full of intrigue and result in my getting involved with major smuggling cases in South Carolina involving corruption in marijuana smuggling with one of the biggest marijuana cases nicknamed The Company initiated by South Carolina State Law Enforcement Department Narcotics Squad (SLED), which resulted in the arrest of the Chairman of the Democratic Party and thousands of pounds of Marijuana being seized. There were numerous historical cases that were made which had major impacts against politicians and law enforcement Chiefs, Sheriffs and state law enforcement agencies' narcotics agents.

As a result of our efforts in South Carolina, A group of lawyers and state politicians attempted to conspire to have me and my family killed. The book will talk about these cases in full. After being transferred to Atlanta, Georgia, in 1981, I was assigned to this office as the Group Supervisor for Enforcement.

The RDE with the DEA, in Georgia, along with the FBI, GBI, TBI, Cobb County Sheriff Department Agents, resulted in our making the largest cocaine conspiracy in the history of the United States called

Operation Southern Comfort. With our team, we became transporters of cocaine for members of the U.S. mob located in Medellin, Columbia.

This investigation took me along with one DEA agent and a U.S. marshal to Colombia and resulted in our being physically involved with the removal of the U.S. broker for the mob, Harold Rosenthal, who was working for Pablo Escobar. We worked with our Medellin country attaché and the Columbian DAS and planned for 12 days the arrest and covert removal of Rosenthal on the street of Medellin. This case involved the transport of thousands of kilograms of cocaine to Georgia for the mob and led to the arrest of 52 defendants.

For this case, the President of the United States, Ronald Reagan, authorized the administrator of the DEA, Jack Lawn, and five of us from Atlanta to be honored and be the recipients of the Ross Perot Texas War on Drugs Award and be presented with a Colt Combat Masterpiece .45 Caliber pistol, serial numbers one of five made.

Colt Combat Masterpiece .45 Caliber pistol

In addition, in Georgia, we arrested Sheriffs and Police Chiefs and judges in drug smuggling operations. I was involved in the shooting of a defendant in Marietta, Georgia, and assigned to the new formation of the Presidential Task Force for the Organized Crime Drug Enforcement Task Force OCDETF as the DEA Coordinator.

The Ride will also take the readers to Washington, D.C where I worked in our DEA Headquarters as an Internal Affairs Inspector, and staff coordinator in foreign operations and cocaine operation.

My final Ride ended as an assistant special agent in charge (ASAIC) at the DEA Miami field division. I was involved in many cases that will keep you intrigued and show you what narcotics agents' lives are really like.

AFTERWORD

The Police Judiciaire has invited my DEA colleagues and me to be V.I.P. guests for the 50th Anniversary celebration of the Joint Cooperation and Assistance between DEA and the French Police that led to the dismantling of the famous French international heroin organization known as The French Connection which was the source of heroin supplies to the United States and Canada.

The celebration has been postponed until November, 2020 at the Port of Marseille, France. I am honored to be a part of this occasion, and our reunion with our French colleagues will be a memorable affair.

I know that we all will remember many of our deceased colleagues who played an integral part in this historic narcotics battle.

ABOUT THE AUTHOR

This is the story of a French-Canadian boy whose name is Pierre "Pete" Charette, born in Valleyfield, Quebec Province, and who became a historical figure in the war on drugs in the United States and Europe. His adventures spanned a heart-pounding 33 years as a police officer, undercover detective and DEA Special Agent throughout the United States and around the world. It chronicles Charette's fascinating, high-stakes and impactful career first-hand. It includes some of the most famous cases ever developed by him, his colleagues and the DEA.

His investigative ability and imagination in numerous undercover roles, took him from the United States into the French criminal underworld (including the French Connection), the Iron Curtain, and across the planet to untangle and uncover some of the largest criminal organizations and to arrest major domestic and international drug traffickers and their criminal organizations. His life is filled with cunning intrigue and white-knuckle courage, risking his life on numerous occasions, in order to effect the arrest of these major international drug traffickers.

Throughout his career, this special agent received numerous awards for his bravery and accomplishments in the war on drugs against the United States. In this book, Charette offers first-hand accounts of investigations that have paved the path for the development of new and innovative techniques for undercover work and investigations in narcotic enforcement.

CPSIA information can be obtained
at www.ICGtesting.com
Printed in the USA
BVHW041230021022
648343BV00001B/2